CONFERENCE PROCEEDINGS

New Opportunities and Challenges for Taiwan's Security

Roger Cliff, Phillip C. Saunders, Scott Harold

RAND NATIONAL DEFENSE RESEARCH INSTITUTE

INSS
INSTITUTE FOR NATIONAL STRATEGIC STUDIES

The research described in this report was conducted within the RAND National Defense Research Institute, a federally funded research and development center sponsored by the Office of the Secretary of Defense, the Joint Staff, the Unified Combatant Commands, the Navy, the Marine Corps, the defense agencies, and the defense Intelligence Community under Contract W74V8H-06-C-0002.

Library of Congress Control Number: 2011924227

ISBN: 978-0-8330-5149-3

Published 2011 by the RAND Corporation
1776 Main Street, P.O. Box 2138, Santa Monica, CA 90407-2138
1200 South Hayes Street, Arlington, VA 22202-5050
4570 Fifth Avenue, Suite 600, Pittsburgh, PA 15213-2665
RAND URL: http://www.rand.org/
To order RAND documents or to obtain additional information, contact
Distribution Services: Telephone: (310) 451-7002;
Fax: (310) 451-6915; Email: order@rand.org

Preface

This volume is the result of the conference "Cross-Strait Relations: New Opportunities and Challenges for Taiwan's Security," held November 7, 2009, at National Defense University in Washington, D.C. The conference was jointly sponsored by the RAND Corporation, the Institute for National Strategic Studies (INSS) at National Defense University, and the Council for Advanced Policy Studies (CAPS) in Taipei. It was the 21st annual conference on China's People's Liberation Army (PLA) cosponsored by RAND and CAPS.

The 2009 conference examined how a range of political, economic, and military aspects of the relationship between mainland China and Taiwan are likely to shape the challenges and opportunities for Taiwan's security over the next decade. Leading experts on political and military issues from both the United States and Taiwan were asked to write short (five to six pages, single-spaced), incisive, policy-relevant papers on a range of topics related to four broad issues: the opportunities created by improved cross-Strait relations and what further progress will be supported by domestic politics on both sides of the Strait; the potential for confidence-building measures (CBMs) to play a role in managing or reducing cross-Strait tensions; the military balance and the impact of changes in key Chinese and Taiwanese military capabilities; and two possible alternate futures: one in which positive trends in cross-Strait political relations continue and another in which improvements in relations are reversed, including how and why these futures might come about.

After the conference, the contributors were asked to revise their papers in response to questions and suggestions that were raised during the conference or subsequently conveyed by the editors of this volume. This volume presents the revised versions of those papers as well as a brief introduction by the editors. It should be of interest to analysts and policymakers interested in developments and policy initiatives that could affect cross-Strait relations and Taiwan's security, including those interested in how CBMs could affect the China-Taiwan relationship.

This research was conducted within the International Security and Defense Policy Center of the RAND National Defense Research Institute, a federally funded research and development center sponsored by the Office of the Secretary of Defense, the Joint Staff, the Unified Combatant Commands, the Navy, the Marine Corps, the defense agencies, and the defense Intelligence Community.

For more information on the International Security and Defense Policy Center, see http://www.rand.org/nsrd/about/isdp.html or contact the director (contact information is provided on web page).

Contents

Figure and Tables

Summary

On November 7, 2009, the RAND Corporation, the Institute for National Strategic Studies (INSS) at National Defense University, and the Council for Advanced Policy Studies (CAPS) in Taipei held the conference "Cross-Strait Relations: New Opportunities and Challenges for Taiwan's Security" at National Defense University in Washington, D.C. The goal of the conference was to consider how a range of political, economic, and military factors are likely to shape Taiwan's security over the coming decade. Phillip Saunders took the lead in developing the agenda for the conference, and INSS took responsibility for the organizational and logistic arrangements after Typhoon Morakot forced a relocation from the conference's traditional setting, in Taiwan.

The conference brought together leading experts on political and military issues from both the United States and Taiwan and featured four panels. The first grappled with the opportunities created by improved cross-Strait relations and assessed what the domestic politics on both sides of the Strait are likely to support in terms of the current agenda. The second panel considered the potential for confidence-building measures (CBMs) to play a role in managing or reducing cross-Strait tensions. The third panel assessed key aspects of the cross-Strait military balance, with a focus on important conceptual questions and the impact of changes in specific Chinese and Taiwanese military capabilities. The fourth panel examined two alternate futures: one in which positive trends in cross-Strait political relations continue and another in which improvements in relations are reversed. It then explored how and why these futures might or might not come about.

Given the speculative nature and topicality of the subject, the presenters were asked to write short (five to six pages, single-spaced) papers. After the conference, they were asked to revise their papers in response to comments provided by the panel discussants and the editors of this volume. This volume presents the revised papers. Roger Cliff, assisted by Phillip Saunders and Scott Harold, took the lead in editing the papers and arranging for their publication.

The first panel, on the implications of recent improvements in cross-Strait relations, featured two papers. The first, by Alan Romberg of the Stimson Center, describes Beijing's perspective on the recent improvements in cross-Strait relations. Romberg finds that, at least in the medium term, cross-Strait tensions should remain low, possibly even resulting in a peace accord at some point. Until formal unification is achieved, however, Taiwan's independence will remain a mainland concern, and Beijing will therefore continue to maintain the military capability to deal with it. In response, Taiwan will continue to improve its defensive capabilities, and the United States will continue to sell arms and provide other military assistance to Taiwan. Nonetheless, it is possible that the growth of China's military power could cause growing alarm in Taiwan and undermine the formal structures of cross-Strait peace.

The second paper, by Scott Kastner of the University of Maryland, analyzes the security implications of increasing economic integration between Taiwan and mainland China. Kastner finds that the consequences of growing economic interdependence are far from straightforward. Although it is possible that closer economic links will reduce the danger of military conflict in the Taiwan Strait, it is not a given that this will happen. Moreover, regardless of the objective truth, the perceived security implications of increased economic integration with the mainland are highly contentious in Taiwan. Thus, it is unlikely that a consensus can be achieved in Taiwan in support of policies to further increase this integration.

The second panel, on the potential role of CBMs in improving cross-Strait stability and security, included three papers. The first, by Bonnie Glaser of the Center for Strategic and International Studies, analyzes China's experience in implementing CBMs with its other neighbors and seeks insights into how China might approach CBMs with Taiwan, as proposed by Chinese president Hu Jintao in December 2008. Glaser finds that common elements are likely to include the importance Beijing attaches to agreement on principles, its reliance on creating high-level political understandings prior to negotiating CBMs, and its preference for reciprocal force adjustments and constraints as opposed to unilateral actions. Nonetheless, the special circumstances of the cross-Strait relationship limit the applicability of China's experiences with its other neighbors.

The second paper of the panel, by Kwei-Bo Huang of National Chengchi University in Taiwan, describes Taiwan's view of the opportunities, obstacles, and challenges presented by cross-Strait CBMs. Huang finds that cross-Strait CBMs will help Taiwan achieve its strategic objectives of peace and stability in the Taiwan Strait, economic development and prosperity, enhanced relations with major powers, and participation in international organizations. Such developments will likely occur at a slow and cautious pace, however, due to the delicacy of the Taipei-Beijing relationship.

The final paper of the panel, by Steven Goldstein of Smith College, assesses the feasibility and utility of CBMs. Goldstein examines whether CBMs have historically played a constructive role in the reduction of tensions between international actors and analyzes the principal elements of Beijing's approach to cross-Strait confidence building. He concludes that formal CBMs are currently not only unlikely but also unnecessary and possibly even harmful to cross-Strait peace and stability.

The third panel examined the effect of changes in the military balance on cross-Strait relations. The first paper, by Christopher Twomey of the Naval Postgraduate School, analyzes the effects of China's increased military capabilities on politics and policy in Taiwan, as well as on U.S. policy toward Taiwan. Twomey first assesses the current balance of power among China, Taiwan, and the United States, then analyzes how successful each has been in achieving its goals in the Taiwan Strait. He concludes that the "substantial military capability enhancements by the [People's Republic of China] have not led to commensurate gains" in pursuit of its goals.

The second paper of the panel, by Bernard Cole of the National War College, reviews improvements in mainland China's naval capabilities from 2000 to 2010 and compares them to changes in Taiwanese and U.S. naval capabilities and posture over the same period. Cole finds that the Chinese navy's relative ability to execute a range of maritime missions has significantly improved over the past ten years and will very likely continue to improve in the years ahead. He concludes that Taipei must therefore resume making significant investments in improving its defensive maritime posture and that Washington must also increase its emphasis on Asia if it is to ensure that it retains the capability to intervene decisively in a Taiwan scenario.

The third paper of the panel, by David Shlapak of RAND, examines the potential impact of Chinese conventional strike capabilities in a cross-Strait battle. Shlapak finds that these capabilities pose a serious and growing threat to the Taiwanese and U.S. air bases that would be needed to defend Taiwan. However, he identifies three promising means by which Taiwan and the United States might ameliorate this threat: ballistic missile defense systems, greater reliance on passive defenses, and dispersing Taiwan's fighter force across a large number of smaller air bases and highway strips.

The final paper of the panel, by Albert Willner of CNA, looks at the problem from the opposite perspective of the previous two papers and assesses the implications of recent and planned changes in Taiwan's defense posture. Willner finds that, while these changes are intended to make Taiwan's military more streamlined, efficient, and responsive to the people it defends, for political and budgetary reasons, many of the planned changes are unlikely to be implemented in the way that was originally envisioned. He recommends that the proposed changes to the defense posture be augmented by a vigorous and persuasive campaign to inform the Taiwanese public about continued threats to Taiwan.

The fourth and final panel of the conference explored longer-term (five to ten or more years in the future) challenges to security in the Taiwan Strait and possible responses to those challenges. The first paper, by Fu-Kuo Liu of National Chengchi University's Institute of International Relations, evaluates Taiwan's security challenges, strategic preparedness, and prospects for U.S.-Taiwan security cooperation. Liu finds that cross-Strait tensions have diminished significantly since 2008 but that Taiwan still faces three challenges: the potential effect of political transition in either Taiwan or mainland China, questions as to whether Beijing can be convinced to give up the option to use force against Taiwan, and challenges to Taiwan's ability to foster a closer political and security relationship with the United States.

The second paper of the panel, by Michael McDevitt of CNA, analyzes the implications for the United States of different development paths for the China-Taiwan relationship. He assesses that developments that reduce the possibility of a U.S.-China conflict over Taiwan are in the interest of the United States and, thus, expresses concern that a combination of impatience and overconfidence by Beijing could result in conflict. For this reason, he believes that the United States must continue to maintain the military advantage over China, even if it leads to greater tensions than might otherwise be the case.

The third paper of the panel, by Michael Glosny of the Naval Postgraduate School, examines the potential implications of deepened cross-Strait rapprochement for China's relations with the rest of Asia and the United States. Glosny argues that deeper rapprochement across the Strait will produce new uncertainties and apprehension in Asia and the United States over how an unconstrained China will use its increased power. The subsequent direction of PLA modernization, however, can either help alleviate these concerns or further exacerbate them, triggering strong countervailing balancing responses from the United States and within the region.

The final paper of the panel, by Michael Lostumbo of RAND, describes potential changes to Taiwan's defense program that would help deter an attack by exploiting operational challenges that mainland China's military would face in executing such an attack. Lostumbo identifies anti-ship cruise missiles, anti-armor munitions, and mines carried by missiles, rockets, or fired from artillery guns as promising defense acquisition candidates. He also recommends a strategy in which Taiwan uses its surface-to-air missiles for only brief periods, to protect its other forces when they are conducting offensive operations against mainland forces. He asserts that such changes can serve as powerful deterrents to Beijing belief that it can achieve an easy victory over Taiwan.

Acknowledgments

This research was cosponsored by the Institute for National Strategic Studies. The mission of INSS is to conduct strategic studies for the Secretary of Defense, the Chairman of the Joint Chiefs of Staff, and the Unified Combatant Commands; to support the national strategic components of the academic programs at National Defense University; and to provide outreach to other U.S. government agencies and the broader national security community. The military and civilian analysts and staff at INSS and its subcomponents execute their mission by performing the following functions: research and analysis, publication, conferences, policy support, and outreach.

Abbreviations

ADB	Asian Development Bank
APEC	Asia-Pacific Economic Cooperation
ARATS	Association for Relations Across the Taiwan Strait
ASBM	anti-ship ballistic missile
ASEAN	Association of Southeast Asian Nations
BMD	ballistic missile defense
CAPS	Council for Advanced Policy Studies
CBM	confidence-building measure
CCP	Chinese Communist Party
CEP	circular error probable
CSBM	confidence- and security-building mechanism
DDG	guided-missile destroyer
DPP	Democratic Progressive Party
ECFA	Economic Cooperation Framework Agreement
EEZ	exclusive economic zone
FFG	guided-missile frigate
FTA	free-trade agreement
HAS	hardened aircraft shelter
IJN	Imperial Japanese Navy
INSS	Institute for National Strategic Studies
JASSM	joint air-to-surface standoff missile
JWG	joint working group
KMT	Kuomintang
LACM	land attack cruise missile
LHD	amphibious assault ship
LPD	landing platform dock
LST	landing ship tank
LY	Legislative Yuan
MND	Taiwan Ministry of National Defense
NATO	North Atlantic Treaty Organization
NCO	noncommissioned officer
NDR	National Defense Report
OSCE	Organization for Security and Co-Operation in Europe

PGM	precision-guided munition
PLA	People's Liberation Army
PLAAF	People's Liberation Army Air Force
PLAN	People's Liberation Army Navy
PRC	People's Republic of China
QDR	Quadrennial Defense Review
RAS	replenishment at sea
ROC	Republic of China (Taiwan)
ROE	rules of engagement
ROK	Republic of Korea
RPG	rocket-propelled grenade
SAM	surface-to-air missile
SEF	Straits Exchange Foundation
SLOC	sea line of communication
SRBM	short-range ballistic missile
SSBN	ballistic missile submarine
TSU	Taiwan Solidarity Union
UAV	unmanned aerial vehicle
WHA	World Health Assembly

1. Recent Developments in Cross-Strait Relations and Their Security Implications: PRC Perspectives

Alan D. Romberg

Basis of Improvements

From Beijing's perspective, two main factors have contributed to the recent improvement in cross-Strait relations: Hu Jintao's policy of greater patience, with its focus on blocking independence rather than promoting reunification, and Ma Ying-jeou's accession to the presidency in Taiwan.

The former was, in part, a product of necessity. Not only was it increasingly evident over the Chen Shui-bian years that "peaceful reunification" was not possible anytime soon, but if Beijing allowed itself to be provoked into military action by statements and policies emanating from Taipei, it would have been at war in short order. As a result, it needed to slow down and get out of the *sine die* clause that suggested that Beijing would go to war if Taiwan put off negotiating peaceful reunification indefinitely, as well as other deadline traps the mainland had set for itself under Jiang Zemin. Under Hu Jintao's leadership, the mainland subtly shifted its stance on conflict with Taiwan to the standard of absolutely rejecting *de jure* independence, which eventually came to mean constitutional change in Taiwan's status, while resolving to merely be difficult over developments short of that.

Beyond that, however, perhaps reflecting a renewed sense of confidence that time was on its side, the People's Republic of China (PRC) under Hu has been willing to see reunification postponed indefinitely as long as the door is left open to that ultimate outcome and independence is not looming. This approach was codified in the Anti-Secession Law of March 2005 and was applied during a moment of substantial tension when the United Nations referendum was put on the ballot in March 2008.

The approach was not a passive one, even when Taiwan was governed by Chen Shui-bian. Though establishment of formal links proved infeasible due to a mutual lack of trust as well as some political gamesmanship on both sides, various cross-Strait relationships were created, ranging from substantial trade and investment ties to high-level party-to-party links between the KMT (Kuomintang) and CCP (Chinese Communist Party) during the period 2000–2008. By the end of Chen's tenure, somewhere between 1 and 2 million Taiwan citizens, representing 5 to 10 percent of the island's entire population, were living more or less full time on the mainland.

One has to presume that not everyone on the mainland, even at the Politburo level, was fully convinced of the wisdom of this approach. But Hu was able to pursue these ties even during Chen's administration because he "fireproofed" himself in two ways.

First, he wrapped himself in the cloak of the "one China principle" and the goal of reunification. The latter remained the unalterable objective, and in the meantime, everything that was done had to be within the framework of the former. It was obvious that Taipei didn't go along with either part of this formula, but as long as Beijing could justify each step as consistent with—or at least *not inconsistent* with—the "one China principle" and not closing the door on reunification, it was good enough for the mainland.

The second way in which Hu fireproofed himself was by making clear that he would crush any movement toward independence, under any name. This was not a new position, but combined with the other elements of his approach, it underscored both the firmness of his position against separatism and the strict limits he placed on what would lead to military confrontation.

The "other" (non–Article 8) provisions of the Anti-Secession Law articulated what has, with increasing clarity, come to form the heart of Beijing's approach to Taiwan: to reach out and form a vast web of mutually beneficial relationships. While hopefully setting the scene for peaceful reunification, these relationships were designed for the long period before that goal could ultimately be achieved, seeking to consolidate opposition within Taiwan to unilateral steps toward independence on an affirmative basis rather than merely out of fear of the consequences of stepping over red lines.

These positions, of course, came to have much greater salience once Ma Ying-jeou and the KMT took full control of the government, and Chen Shui-bian and the Democratic Progressive Party (DPP) were consigned (at least temporarily) to the political wilderness. Ma was forced by the realities of Taiwan politics to set aside the KMT doctrine on ultimate unification with a democratic, market-oriented mainland run under the rule of law, and to state that final decisions on Taiwan's relationship with the mainland were up to the people of Taiwan. Nonetheless, even though it was obvious that unification was not an option for the foreseeable future, both because of his party's formal doctrine and because of his own "mainlander" roots, he had to take the unusual step of affirmatively foreswearing even discussing it during his term of office.

The unification issue aside, however—and, as will be discussed later, it is clear that some on the mainland have not set it aside—Ma's basic approach to cross-Strait relations accorded very well with Hu's. Although Ma insists on the sovereign independence of the Republic of China (ROC) as reflected in the ROC constitution, he wanted to take the irresolvable sovereignty issue off the table both in direct cross-Strait dealings and in his efforts to obtain greater "international space" for Taiwan. Beijing welcomed the relief from Chen Shui-bian's insistent efforts to gain recognition for Taiwan in the international community as a separate, sovereign entity, and it welcomed Ma's stated willingness to work with Beijing on realizing Taiwan's international aspirations rather than, as both Lee Teng-hui and Chen Shui-bian had done, merely insisting.

Ma's pragmatism in these respects has caused him a certain level of domestic political grief, but it has been crucial for obtaining PRC cooperation in working with him not only to realize the World Health Assembly (WHA) observership goal laid out as a joint objective as early as April 2005 when Lien Chan and Hu Jintao adopted their five-point consensus, but also to expand to an even more ambitious agenda.

Sustainability

On the one hand, there is every reason to assume that, whatever the temporary ups and downs this process may encounter, the basic trend is set. Continuing on the present course is clearly in the interests of both sides—at least economically and, arguably, in political and security terms as well, though we will return to this issue—as seen not only by the authorities but also by the public on both sides of the Strait. From a PRC perspective, the pragmatic cooperation currently being pursued promotes ultimate peaceful reunification while lessening independence demands and forestalling conflict. In so doing, it also largely removes a thorn in the side of Sino-American relations, permitting smoother, more far-ranging cooperation on a broad range of issues important to Beijing.

That said, the current approach is not without uncertainties and risks. Even if sustained, it will not necessarily remove all of the problems inherent in having Taiwan remain separate from the mainland, including the U.S. security relationship with the island (especially U.S. arms sales to Taiwan) and the impact of that relationship on PRC strategic relations with the United States. And while it potentially can help to—perhaps quite significantly—tip the scales against independence, even there it does not guarantee anything.

As PRC officials and analysts are quick to point out, Taiwan's robust democracy could bring the DPP back into office. This is especially a concern if Ma continues to be seen as inept in responding to the needs of the people of Taiwan, whether the result of the burdens of economic downturn, the effects of natural disasters, or the perceived costs of his cross-Strait and foreign (especially U.S.) policies. Public opinion polls, plus the attitudes of all major countries in the world, strongly suggest that the mainland vastly overstates the risk of any Taiwan leader being successful in promoting *de jure* independence or Taiwan's acceptance as a sovereign entity in the international community. But until the day of unification, it will remain a PRC concern.

One consequence is that, even if tensions remain low, the formal state of hostilities ends, a peace accord is reached, and a political framework for long-term peace and stability across the Strait is created, the People's Liberation Army (PLA) will maintain the capability to deter and, if necessary, defeat any efforts by Taiwan to formalize its independence. And that means that Taiwan will need to maintain a sufficient level of self-defense capability to make the cost of any use of force against the island very high, including a sufficient force to enable Taipei to hold out until U.S. forces could come to the rescue. This imperative, in turn, means that the United States will, in all probability, continue to sell defensive arms to Taiwan and maintain the other aspects of its security relationship with Taiwan. These steps will help ensure, on the one hand, that military force will not be threatened or used by the mainland and, on the other hand, that Taipei feels sufficiently confident to negotiate steps with Beijing that can contribute to long-term peace and stability. The net effect on PRC calculations about the success of its cross-Strait policies is hard to determine in the abstract.

Another uncertainty is the gnawing sense among many in Beijing that Ma may be strongly opposed to *de jure* independence but that he is consolidating *de facto* independence, or "peaceful separation" as it is increasingly being called. But the ironic fact is that Ma's ability to continue to move along the course he and Hu Jintao have laid out requires that the Taiwan public have confidence that its future is not being determined, willy-nilly, by growing interdependence with the mainland. This creates a dilemma for Beijing: consolidation of the sense of *de facto* separate status is actually required if further progress is to be made.

One can square that circle if one thinks far enough into the future about the likely outcome of the current relationships—and if one is willing to think flexibly enough about definitions of such concepts as "one China," "reunification," and "sovereignty." However, applying such farseeing approaches to the mainland's Taiwan policy is in fact very hard for many in Beijing. Thus, coping with these kinds of concerns will not be easy.

In considering what arrangements the PRC should seek to fashion in the short to medium term, one needs to take into account the democratic reality of Taiwan in another sense. Any cross-Strait agreements reached need to be sustainable across changes in administration in Taipei in the years ahead. This includes transitions to other KMT governments that might follow Ma but also, and probably even more importantly, the need to be sustainable over transitions to future DPP governments and future Legislative Yuans.

Thus, for example, although some on the mainland would like to use the vehicles of military mutual trust mechanisms and, especially, a peace accord to try to force Taiwan to adopt a more explicit formula on "one China" going beyond the "1992 Consensus," any attempt to do so would very likely end in failure, setting back not only political but also economic relations. There are many on the mainland who understand this and would have Hu (and his successors) avoid any such self-defeating effort. But the pressure to move in this direction is insistent and, when one thinks of consolidating the status quo, one needs to think about how to continue fending off such counterproductive lines of attack.

We also see growing PRC pressure for "reciprocity" in cross-Strait arrangements. As discussed below, this is quite evident in the handling of the Economic Cooperation Framework Agreement (ECFA) that the two sides negotiated over several months, as well as in a number of mainland articles and speeches about the way to approach military mutual trust-building measures and mechanisms. This is not illogical, and, politically, a certain degree of reciprocity is probably necessary to ensure the continuing support of important PRC constituencies. But taken too far, it will undermine the perceived beneficial effects in Taiwan and subvert Hu's long-range strategic vision of cross-Strait relations.

Perhaps not so coincidentally, the resentment at being presented by Ma with *faits accomplis* to which Beijing has been "expected" to adjust has not diminished and probably has contributed to at least some of the pushback on ECFA and in other areas.[1] Strategic thinking in Beijing has largely overridden the irritation, but Ma will need to be careful that he doesn't exceed Beijing's patience.

Overall, across the period of Ma's tenure, the mainland has gained some confidence that he is, as promised, not going to pose a direct challenge on the issue of sovereignty and that he has not "assumed" too much by way of PRC tolerance on "international space," instead moving rather cautiously. Indeed, from the PRC's perspective, one problem has been Ma's reluctance to move as quickly on issues related to political dialogue as Beijing wants.

All of that said, while nothing is preordained, the likelihood is that there will be further progress.

---

[1] Examples of such steps include Ma's insistence on the July 4 start date for weekend charters in 2008, his call for a "diplomatic truce," his assertion that both sides adhere to "mutual non-denial," and his unilateral shift from a *Comprehensive* Economic Cooperation Agreement, which Hu had endorsed in his December 31, 2008, speech, to an Economic Cooperation Framework Agreement.

Key Issues on the Agenda

Although, as noted, Ma has made clear that even discussing "unification" during his term of office is off the table, in his inaugural address he did not shrink from the idea of political, including security-related, dialogue: "We will also enter consultations with mainland China over Taiwan's international space and a possible cross-Strait peace accord."

In fact, it can be argued that Ma hoped to proceed with a peace accord even in his first term. As domestic political reality caught up with him, however, it appears that he put it off until after his reelection. Although some well-informed PRC observers state that completing a peace accord before he leaves office is not a high priority for Hu Jintao, others disagree. The latter group argues that anything major not completed by the fall of 2012, when Hu steps down from his party leadership position, will likely remain uncompleted for several years. Not only is there no guarantee that the next leader will share Hu's enthusiasm for approaching Taiwan in accordance with present guidelines, but he will necessarily be focused on consolidating his power and influence in other, more pressing areas. And in that case, the air could go out of the cross-Strait balloon, with unpredictable effects on Taiwan's domestic politics and, hence, on the course of cross-Strait relations.

Experts on both sides have pointed to the roughly six-month "window of opportunity" between Ma's (possible) reelection in March 2012 and Hu's departure. But the reality is that, if the fundamental groundwork has not been laid before then, the period will likely be far too short to put major new initiatives into place.

To some extent, it may be this consideration that has led Beijing to argue for the very preliminary phases of political dialogue even now. The logic is that military mutual trust measures and mechanisms must be preceded by the creation of greater political trust, and that requires a long period of exchanges and experience, starting from such things as meetings between retired military officers and "track II" dialogues. Although some activities along both lines are proceeding even today and are certainly known to both governments, they do not have official sanction.

Despite—or perhaps because of—mutual agreement that economic issues should precede political/security ones, and that easy issues should be tackled before more difficult ones (and Ma's third provision: that urgent issues should precede those that can wait), Taipei perceived the PRC's proposals for political dialogue as pressure. Although some nongovernment specialists don't deny that Beijing was applying pressure, responsible mainland government officials do. The latter argue that the relationship cannot be sustained over the long term by economic agreements alone. As seen in the Chen Shui-bian era, even when there is very substantial economic interaction, with huge financial resources and large numbers of people involved, if the relationship does not have a political underpinning, it can go badly off the tracks. Moreover, they argue, even economic relationships themselves will be threatened eventually if a climate of reliable peace and stability is not created. So the point is, they say, that political dialogue at some point is not a luxury but a necessity.

That being said, the number of references to political dialogue dropped substantially after Taipei's concerns were brought more clearly to Beijing's attention in early fall 2009.[2] So perhaps Ma's concern about the counterproductive effect of the PRC's insistent references to the subject registered.

On the other hand, the PRC view of this is logical from where it sits, and one should not expect the issue to go away.

Whenever such dialogue does take place, one possible showstopper would be if, as discussed earlier, the mainland insists that Taiwan endorse a more explicit formulation on "one China." Taipei officials are convinced that this will be the first topic Beijing puts on the table when the two sides sit down to discuss a peace accord or even confidence-building measures (CBMs).

As suggested earlier, any attempt by Beijing to strong-arm Taipei on this issue will likely doom the entire endeavor to failure and could very well set overall relations back. Although those managing the PRC's Taiwan policy now seem to understand this, whether the internal political dynamic on this issue within the PRC—one that by its very nature will involve the PLA, reported to be among the greatest skeptics about the appropriateness of Hu's approach—will lead to a successful outcome remains to be seen. Timing—that is, whether the effort is made before Hu steps down and the context in terms of cross-Strait and Sino-American relations—could be crucial.

Domestic Support

As just suggested, not all aspects of Hu's approach are universally applauded. The military on the mainland, just as the military on Taiwan, appears to take a harder-line, more skeptical view. One area of skepticism has to do with unilateral concessions. In particular, some have suggested that going along with Ma's stated "precondition" for negotiating a peace accord (i.e., that the short-range missiles opposite Taiwan must be drawn down) is unacceptable. Perhaps, they say, the missiles could be moved or otherwise reduced, but only as the product of a negotiation in which each side makes concessions. In this case, the reciprocal concession from Taiwan that such analysts have in mind seems to be related to U.S. arms sales and other security relations with Taipei.

Moreover, as the ECFA experience shows, economic constituencies on the mainland are also becoming more insistent on reciprocity. It is clear that Taipei will not open its market to all PRC agricultural or even manufactured products, that it will limit mainland services in Taiwan in various ways, and that blue-collar labor, especially, will not be welcome to work on the island, even in PRC-invested firms. Hu is likely to be able to deal with the complaints, but as with everything else, that could well depend on other aspects of the broader context.

---

[2] The only reference in late 2009 by the Taiwan Affairs Office, for example, was in response to a question at the regular press briefing on October 14. The questioner referred to Ma's National Day speech, in which he pointed to the continuing military threat from the mainland. The spokesman said, "Regarding the military issue between the two sides of the Strait, we already made it clear long ago, that is, we hope that the two sides of the Strait will further strengthen exchanges and that the solution to the military issue between the two sides of the Strait should proceed with the exploration and establishment of a military mutual trust mechanism."

The most serious problem from domestic critics could come in the form of sustained opposition to making "concessions" to Taiwan without linking them to PRC gains on the sovereignty issue and unification. As opposed to the reciprocity issues just discussed, any attack from this angle would raise questions about Hu's entire strategy toward Taiwan, not just his tactics. Beyond the very serious implications they could have for cross-Strait relations, and potentially for Sino-American relations, developments in this regard could be an important indicator of Hu's relative strength during the remainder of his tenure.

In all these respects, if Ma seems to be in real political trouble—meaning a level of problems well beyond anything we have seen to date—then it is possible that mainland skeptics will speak with a louder voice, questioning the point of making "concessions" to Taipei when the prospects for a DPP return to power seem all the greater. The irony, of course, is that this could become a self-fulfilling prophecy, as PRC reticence would only contribute to the possibility of a DPP victory. But be that as it may, it could become the relevant dynamic.

Bargaining Positions/Increasing Cooperation

All of this points to the question of *how* the two sides seek to deal with each other. Thus far, for the most part, the mainland has kept to the high road, playing the long game. That is, even if it appears that Beijing is taking most of the initiatives and making most of the compromises, it has been seen as serving the PRC's short-term interest in blocking the DPP (and supporting Ma) and its "medium-term" (maybe several-decades-long) interest in consolidating peace and stability and putting the independence issue to bed, as well as, especially, its long-term interest in promoting peaceful reunification.

From that perspective, tit-for-tat bargaining has not been the essential negotiating framework. Despite the increasing element of reciprocity in PRC positions on some issues, overall, it still does not appear to be the driving force. And although, as suggested earlier, there is not likely to be a change in this approach, one would be foolish to rule it out if there are major changes in the context—in Taiwan, on the mainland, or in the international community.

In addition, whether there will be substantially greater "proactive" cooperation is also a bit dubious. There could be some, especially in such areas as joint exploration/exploitation of seabed resources, etc. (i.e., things essentially confined to a cross-Strait context). Internationally, however, while not impossible, substantial cooperation seems much less likely.

One question is whether the "diplomatic truce" can hold. Viewed objectively, it should. It serves the interests of both sides. But that will require that Hu's strategic vision of cross-Strait relations continues to dominate, and we have already alluded to several factors that could upset that. Moreover, especially after Hu steps down, a new leader might find that picking off two or three of Taiwan's diplomatic partners is a reasonably cheap and (he would hope) not-too-destabilizing way of showing his toughness early in his tenure. What the unintended consequences of such a move might be, however, are open to speculation.

In any event, to the extent that issues of sovereignty can be avoided, as well as disputes over who is the superior and who is the inferior partner in any given endeavor, perhaps some other cooperation might be possible. But it is not likely to be of major significance in the near to medium term.

Security Implications

One obvious implication is that tensions should remain low, perhaps extending to CBMs and the like, and possibly even extending to a peace accord. If the latter—the essential core of which would be an exchange of Taiwan's commitment not to move to *de jure* independence so long as the PRC does not use force and the PRC's pledge not to use force so long as Taiwan does not move to independence—then there should be reasonable confidence that confrontation and war can be ruled out.

But as we've said, until the day of unification, Taiwan independence will remain a mainland concern and, thus, so will the maintenance of the military capability to deal with it. In turn, Taiwan will seek to maintain a reasonably robust defense, and the United States will help in that regard. How comfortable all three parties are that a sustainable political framework exists for the peaceful development of cross-Strait relations will be a central determinant of whether these efforts by all three can be held to a minimum.

Even if confidence is high and deployments (including arms sales) are altered in a major way, surely the PLA will continue apace to modernize and expand its military capabilities across the board. Just because the Taiwan issue has been a galvanizing factor in modernization so far does not mean that it will be a necessary factor to sustain the effort into the future. Nonetheless, in light of PLA growth, policies of mutual reassurance across the Strait could be compromised so that suspicion and agitation continue to bubble beneath the formal structures of cross-Strait peace.

To sum up, overall, one has to say that the trends right now are very positive. But one needs to temper this with a significant dose of realism about the continuing sense of mutual unease about the fact that the two sides have very different long-term ambitions.

2. The Security Implications of China-Taiwan Economic Integration

Scott L. Kastner

Prior to the election of Ma Ying-jeou as Taiwan's president in 2008, the phrase "hot economics, cold politics" succinctly summarized the nature of the China-Taiwan relationship. Despite hostile political relations and occasional crises, economic ties grew rapidly beginning in the late 1980s; by the early 2000s, China had become Taiwan's largest trading partner. Since Ma's election, however, the political relationship has improved dramatically. The two sides are engaged in regular dialogue and have reached numerous agreements on such issues as direct flights across the Taiwan Strait and allowing Chinese tourists to visit Taiwan; both sides have even indicated some interest in trying to reach a peace accord.[1]

Whether the détente in cross-Strait relations is a permanent thaw or merely a temporary warming remains unclear. The People's Republic of China (PRC) continues to modernize its military capabilities, and it has not stopped adding to, much less reduced, the large number of missiles deployed in range of Taiwan. In addition, Ma Ying-jeou's job approval ratings have been lackluster since 2009, meaning that the island's future political direction is uncertain.[2] Given the continuing Chinese threat and the potential that Ma's soft approach to cross-Strait relations could be replaced in 2012 if the Democratic Progressive Party (DPP) were to return to power, the impact of underlying trends—especially the deepening of cross-Strait economic integration on cross-Strait security relations—remains important for scholars to understand. For instance, does deepening economic integration help reduce the likelihood of a future military confrontation? Does Taiwan's growing economic dependence on the PRC undercut the island's security, perhaps making it less able to resist unification on the PRC's terms? This paper explores these topics. It begins with a short overview of cross-Strait economic ties.

Trends in Cross-Strait Economic Integration

Economic ties between the PRC and Taiwan have grown rapidly over the past two dozen years. Trade across the Taiwan Strait ballooned from less than US$1 billion per year in the mid-1980s to over US$100 billion by 2007.[3] Estimates of Taiwan's investments in the PRC since the 1980s run as high as US$150 billion.[4] The PRC has

---

[1] Phillip C. Saunders and Scott L. Kastner, "Bridge over Troubled Water? Envisioning a China-Taiwan Peace Agreement." *International Security*, Vol. 33, No. 4, Spring 2009.

[2] A January 2011 Global Views Survey Research Center poll found a 40-percent approval rating and a 47-percent disapproval rating. This actually represents a significant improvement from earlier polls. See Global Views Survey Research Center, "Survey on President Ma Ying-jeou's Approval Rating," January 21, 2011.

[3] Unless otherwise noted, cross-Strait trade and investment statistics are based on Taiwan's Mainland Affairs Council estimates of trade and investment flows between Taiwan and mainland China (excluding Hong Kong), reported in *Liang'an Jingji Tongji Yuebao* [*Cross-Straits Statistics Monthly*], various issues.

[4] Jonathan Adams, "Exuberance in Taiwan as Ties with China Warm," *New York Times*, May 13, 2009.

replaced the United States as Taiwan's largest trading partner and is, by far, the primary destination of the island's outbound foreign direct investment. Economic integration across the Taiwan Strait has proceeded despite persistent tensions in China-Taiwan relations. Indeed, cross-Strait trade accelerated even as China-Taiwan political relations deteriorated markedly during the Chen Shui-bian presidency (2000–2008).

Both Chen and his predecessor, Lee Teng-hui (1988–2000), were deeply skeptical of the political and economic benefits of expanding economic ties with the PRC. As cross-Strait trade and investment flows grew rapidly during the 1990s, the Lee administration adopted policies to slow the pace of cross-Strait economic integration. Although early Taiwan investors in China tended to be labor-intensive industries moving outdated production facilities to the PRC in order to take advantage of cheaper labor costs, by the 1990s, many of Taiwan's larger, more advanced firms were also eyeing the rapidly growing mainland market.

In response, the Lee administration banned individual investment projects in China that exceeded US$50 million and also placed restrictions on the types of facilities in which Taiwanese companies could invest. Furthermore, Lee maintained longstanding prohibitions against direct trade or travel across the Taiwan Strait. The Chen administration relaxed some of these restrictions. For instance, the US$50 million cap on individual investment projects was scrapped, and Chen also relaxed some of the restrictions in place on high-technology investments in China. Yet significant barriers remained in place under Chen, including the ban on direct travel and shipping linkages, tight regulations on cutting-edge technology investments, and prohibitions on most kinds of potential PRC investments in Taiwan.[5]

In contrast to the Chen and Lee administrations, the Ma Ying-jeou (2008–present) administration unambiguously welcomed cross-Strait economic integration. Since Ma has been president, his government has signed numerous economic agreements with Beijing. These agreements have—among other things—opened direct shipping and air transport links with the PRC, opened Taiwan to PRC tourists, and increased financial cooperation between the two sides. Taiwan has also relaxed restrictions on many kinds of PRC investments in the island. Despite the change in policy, cross-Strait trade dropped sharply in 2009 as a consequence of the global recession, declining nearly 18 percent from the previous year. But growth in cross-Strait trade resumed in the fall of 2009.

The Ma administration inked a far-reaching Economic Cooperation Framework Agreement (ECFA) with the PRC last year. The agreement provides a roadmap for further liberalization in cross-Strait trade and economic flows and includes an extensive "early harvest" list of goods subject to accelerated tariff-reduction schedules. Ma administration officials have emphasized that the ECFA will keep Taiwan's exports from being at a disadvantage

---

[5] For discussions of the evolution of Taiwan's economic policies toward the PRC under the Lee and Chen administrations, see, for instance, Scott L. Kastner, *Political Conflict and Economic Interdependence Across the Taiwan Strait and Beyond*, Stanford, Calif.: Stanford University Press, 2009, and Murray Scot Tanner, *Chinese Economic Coercion Against Taiwan: A Tricky Weapon to Use*, Santa Monica, Calif.: RAND Corporation, MG-507-OSD, 2007.

relative to those of other countries and regions moving forward with free-trade agreements (FTAs) with China, such as ASEAN (the Association of Southeast Asian Nations).[6] Daniel Rosen writes, however, that Taiwan's primary gains from an ECFA would arise not from liberalized trade opportunities with its neighbors but from improved allocation of capital within Taiwan, stemming from improved competition from China made possible by reductions in barriers to cross-Strait economic integration. An ECFA would also be beneficial to Taiwan to the extent that it opens the door for Taiwan to sign FTAs with other countries in the region; currently, concern over offending the PRC has discouraged other major countries from seriously considering signing FTAs with Taiwan.[7] Whether an ECFA would really change that dynamic, however, remains to be seen.

The remainder of this paper briefly explores some of the different political/security consequences of cross-Strait economic integration. It focuses, in particular, on two questions: Does economic integration make military conflict less likely? And, does economic integration have significant implications for Taiwan's security?

Does Economic Integration Between China and Taiwan Reduce the Likelihood of Military Conflict?

Economic integration is believed by many observers to have a stabilizing impact on cross-Strait security relations, and for this reason, the U.S. government has generally encouraged China-Taiwan economic cooperation.[8] For instance, in testimony before Congress in April 2004, then–U.S. Assistant Secretary of State James Kelly argued that U.S. policy had helped create an "environment in which cross-Strait people-to-people exchanges and cross-Strait trade are flourishing and creating, we hope, the necessary conditions for peaceful resolution of cross-Strait differences."[9] In a similar vein, a U.S. State Department spokesman quoted in the *Taipei Times* on February 1, 2006, summarized U.S. policy concerning cross-Strait economic integration as follows: "We support expansion of transportation and communication links across the Strait aimed at increasing political, economic, social and cultural exchanges with a view to increasing mutual understanding and diminishing the chances of miscommunication or misunderstanding."

In theory, economic integration between China and Taiwan can reduce the likelihood of a cross-Strait military confrontation in at least three ways.[10]

---

[6] This section is based on author's interviews with officials, spring 2009.

[7] Daniel Rosen, "What Are the Implications of Taiwan-China Economic Liberalization?" Washington, D.C.: Center for Strategic and International Studies, Freeman Report, September 2009.

[8] This section draws heavily on material presented in Kastner, 2009, Chapter 6, and Scott L. Kastner, "Does Economic Integration Across the Taiwan Strait Make Military Conflict Less Likely?" *Journal of East Asian Studies*, Vol. 6, No. 3, Fall 2006.

[9] Kelly's prepared statement further noted, "In the absence of a political dialogue, we encourage the two sides to increase bilateral interactions of every sort. Clearly, there would be economic benefits for both sides by proceeding with direct aviation and shipping links. The increasing people-to-people contacts may also ease tensions."

[10] The three mechanisms described here are drawn from existing international relations literature on trade and conflict. For a more detailed description of each mechanism, and more references to specific literatures, see Kastner, 2009, Chapter 6.

First, economic integration can raise the costs of military conflict for both sides; at a minimum, serious military conflict would most likely lead to a prolonged interruption in cross-Strait trade, and it is easy to imagine more dire, and long-term, consequences.[11] That Taiwan and China have become deeply embedded in global information technology supply chains serves to magnify the potential costs of a disruption in cross-Strait trade, and indeed means that such a disruption would potentially have profound effects on the global economy more broadly.[12] As the costs of military conflict increase, it is possible that leaders on both sides will be more cautious about using force or adopting policies that could risk escalation.[13]

Second, economic integration can potentially foster a transformation in the policy preferences of the two governments, especially in Taiwan, which is much more dependent on the relationship.[14] In particular, a growing number of Taiwanese have a direct stake in a stable cross-Strait economic relationship. In turn, actors in Taiwan who benefit from cross-Strait economic exchange may be less likely to support candidates who will emphasize sovereignty-related issues, fearing that such candidates will provoke conflict with Beijing. Economic integration, in other words, may facilitate some convergence in the preferences of the governments in Taipei and Beijing over sovereignty-related issues; conflict, in turn, becomes less likely as countries come to share more similar underlying preferences.

Third, cross-Strait economic integration may make it easier for Beijing to coerce Taiwan or to signal resolve credibly without resorting to military measures.[15] Leaders in Taiwan may have some uncertainty concerning PRC resolve to use military force should Taiwan take concrete steps to consolidate its sovereign status; PRC threats in this regard are inherently suspect, since talk is relatively cheap. War could result if Taiwan concludes that a truly resolved PRC is bluffing. But economic integration gives Beijing a way to communicate its resolve more credibly if Taipei tests it: In particular, China can impose economic sanctions, which demonstrate a willingness to

---

[11] For an example of this sort of "opportunity-costs" argument linking conflict and trade, see Solomon William Polachek, "Conflict and Trade," *Journal of Conflict Resolution*, Vol. 24, No. 1, March 1980. For a critique, see Jack S. Levy, "Economic Interdependence, Opportunity Costs, and Peace," in Edward D. Mansfield and Brian M. Pollins, eds., *Economic Interdependence and International Conflict: New Perspectives on an Enduring Debate*, Ann Arbor, Mich.: University of Michigan Press, 2003.

[12] On this point, see Stephen G. Brooks, *Producing Security: Multinational Corporations, Globalization, and the Changing Calculus of Conflict*, Princeton, N.J.: Princeton University Press, 2007; see also Thomas L. Friedman, *The World is Flat: A Brief History of the Twenty-First Century*, New York: Farrar, Straus and Giroux, 2005.

[13] It is worth emphasizing that the economic consequences of a cross-Strait military conflict would almost certainly extend far beyond cross-Strait economic ties. Indeed, such a conflict would likely have a significant impact on both sides' broader links with the global economy. Thus, as China becomes more integrated into global markets, a cross-Strait conflict will potentially have more significant, and devastating, consequences for China's continued economic development.

[14] On engagement policies that seek to harness such transformative effects, see Miles Kahler and Scott L. Kastner, "Strategic Uses of Economic Interdependence: Engagement Policies on the Korean Peninsula and Across the Taiwan Strait," *Journal of Peace Research*, Vol. 43, No. 5, September 2006.

[15] For an argument linking economic integration to improved signaling efficiency, see Erik Gartzke, Quan Li, and Charles Boehmer, "Investing in the Peace: Economic Interdependence and International Conflict," *International Organization*, Vol. 55, No. 2, Spring 2001.

pay high costs to block Taiwan independence. In essence, economic integration may reduce the likelihood of war because it provides Beijing with ways to punish Taiwan without resorting to military violence.

Economic integration can thus potentially lead to a reduced likelihood of cross-Strait military conflict through several distinct processes. However, such an effect should not be assumed to hold true. Before concluding that China-Taiwan economic integration does reduce the danger of war, it would be important to confirm that one or more of these causal processes is, in fact, playing out in the Taiwan Strait. Indeed, there are some reasons for skepticism. For instance, deepening economic integration has not reversed a general upward trend in the percentage of Taiwan's citizens who self-identify as "Taiwanese" (as opposed to identifying as either "Chinese" or "both Chinese and Taiwanese"). Similarly, public opinion polls in Taiwan suggest declining support for unification, even as a long-term solution.[16] While it is important to be cautious in drawing inference from these trends (for instance, perhaps the trends would be even more pronounced if not for deepening economic integration), they do nonetheless suggest that some caution is also warranted in speculating that cross-Strait economic ties will ineluctably lead to a fundamental transformation in Taiwan's foreign policy preferences.

Moreover, it is quite possible that economic integration can actually be destabilizing in certain contexts. For instance, if economic integration does indeed raise the costs of war for Beijing, then Taiwan's president may be tempted to "push the envelope" on sovereignty issues farther than he otherwise might. And to the extent that economic integration is expected to generate the sort of transformative effects on Taiwan's policy preferences noted above, a pro-independence leader of Taiwan may be more likely to conclude that "time is not on our side." Fearing that support for consolidation of Taiwan's sovereignty will only decline in the future, he may calculate that action is needed in the short term, potentially increasing cross-Strait tensions as a result. Finally, while economic integration may give Beijing an increased ability to punish Taiwan without using military force, the PRC would also face significant constraints in this regard. Sanctions, for instance, would impose considerable economic costs on China as well as Taiwan. Sanctions also have the potential to backfire because they would harm most the very actors—such as the Taiwan business community—that already have a strong stake in a stable and peaceful relationship with China.[17]

Does Economic Integration Harm Taiwan's Security?

Even if we accept that economic integration across the Taiwan Strait does indeed reduce the potential for military violence, the implications for Taiwan's security require further examination. Indeed, some of the potentially

---

16 In regular polls commissioned by Taiwan's Mainland Affairs Council, the percentage of respondents saying that they support the status quo for now and unification later has remained under 10 percent in recent years (after hovering between 14 and 21 percent in the early 2000s). Support for immediate unification has been consistently minimal. Poll results for the last ten years are available online at http://www.mac.gov.tw/public/MMO/MAC/9809e_1.gif.

17 For a thorough discussion of some of the difficulties China would likely face in trying to use economic coercion against Taiwan, see Tanner, 2007.

stabilizing effects of economic integration are stabilizing precisely because they constrain Taiwan's options or magnify China's coercive capacities vis-à-vis the island. For instance, that the PRC can now impose costly economic sanctions against Taiwan may make it less likely that China will have to resort to military options in efforts to coerce or signal resolve toward Taiwan. But this should hardly make Taiwan feel more secure: On the contrary, economic integration in this scenario makes it possible for Beijing to exercise influence over Taiwan more efficiently.

Whether cross-Strait economic integration is, on balance, harmful or beneficial (or neither) to Taiwan's security is a controversial issue on the island. Many, especially within the DPP-centered "pan-Green" coalition, are deeply pessimistic about the security implications of Taiwan's growing economic dependence on the PRC. These observers worry, in particular, that Taiwan's economic dependence on China makes it more vulnerable to PRC economic statecraft. That PRC officials and scholars openly acknowledge the political motivations of PRC efforts to expand cross-Strait economic interactions intensifies these concerns. And Beijing has certainly shown some willingness to politicize economic ties. For instance, after the 2000 and 2004 Taiwan elections, some pro-DPP businesses operating in China were harassed.[18] More recently, Chinese officials have encouraged mainland tour groups to cancel trips to southern Taiwan after local leaders invited the Dalai Lama to visit and hosted a film festival that screened a documentary about Uighur activist Rebiya Kadeer.[19] Whether or not these sorts of efforts are successful, at a minimum they intensify concerns among many Taiwanese about the political consequences of expanded economic linkages with the PRC. As DPP Chairwoman Tsai Ing-Wen has put it, "China has maintained a consistent economic strategy against Taiwan that involves making it part of the greater China economic sphere and enslaving Taiwan to China's economy."[20]

There are other potential security pitfalls associated with Taiwan's economic ties to China. For instance, the flow of Taiwanese technology and know-how to the PRC helps make the PRC stronger economically and, indirectly, militarily. Some have suggested that increased personnel flows across the Taiwan Strait may make PRC espionage against Taiwan easier.[21] And, from the standpoint of those favoring a formally independent Taiwan, the possibility that economic integration might transform Taiwan's domestic political dynamics would certainly be seen as a negative security consequence of cross-Strait economic linkages.

Others in Taiwan, including President Ma Ying-jeou, are more optimistic concerning the security implications of China-Taiwan economic ties. Ma believes that economic integration can have more balanced, and

---

[18] Elsewhere (*Political Conflict*, 2009, Chapter 5), I argue that China seems reluctant to push harassment of pro-DPP businesses too far. See also Tanner, 2007, on this case.

[19] "China Tells Tourists to Boycott Taiwan City over Dalai Lama: Report," Agence France Presse, September 17, 2009.

[20] Tsai Ing-wen, "CECA Comes with Big Hidden Costs," *Taipei Times*, March 1, 2009.

[21] See, e.g., J. Michael Cole, "Paradigm Shift: Expanded Opportunities for Chinese Espionage Against Taiwan," Taipei: MacArthur Center for Security Studies, October 19, 2009.

positive, transformative effects on the cross-Strait relationship; in particular, increased contacts and exchange can help to build trust and understanding. As he put it in a 2008 interview, "Only by more contact, more understanding, more exchange [can] we reduce the historical hostilities across the Taiwan Strait."[22] Officials in the Ma administration also believe that failure to normalize cross-Strait economic ties (and failure to reach an ECFA with Beijing) make Taiwan more vulnerable to economic marginalization: As countries in East Asia move toward regional integration, Taiwan will be shut out, unable to sign FTAs with other major states, such as the United States or Japan.[23] Likewise, continued barriers to cross-Strait trade may act as a drag on long-term economic growth in Taiwan, which over time will influence Taiwan's security, since military power ultimately rests on a strong economy.[24]

The considerable disagreement in Taiwan about the security consequences of deepening cross-Strait economic integration ultimately arises from a number of sources.

First, economic integration has differential effects on Taiwan's security; some consequences are clearly negative, others positive. Sorting through the relative importance of these different effects is complicated, and people are likely to reach different conclusions.

Second, whether an actor views cross-Strait economic integration as helping or hurting Taiwan's security may hinge, in part, on that actor's preferences regarding the cross-Strait sovereignty dispute.[25] Suppose, for instance, that economic integration both makes it harder for pro-independence candidates to be elected in Taiwan and makes the PRC more reluctant to initiate military conflict. Taiwan's citizens who are happy with the cross-Strait status quo would probably see such an outcome in a positive light—as contributing to peace while not undercutting the autonomy Taiwan currently enjoys. But Taiwanese hoping for formal independence may view such an effect more negatively.

Finally, cross-Strait economic ties also have strong distributional consequences in Taiwan. Those who stand to be hurt by economic integration (including some farmers, unskilled laborers, and perhaps even some skilled workers in industries relocating to the PRC) should naturally be inclined to emphasize the negative security consequences; those who gain most directly (especially owners of mobile capital, but many others too) should be expected to accentuate the positive. Given these different sources of disagreement concerning the security

---

[22] Ma also argued that "when you have more trade, more investment, more contact—cultural, educational—particularly among the young people, when they make friends with their contemporaries on the other side of the Taiwan Strait, I'm sure friendship, . . . cooperation instead of hostility, will grow." See "An Interview with President Ma Ying-jeou," *New York Times*, June 19, 2008.

[23] See, for example, "ECFA with China to Help U.S. FTA: Yuan," *China Post*, April 16, 2009.

[24] See Rosen, 2009, on this point.

[25] This point is developed at greater length in Scott L. Kastner, "Drinking Poison to Quench a Thirst? The Security Consequences of China-Taiwan Economic Integration," paper presented at the Association for Asian Studies annual meeting, Philadelphia, Pa., March 2010.

consequences of China-Taiwan economic integration, consensus on the issue is likely to prove difficult. This is especially the case because there is a clear partisan dimension to the disagreement.

Conclusion

Despite what, at times, has been a hostile political relationship, economic integration across the Taiwan Strait has proceeded rapidly since the 1980s, the recent global slowdown notwithstanding. While China-Taiwan relations have improved substantially since Ma Ying-jeou took office last year, the potential for renewed tension certainly exists. As such, an understanding of the political consequences of China-Taiwan economic integration remains important. As this paper makes clear, however, these consequences are far from straightforward. Two points are worth emphasizing. First, although there are several plausible ways in which expanding cross-Strait economic links can reduce the danger of military conflict in the Taiwan Strait, there are also reasons to be cautious in assuming that these causal processes will actually materialize. Second, whether economic ties with China have a net positive or negative effect on Taiwan's security is the subject of some controversy in Taiwan. This controversy stems, in part, from the differential security-related effects of economic integration. But because the controversy involves an issue with significant distributional consequences, and because an actor's views on the subject are likely to be conditioned by that actor's views on the cross-Strait sovereignty dispute, consensus is unlikely.

3. China's Approach to CBMs with Taiwan: Lessons from China's CBMs with Neighboring Countries

Bonnie S. Glaser

Chinese military researchers emphasize that the cross-Strait mechanism of mutual trust in the military and security fields proposed by Chinese Communist Party (CCP) General Secretary Hu Jintao in December 2008 is a special arrangement based on the special circumstances in relations between Taiwan and the mainland. This reflects Beijing's concern that confidence-building measures (CBMs) between the two sides of the Strait not be used to legitimize the existence of Taiwan as a separate, sovereign state. Nevertheless, the Chinese recognize that there are useful experiences to be gleaned from the use of CBMs in other parts of the world and from China's own experiences in implementing CBMs with its neighbors. They accept that the main objective of CBMs, broadly defined, is to ease tensions and improve mutual trust, while in the narrow military sense these measures serve to minimize the risk of accidental conflict and enhance security.

An examination of China's experiences in implementing military CBMs with other nations may provide some insight into how it will approach building confidence in the military realm with Taiwan. However, it is important to distinguish between areas where the Chinese may employ approaches similar to those applied elsewhere and areas where they will seek to apply creative ideas that are unique to the Taiwan situation.

Comparisons with China's Other CBM Experiences

China has viewed military CBMs as part of a broader endeavor to improve overall political relations with many of its neighbors, including India, Vietnam, Russia, and the other members of the Shanghai Cooperation Organization (Kazakhstan, Kyrgyzstan, Tajikistan, and Uzbekistan). There is no case in which Beijing has pursued military CBMs outside the context of a larger reconciliation effort. Similarly, China seeks to pursue CBMs with Taiwan as part of its policy to promote peaceful development across the Strait and improve cross-Strait relations.

In the case of China's neighbors, CBMs were proposed, discussed, and negotiated only after a considerable amount of progress was achieved in improving political relations. Even though improvement in cross-Strait relations thus far has been mostly in the economic realm and not the political arena, Beijing is nevertheless eager to promote military CBMs with Taiwan. In fact, in contrast to the pattern established in its relations with its neighboring countries, the mainland proposed establishing a "mechanism of mutual trust in the military field" with Taiwan in May 2004, according to a statement issued by the Taiwan Affairs Office, at a time when cross-Strait ties were tense.[1] However, no progress was made toward opening talks with Taiwan during Chen Shui-bian's presidency.

---

[1] As published by Xinhua, May 16, 2004.

Since the election of Ma Ying-jeou as president and the resumption of contacts between the two quasi-official entities, the Straits Exchange Foundation (SEF) and the Association for Relations Across the Taiwan Strait (ARATS), establishing military CBMs has been accorded high priority by Beijing. In a December 2008 speech, CCP General Secretary Hu Jintao stated,

> To help stabilize the situation across the Taiwan Strait and alleviate military and security concerns, the two sides of the Taiwan Strait can choose the right time to carry out contacts and exchanges on military issues and explore the question of setting up a mechanism of mutual trust in military and security affairs.[2]

The process of discussing and negotiating military CBMs with Taiwan is likely to be slow and incremental, though it will probably not be as prolonged as some of China's other CBM agreements. In the Russian case, for example, it took the two sides 21 years from the time of their initial agreement on "basic principles" before the first CBM agreement was signed in 1990. Similarly, it took 14 years of negotiations for India and China to reach their landmark CBM agreement in 1993. In the Taiwan case, it is more likely that Beijing will seek to implement CBMs on a case-by-case basis, building on each experience piecemeal, rather than negotiating a detailed, comprehensive accord as was done with Russia and India.

As in past efforts to negotiate CBMs with neighboring countries, China hopes to further improve political relations and to establish contacts and build trust between the adversarial militaries. In addition, Beijing aspires to achieve several goals that are specific to its relationship with Taiwan. It seeks to weaken Taiwan's security ties to the United States and reduce or eliminate U.S. arms sales to Taiwan. It also aims to incorporate the Taiwan military into its united front policy that seeks to broaden support for closer ties with the mainland while isolating the die-hard pro-independence forces. A longer-term objective in pursuing cross-Strait CBMs is to promote the reunification of Taiwan with the motherland.

From Beijing's perspective, CBMs require a political foundation. In contrast with Western experiences in confidence building that have emphasized a bottom-up approach, in which preliminary trust-building measures lay the groundwork for more advanced steps, the Chinese prefer a top-down approach in which political principles are agreed upon first. Without concurrence on broad strategic principles, the Chinese are unlikely to proceed with implementing CBMs. Such a top-down model has been followed in China's relations with many of its neighbors, including Russia, the former Soviet states along China's Central Asian borders, Vietnam, and India. For example, China and India agreed to base their relationship on the Five Principles of Peaceful Coexistence. Beijing will also likely seek agreement with Taiwan on principles to guide their relationship. At the 17th Party Congress, General Secretary Hu Jintao stated, "On the basis of the one China principle," the two sides should discuss a formal end to the cross-Strait state of hostility, reach a peace accord, and build a framework for the "peaceful development of

---

[2] As published by Xinhua, December 31, 2008.

cross-Strait relations."[3] Hu renewed this appeal in his December 2008 address. However, his proposal to hold discussions on establishing a mechanism of mutual trust was not conditioned specifically on mutual agreement on the one China principle. Although many Chinese researchers maintain that Taipei's acceptance of the one China principle is a prerequisite for cross-Strait CBMs, Beijing may be willing to negotiate some CBMs on the basis of the 1992 consensus. Following its experiences with its neighbors, as well as with Taiwan, China will likely promote adhering to the principle of seeking common ground while reserving differences.

Breakthroughs in establishing CBMs with China's neighboring countries frequently resulted from high-level visits to or from China by heads of state or ministers responsible for foreign affairs or defense. In many of these cases, the high-level meeting included the signing of an important document that raised the political relationship to a new stage. For example, the meeting between Deng Xiaoping and Mikhail Gorbachev in 1989 normalized the Sino-Soviet relationship and provided the impetus for negotiations to resolve the border dispute and implement CBMs. In the case of India, a summit between Prime Minister Rajiv Gandhi and Deng Xiaoping in 1988 laid the foundation for the establishment of the joint working group (JWG) to promote cooperation in the military sphere. Between 1989 and 2003, 14 JWG meetings were held and produced several important Sino-Indian CBM agreements.

Beijing may seek to hold a meeting between Hu Jintao and Ma Ying-jeou, in their capacities as chairmen of their respective political parties, and use such a meeting to kick-start a CBM process with Taiwan. A joint statement might be agreed upon at a Hu-Ma meeting that would signify an increase in political trust and, in turn, allow CBM negotiations to begin. Since Ma was sworn in as KMT chairman on October 17, 2009, Chinese analysts have begun to push for such a meeting to take place.[4]

China's experiences in implementing CBMs with its neighbors suggest a preference for bilaterally negotiated constraint measures or force reductions, rather than unilateral measures. Decisions to pull back Chinese forces from the border with Russia, for example, were concluded through negotiations. Similarly, restrictions in the scale, geographic limits, and numbers of troop exercises were agreed upon in 1996 with Russia, Kazakhstan, Kyrgyzstan, and Tajikistan, which, along with China, were the Shanghai Five, the precursor to the Shanghai Cooperation Organization. Reductions of troops and armaments as well as constraints on troop deployments and maneuvers along China's border with India were also reached through bilateral agreements between Beijing and New Delhi.

Chinese military researchers suggest that adjustments in military deployments against Taiwan will not be carried out unilaterally, but rather will require reciprocal measures by the Taiwan military. For example, Major

---

3 "Full Text of Hu Jintao's Report at 17th Party Congress," Xinhua, October 24, 2007.
4 For example, Liu Guoshen, director of the Institute of Taiwan Studies, said that Beijing had indicated its willingness to hold a meeting between Hu Jintao and Ma Ying-jeou in their capacity as CCP and KMT leaders and hoped that the meeting would be held in Taiwan, according to *Hsiang Kang Shang Pao* (Hong Kong), October 23, 2009.

General Luo Yuan of the Academy of Military Sciences has stated that "military adjustment should be equal and a mutual action. When the mainland adjusts its military deployment, Taiwan should also adjust its military deployment."[5] Although some Beijing-owned Hong Kong media outlets have suggested that China will pull back some short-range ballistic missiles deployed opposite Taiwan,[6] the mainland seems reluctant to act unilaterally. Some Chinese researchers have suggested that Taiwan should withdraw its troops and missiles from the offshore islands as a reciprocal step.

Also worth noting are China's experiences in implementing CBMs with its neighbors that are *not* likely to be applied in the pursuit of CBMs with Taiwan. For example, demarcation and recognition of borders were important prerequisites for progress on CBMs with the former Soviet Union and India. In the case of the former Soviet Union, specific CBMs were agreed upon that required both countries to pull back troops and weapons to specific distances from the border. With India, agreement on the Line of Actual Control was crucial prior to discussion of border management measures and military CBMs, including advance notification of military exercises, separation and standoff agreements, management of airspace, military restraint measures, and communication measures.

It is unlikely, however, that China will agree to recognize the centerline in the Taiwan Strait, even though it has tacitly accepted it for six decades as an operational dividing line that is deliberately rarely crossed and then only to send a political warning. Taiwan's 2006 National Security Strategy proposed that the two sides establish a buffer zone along the centerline to prevent inadvertent contact between the two militaries. Such a suggestion is anathema to the mainland, which insists that there cannot be a centerline over a body of water that belongs to China.

Another difference between China's experiences in implementing CBMs with its neighbors and its likely approach to Taiwan is on the question of making a commitment not to use force. Beijing included language on the non–use of force in its agreements with Russia, the Central Asian Republics, and India in order to promote its CBMs with these countries. However, in Taiwan's case, Beijing has consistently declared that it will not renounce the use of force to reunify Taiwan with the mainland. Chinese military researchers have not ruled out an eventual pledge to not use force but insist that it would have to be part of a comprehensive understanding with Taiwan in which Taipei forswears independence and recognizes the "one China principle."

Conflict avoidance was an important objective in China's negotiation of CBMs with both Russia and India, countries with which China had engaged in armed conflict. The goal of conflict avoidance is a much lower priority for China in its consideration of CBMs with Taiwan, however. This is primarily because both sides have established unilateral rules of engagement (ROE) that are clearly understood by the other side. Taiwan's air force is

5 Luo Yuan, "Cross-Strait Military Mutual Trust Needs to Analyze and Solve Three Mysterious Ideas," Zhongguo Pinglun Tongxun She (China Review News Agency), August 12, 2009b.
6 Lin Chuan, "Both Sides of the Taiwan Strait Wish to Establish a 'Mechanism of Mutual Trust' in Military and Security Affairs," Zhongguo Pinglun Tongxun She (China Review News Agency), January 5, 2009.

under guidance to absorb the first strike, for example. People's Liberation Army (PLA) Air Force ROE are not publicly declared but almost certainly exist. Chinese military officers claim that there is a low probability of an incident in the Strait unless it is preplanned.

Whereas military CBMs were formally negotiated between the militaries of China and its neighbors, the Chinese are seeking to begin discussions with Taiwan on CBMs through informal channels. Mainland officials and scholars have proposed convening track II meetings to explore a possible CBM agenda.[7] They have also proposed exchanging delegations composed of retired military officers. The Chinese propose engaging Taiwan's military officers in discussions of shared military culture, their common experiences in fighting the Japanese in the 1940s, and ways in which the two militaries can promote their shared territorial claims in the South China Sea and East China Sea. This focus on culture, history, and common stances reflects Beijing's interest in promoting common bonds of identity between the two militaries in support of reunification.[8]

Specific CBM Proposals

In developing specific CBM proposals for Taiwan, China may draw on some of its experiences in implementing CBMs with its neighbors. For example, China may agree to establish communication mechanisms between the Chinese and Taiwan militaries, especially since this type of CBM is almost certain to be a high priority for Taipei. It is more likely that Beijing would agree to setting up operational hotlines with Taiwan's naval and air force commanders, similar to those that China established with the Republic of Korea (ROK) in 2008, than that rather than hotlines between heads of state, such as China set up with the United States and Russia in 1998. In the PRC-ROK case, a hotline was set up between the command-and-control centers of the two countries' main naval and air force centers—Qingdao and Jinan in China and Pyeongtaek and Taegu in South Korea. The main purpose of the hotline was to promote real-time exchanges of information about unidentified aircraft and vessels approaching the territorial air and maritime space around the Korean Peninsula.

The mainland and Taiwan could establish hotlines to enable direct communication about air and naval activities in the Taiwan Strait. Such a channel would be especially useful for maritime search-and-rescue operations. Cooperation in maritime rescue operations already takes place, and its effectiveness would undoubtedly be enhanced by the existence of such a hotline. In 2002, joint rescue operations by Taiwan and the mainland provided assistance to the victims of a China Airlines crash in the Taiwan Strait.[9] More recently, in response to a distress call sent out on October 4, 2009, by the Panama-registered cargo ship *Eufonia*, which was located near the

---

[7] Luo Yuan, "Chance to Establish Cross-Strait Military Security Mutual Confidence Building System Should Not Be Missed," *Guoji Xianqu Daobao Online*, January 5, 2009a.

[8] Luo Yuan, 2009a.

[9] Chuyngly Lee, "Maritime Confidence Building Measures Across the Taiwan Strait: Technical Collaboration for Human Security at Sea," Albuquerque, N.M.: Sandia National Laboratories, Cooperative Monitoring Center Occasional Paper No. 26, SAND 2003-0753, March 2003.

middle of the Taiwan Strait, the Republic of China (ROC) Coast Guard Administration dispatched crews and worked in parallel with ships dispatched by the mainland to rescue the crew.[10]

A first step could be to formalize the informal communication mechanisms that already exist between the two sides. For example, a civilian hotline between the Taipei-based China Rescue Association and its mainland counterpart, the China Marine Rescue Center, has been in place since November 1997 to facilitate marine rescue work in the Taiwan Strait. Under the agreement, when accidents occur in the Strait involving the ships from both Taiwan and the mainland, the ships in distress and the rescuing ships may use the hotline to request assistance and ask for permission to enter the waters and harbors of the other side. The hotline operates 24 hours a day.

China could also draw on its experience in the Shanghai Cooperation Organization as well as with India and agree to reciprocally provide advance notification of major troop movements and large-scale military exercises. Notification mechanisms are important transparency measures that can help eliminate fears that an exercise may be part of preparations for war. Taiwan has made public its annual schedule of naval exercises for more than a decade. China might consider advance notification of exercises in the Nanjing and Guangzhou military regions opposite Taiwan, as well as naval vessel movements. As a mutual transparency measure, China and Taiwan could formally notify each other through SEF and ARATS.

Finally, Beijing has shown a willingness to employ declaratory CBMs, most commonly in the nuclear field. China has unilaterally declared, for example, that it would not use nuclear weapons first and would not use or threaten to use nuclear weapons against non-nuclear states or nuclear-free zones. In bilateral accords with Russia and the United States in 1994 and 1998, respectively, China agreed not to target those countries with nuclear weapons in exchange for a reciprocal pledge. Beijing could issue declaratory statements that it has no intention to use nuclear weapons against Taiwan. It could also pledge to not use force as long as Taiwan does not declare independence.

Limited but Instructive Lessons

China's approach to discussing military CBMs with Taiwan will, in all likelihood, be based on the special circumstances that prevail in the cross-Strait relationship. Avoiding agreements that imply Taiwan's existence as a separate, sovereign entity will be a high priority. As noted at the beginning of this paper, the main objective of CBMs can be to ease tensions and improve mutual trust, or simply to minimize the risk of accidental conflict. For Beijing, trust building is likely to be a more important objective than conflict avoidance. Delineation of borders, which were crucial precursors to CBM agreements with some of China's neighbors, will not factor into Beijing's CBM plans with Taiwan. Nevertheless, China's experience in negotiating and implementing military CBMs with its neighbors can provide some insights into how it may approach discussion and development of a road map for confidence building with Taiwan. Some of the lessons that can be applied include the importance China attaches

---

10 "Panamanian Ship's Captain, 2 Crew Member [sic] Rescued," Central News Agency, October 5, 2009.

to agreement on principles, its reliance on high-level meetings to create political understandings prior to negotiating CBMs, and its general preference for bilateral force adjustments and constraints over unilateral measures. Specific CBMs that have been implemented between China and its neighbors may also provide useful models for the cross-Strait situation, such as operational hotlines and transparency measures.

4. Cross-Strait CBMs: Taiwan's Views on Opportunities, Obstacles, and Challenges

Kwei-Bo Huang

This paper begins by discussing the role that confidence-building measures (CBMs) play in general in achieving peace between adversary states, as well as by examining and assessing briefly the strategic context in which the Republic of China (ROC, hereafter Taiwan) exists. Understanding Taiwan's strategic context is a prerequisite for understanding how to build helpful, concrete, and effective CBMs between the two sides of the Taiwan Strait. Then, the paper presents a personal view of the potential opportunities, obstacles, and challenges associated with CBMs in the context of better relations between Taiwan and mainland China. It concludes by arguing that cross-Strait CBMs are definitely a positive factor in contributing to peace and stability between the two parties but are likely to develop at a slow and cautious pace, largely due to the delicate Taipei-Beijing relationship that has only recently evolved from confrontation to seeming accommodation.

General Propositions

The Positive Role of CBMs

I agree with Michael Krepon and his colleagues that phased and incremental CBMs are the most conducive to the eventual emergence of a stable and lasting peace between adversaries. Krepon suggests three stages that apply to "phased and incremental confidence building"; they are conflict avoidance, confidence building, and strengthening peace. Conflict avoidance is based on mutual contacts and appropriate communication between conflicting parties. With consensus and healthy interactions between the parties, CBMs will follow. If the obstacles to the prevention of war can be removed, leaders can use existing or newly developed CBMs to strengthen peace.[1]

In addition to political dialogue, socioeconomic interactions, ranging from people-to-people exchanges to stronger economic interdependence, are necessary for CBMs to succeed. In other words, both top-down and bottom-up approaches can pave the way for the emergence of a less harsh environment in which various strata in the two parties' societies proactively or passively accept some sort of peaceful engagements with the other conflicting party.

Effective and significant multilateral efforts to promote CBMs did not take place in the European context until approximately 1975 with the signing of the Helsinki Final Act. These CBMs were aimed primarily at reducing enmity, avoiding miscalculation and misperception, increasing military transparency, and demonstrating self-restraint to enhance mutual trust. As Table 4.1 indicates, CBMs, which have been used for more than three decades, take many different forms nowadays: declaratory, communicative, transparency-enhancing, constraining,

---

[1] Michael Krepon, Khurshid Khoja, Michael Newbill, and Jenny Drezin, eds., *A Handbook of Confidence-Building Measures for Regional Security*, 3rd ed., Washington, D.C.: Stimson Center, 1998, pp. 3–14.

and verification-oriented. With the exception of verification measures, any of the other four types can be undertaken either single-handedly or collectively by the parties to a conflict, with the aim of reassuring the other side.

Table 4.1: CBM Types

CBM Types	Examples
Declaratory measures	• Acceptance of existing borders • Pledge not to attack or use force • Commitment of noninterference in domestic affairs • Pledge of peaceful coexistence
Communication measures	• Hotline agreement • Visits of high-level officials • Establishment of multilateral communication network • Founding of conflict-prevention centers • Obligatory consultation on emergencies or routine assessments
Transparency measures	• Publication of defense white papers • Calendar of military maneuvers or activities • Exchanges of military personnel/students • Advance notification of military maneuvers or movements • Invitation of observers to maneuvers or sensitive facilities • Participation in UN or regional arms registries
Constraint measures	• Demilitarizing, thinning out forces, or establishing nuclear-free zones • Decreasing conventional or nuclear forces • Establishing a code of conduct for military contacts/activities • Deployment limits by numbers, geographical areas, etc. • Maneuvers limits by numbers, geographical areas, etc. • Limits on personnel nationalities, categories, etc.
Verification measures	• On-site inspection • Aerial inspection • Surveillance of ocean resources, military disengagement, etc. • Open skies • Implementation-assessment meetings

Taiwan's Constrained Strategic Context

The primary source of threat that Taiwan faces comes from the ongoing competition between the two sides of the Strait. Taiwan's strategic environment has been shaped mainly by its relationship with mainland China and by relations between mainland China and the United States. Three important additional factors also help define Taiwan's strategic context.

First, the degree of Taiwan's military strategic importance has risen and fallen mainly as a function of the strategic nature of the relationship between Washington and Beijing. A long-time U.S. ally, Taiwan must take the U.S. position in East Asia into account when choosing its military strategy. In addition, Taiwan's arms acquisitions have long been substantially affected by the fierce opposition of mainland China and the political calculations of the United States. Accordingly, Taiwan has long felt militarily insecure, especially in the face of a rapidly growing and modernizing communist regime across the Strait.

Second, in addition to the military threat from mainland China, Taiwan is involved in territorial disputes with Japan, Vietnam, the Philippines, Malaysia, and Brunei. These disputes pose a dilemma for Taiwan: A relatively strong military presence will lead to criticisms from the other countries concerned, and a relatively weak military presence will probably mean that Taiwan will be forced to concede in these disputes. More specifically, the Taiwan-Japan disputes over the Diaoyutai/Senkaku Islands and a small part of the East China Sea loom large and can, from time to time, hinder the positive development of bilateral relations between Taipei and Tokyo. The South China Sea territorial dispute, in which Taiwan claims sovereignty over the entire area, is widely recognized as a significant challenge for those favoring peaceful dispute settlements in East Asia. For Taiwan, constructive measures for dealing with these disputes may help with its international image as a peacemaker in the region.

Finally, Taiwan faces an overwhelming disadvantage in competing against a mainland China that is on the rise while Taiwan remains significantly constrained both politically and economically. Politically, Taiwan's access to international organizations and regimes has been limited, and its relations with countries that do not extend it official recognition remain at the socioeconomic and cultural levels and can hardly be converted to greater political support in major international arenas. Economically, Taiwan's heavy dependence on international trade appears to put it in a weak position inasmuch as the forces of economic globalization and regionalization are evolving in ways that may possibly come to exclude Taiwan. Globally, Taiwan cannot join most of the major international economic and financial regimes; regionally, in organizations in which Taiwan enjoys membership, such as the Asia-Pacific Economic Cooperation (APEC) and the Asian Development Bank (ADB), it often receives differentiated treatment in terms of the use of its national title or the level of officials who represent the ROC government. As such, Taiwan confronts a tough strategic situation in which the room for economic strategies is being compressed by the political pressure of the People's Republic of China (PRC).

Generally speaking, in the face of a rising mainland China, Taiwan has three policy options: inaction, confrontation, and cooperation with policy accommodation. Inaction, meaning indifference to any request from or interaction with mainland China, is not an option because Taiwan cannot afford to engage in wishful thinking about the international arena without considering the so-called "China factor." Confrontation, or assertiveness, has been carried out by former President Lee Teng-hui (after approximately 1999) and former President Chen Shui-bian (roughly 2003–2008) but has proven ineffective to a great extent, in part because mainland China has grown too strong to ignore and in part because Taiwan-U.S. political relations turned sour with the loss of mutual trust among the leaders. As a result, cooperation with policy accommodation appears to be an appropriate option that the Ma Ying-jeou administration can undertake gain a better grasp of mainland China as a window of opportunity that is key to Taiwan's survival and development. In this sense, cross-Strait CBMs can help implement strategic thinking, given the fact that Taiwan is in an inferior strategic position and needs to improve its substantive ties and international image by engaging constructively with mainland China and being a responsible stakeholder in the world.

Cross-Strait CBMs

Since CBMs are generally beneficial to the avoidance of conflict, and since Taiwan's strategic context is severely constrained by its external milieu, there appear to be good reasons for Taiwan to be supportive of cross-Strait CBMs. Although CBMs across the Taiwan Strait have not been put into practice yet, they appear necessary to alleviate the fundamentally hostile situation and to create a stable and prosperous environment for the people on both sides of the Strait. Indeed, there are opportunities for cross-Strait CBMs to be carried out step by step. Still, obstacles and challenges stand in front of both Taiwan and mainland China, despite the fact that cross-Strait relations have been moving in the right direction since May 2008.

Opportunities

The first opportunity comes with the idea of "flexible diplomacy" put forward by President Ma Ying-jeou. Flexible diplomacy stresses the importance of a diplomatic truce between Taipei and Beijing and the necessity of retasking resources that were used to compete with or confront each other to other tasks that both parties feel are urgent to undertake. To facilitate flexible diplomacy, cross-Strait CBMs launched either single-handedly or bilaterally may be used. Following the same line of thought, CBMs, including the diplomatic truce and the mutual nondenial of the ROC and the PRC governments initiated by Taiwan, are expected to play a constructive and stabilizing role in the development of Taipei-Beijing relations.

There are two more prominent opportunities that can increase the likelihood that Taipei and Beijing will discuss and implement CBMs: the realistic nature of the top leaders of both sides of the Taiwan Strait and the new atmosphere of world politics.

The pragmatic orientation of both sides' leaders is easy to discern, although some dogmatic policies may nonetheless prove unavoidable due to the domestic pressures imposed by the opposition in Taiwan and conservatives on the mainland. One of the most salient examples of this is President Ma's consistency in employing the "no unification, no (Taiwan) independence, no use of force" formula based on the "1992 Consensus" as the foundation for the resumption of cross-Strait talks. Similarly, Hu Jintao has strictly employed the so-called "Six Points" framework he laid out on December 31, 2008, delineating principles on cross-Strait relations from political, economic, sociocultural, diplomatic, and military perspectives and aiming to prevent Taiwan's independence rather than seek further unification.

The new atmosphere of world politics extends beyond U.S. accommodation of Russia and mainland China, respectively. In an increasingly interdependent world, cooperation, coordination, threat reduction, and collective security among sovereign states have become more mainstream ideas; meanwhile, norms that strictly uphold state sovereignty as an absolute good are undergoing major transitions. Peter Wallensteen argues that "there has been a definite development in the internationally accepted collective security doctrine," and new concepts like humanitarian intervention and responsibility to protect (R2P) at-risk populations are growing in acceptance.[2] Thus, it is possible that existing conflicts can be limited, in part, through the emergence of new norms that downplay the importance of sovereignty. Although the influence of these developments on mainland Chinese leaders' views on Taiwan policy remains to be seen, one should not discount the force of "international socialization" of mainland China, which may create a positive linkage between mainland China's greater participation in and adaptation to the international society and its policies toward Taiwan.

Flexible diplomacy and the realistic nature of leaders on both sides of the Strait have brought about a decrease in hostility and an increase in the tendency to deescalate. If one observes mainland China's policies with respect to Taiwan in 2009—most notably its decision not to block Taiwan's observership in the World Health Assembly (WHA) and its reaction to President Ma's decision to issue a visa to the Dalai Lama—it seems clear that mainland China has made a deliberate decision to pursue a relatively milder Taiwan policy, though it is not yet clear whether such a decision can continue to develop in a constructive direction. Consequently, it is important for both Taipei and Beijing to begin institutionalizing cooperation through mechanisms that help maintain peace, reduce hostility, prevent escalation or retaliation, and improve understanding and trust.

Obstacles in the Near Term

Despite the opportunities that have arisen since President Ma took office in May 2008, one cannot deny that there are also obstacles to cross-Strait CBMs in the near term, emanating not only from the intricacies of Taipei-Beijing relations but also from certain outside actors with vital or vested interests in the Taiwan Strait.

Among these obstacles are the domestic politics of Taiwan and mainland China. In Taiwan, calls for independence from mainland China still exist and, generally speaking, become stronger as cross-Strait relations become unstable. For example, according to polls conducted by the Mainland Affairs Council of the ROC Executive Yuan, the percentage of people in Taiwan who favored "immediate independence" and "status quo and independence later" grew between August 2003 and roughly September 2004 as former ROC President Chen Shui-bian made his "One Country on Each Side" statement, resulting in a setback in cross-Strait relations. Politicians in favor of Taiwan's independence, particularly those from the Democratic Progressive Party (DPP) and the Taiwan Solidarity Union (TSU), tend to discount the benefits of cross-Strait CBMs, or view mainland China's promotion of such CBMs as a trap. Some news media in support of the DPP and TSU even counteract negotiating efforts made by the Ma administration in an effort to sell Taiwan to the Chinese communists. These approaches have significantly reduced the effectiveness of the government's peace measures aimed at stabilizing and improving cross-Strait relations.

---

[2] Peter Wallensteen, *Understanding Conflict Resolution*, 2nd ed., Los Angeles, Calif.: Sage Publications, 2007, pp. 225, 251.

In mainland China, the influence of hardliners on Taiwan policy is an important obstacle to better cross-Strait ties. The policy preferences of officers and officials from the People's Liberation Army (PLA) and the Ministry of Foreign Affairs, many of whom were indoctrinated with nationalist or irredentist fervor about Taiwan, make it difficult for mainland Chinese authorities to make concessions when Taiwan policy is going to be adjusted in a manner that seems to benefit Taipei. In addition, top leaders in Beijing are also cautious about every policy accommodation or concession to Taiwan because they need to maintain their ruling basis and legitimacy by supporting a Taiwan policy that is perceived to benefit the Chinese Communist Party (CCP).

A second obstacle to the improvement of Taiwan–mainland China relations is the lack of understanding by each about the other's real intentions with respect to cross-Strait CBMs. For Taiwan, not only the opposition parties but the general public more broadly—including some in the ruling party—are skeptical of the seriousness of mainland China's accommodation in its Taiwan policy. Despite the fact that mainland China has shown substantially more political goodwill toward Taiwan recently—for example, implicitly agreeing on a diplomatic truce and compromising on Taiwan's meaningful participation in a very small number of intergovernmental organizations and events—it is often seen as a sugar-coated poison pill by some in Taiwan. Not all government officials in mainland China realize that Taiwan's pursuit of international and diplomatic space (a common request among Taiwan's general public) is not for permanent separation but for Taiwan's self-respect and development. Moreover, mainland officials sometimes overestimate the extent to which Taiwan is a divided society with only pro-Blue and pro-Green citizens and miss the popular nature of the quest for greater international participation and recognition. To overcome this obstacle, there are no special approaches, but continued positive interactions and policy consistency from the mainland will be crucial.

A final obstacle that is vital to the implementation of cross-Strait CBMs has to do with the behavior and policies of third parties that can help develop a win-win-win situation in cross-Strait and regional environments on security-related issues. A key principle of flexible diplomacy is that Taiwan should work on cross-Strait peace and security while cultivating its relationships with the rest of the world in a constructive and responsible way. At the same time, Taiwan will not feel confident in any cross-Strait CBMs if a supportive international environment does not exist. For Taiwan, cross-Strait improvements will amount to little if Taipei's external ties do not also make progress as cross-Strait security-related issues are being discussed. For mainland China, its rigid "one China" principle has prevented the international community from strengthening substantial ties with Taiwan, which will eventually highlight the difficult part of cross-Strait talks on CBMs and make it hard for the Kuomintang (KMT) to persuade the general public in Taiwan to see cross-Strait CBMs in a positive light.

Challenges to Taiwan in the Near Term

Having outlined the opportunities and obstacles for cross-Strait CBMs in the short run, this paper presents two immediate challenges that confront the Ma administration. The first deals with the need to build-up a domestic consensus in support of warmer cross-Strait ties, and the second concerns the importance of retooling public diplomacy to promote Taiwan's idea of cross-Strait peace talks.

The Ma administration needs the general public's consensus to move ahead on cross-Strait CBMs because Taiwan must interact with mainland China from a position of both caution and confidence. Taiwan's attitude and policies toward mainland China have been conditioned by the caution exercised by the Ma administration. This caution stems from at least two facts. First, the interaction between the two sides of the Strait was like a rollercoaster in the past and therefore needs more time to be "upgraded." Second, the majority of people in Taiwan support the status quo and are not used to or do not actively seek rapid changes in cross-Strait relations. As such, a domestic consensus on how to improve cross-Strait ties is absolutely necessary before any major breakthrough in the political relationship between Taipei and Beijing can be pursued in concrete terms. In terms of the confidence Taipei needs in order to make such a breakthrough, it will most likely come from the strong domestic support of a populace that appreciates the KMT's caution in mainland policy. For these reasons, Taiwan's domestic consensus needs to emerge and be nurtured gradually through the use of a cautious mainland policy, as this is crucial for the pursuit of further cross-Strait CBMs.

Another immediate challenge results from the possible misperception by foreign countries of the motives for or implications of improvements in the cross-Strait relationship. This challenge highlights the need for public diplomacy to explain quickly, coherently, and completely the benefits and drivers of the rapid improvements in cross-Strait ties, especially the improvement in political and security relations. As a result of the imbalance in international influence between Taiwan and mainland China, public diplomacy has an important role to play for Taiwan.

Public diplomacy is dialogue-oriented: It involves speaking and listening. Taiwan needs to formulate a plan for familiarizing potential target audiences with the benefits of peace and stability in the Taiwan Strait and the merits of the flexible diplomacy approach of the Ma administration. Some of Taiwan's foreign friends do not understand the basic mainland policy pursued by the KMT and are worried about a closer relationship between the two sides of the Taiwan Strait. In fact, the attempts of the Ma administration to enhance cross-Strait ties both pragmatically and constructively aim simply to bring peace and prosperity, not only to the Taiwan Strait but also to the region. To defend and promote the policy decisions of the Ma administration, improved public diplomacy will be necessary.

Concluding Remarks

Since President Ma took office in May 2008, Taiwan's primary strategic objectives have included preserving peace and stability in the Taiwan Strait, maintaining economic development and prosperity, encouraging cross-Strait dialogue and mutual understanding, enhancing relations with major powers, and participating in international organizations and regional bodies. Cross-Strait CBMs, if carried out sincerely, will help accomplish these goals, both because almost every strategic objective of Taiwan hinges on the peaceful development of cross-Strait relations and because, time and again, the United States and the other powers have expressed their hopes for a stable cross-Strait relationship that can facilitate the peaceful resolution of cross-Strait conflict.

In conclusion, to seize those opportunities and overcome the obstacles, Taiwan, under President Ma's leadership, appears likely to move at a slow, careful pace and adopt a thoughtful approach in transforming the delicate Taipei-Beijing relationship from confrontation to accommodation. Although the opportunities for successfully employing peaceful means, including CBMs, to improve relations between Taiwan and mainland China are still complicated by domestic, cross-Strait, and international contexts, cross-Strait CBMs are beyond all doubt a positive factor contributing to peace and stability in the Taiwan Strait and East Asia more broadly.

5. Cross-Strait CBMs: Like a Fish Needs a Bicycle?

Steven M. Goldstein

As some will undoubtedly note, the title of this paper draws from the famous phrase coined by Irina Dunn, later used by U2 in the song "Throwin' Your Arms Around the World"; it also encapsulates its argument that, at the present time, confidence-building measures (CBMs) across the Taiwan Strait are largely superfluous. By superfluous, I mean to say not only that they are neither necessary nor even possible but that beginning the process of negotiation could well complicate rather than ameliorate cross-Strait tensions.

I begin with a brief exploration of the nature of CBMs as well as the factors, distilled from the experience of their application in other settings, that have conditioned whether or not they have played a constructive role in the reduction of tensions among international actors. This is followed by an analysis of what appear, at the moment, to be the principal elements in the mainland's approach to the issue of cross-Strait trust mechanisms as reflected in public sources.[1] The paper concludes with an assessment of both the possibility and the advisability of promoting the negotiation of cross-Strait CBMs by briefly considering how these elements would affect not only the process of negotiation but ultimately the tenor of cross-Strait relations.

But first, a note about sources. In this paper, I have drawn strictly from materials published in mainland China or in Hong Kong newspapers.[2] There is no assurance that they represent the thinking at the highest levels of leadership. However, public sources are important for four reasons. First, articles by experts might reflect advocacy positions. Second, they equally can reflect what those who specialize in cross-Strait relations, and presumably know best, consider to be official positions. Third, they influence public expectations in China about the process. And finally, to the extent that they are monitored by Taiwan analysts, they can shape Taipei's perceptions and expectations of future negotiating positions.

Confidence-Building Measures: Their Origins and Evolution

Much of the theorizing regarding the nature of CBMs and their possible application is based on attempts to extend their applicability beyond the role that they played during and after the Cold War in the West. It is my sense that this fact has influenced discussions of cross-Strait measures in two ways. First, the dramatic success of the European

---

[1] I make reference to the view from Taipei only insofar as it informs the kind of response that mainland objectives might be expected to receive.

[2] The most useful of these are the articles and monographs that have come out of a Center for Strategic and International Studies project on CBMs, especially essays by Bonnie Glaser and Brad Glosserman. As one might expect, many of the insights they collected on PRC (People's Republic of China) positions are found in the materials analyzed here. Publications of this project include Brad Glosserman, "Cross-Strait Confidence Building Measures," *Issues and Insights*, Vol. 5, No. 2, February, 2005; Bonnie S. Glaser and Brad Glosserman, *Promoting Confidence Building Across the Taiwan Strait*, Washington, D.C.: Center for Strategic and International Studies, September 2008; and Bonnie S. Glaser, "Cross-Strait Confidence Building: The Case for Military Confidence Building Measures," in Chris Fugarino and Donald S. Zagoria, eds., *Breaking the China-Taiwan Impasse*, Westport, Conn.: Praeger, 2003.

effort has often resulted in analysts minimizing the difficulties and dangers of negotiating such agreements in the case of relations between Taiwan and the mainland. Second, there has been an expansion in the definition of CBMs beyond their original focus on military issues in the post–Cold War period, which makes it necessary to define precisely how the term is being used. These two factors explain why the general discussion of these measures that follows might seem, to some, to be excessively pessimistic and narrow in scope.

Beginning with the simple act of establishing a Washington-Moscow hotline following the Cuban Missile Crisis, CBMs evolved dramatically through the Helsinki Final Act of 1975, which stipulated largely voluntary notifications of troop movements and eventually became the basis for the establishment of the Organization for Security and Co-Operation in Europe (OSCE). This body, which has extended its reach all the way to Central Asia, has established a broad range of treaty-based obligations geared toward crisis avoidance and management that have been placed under the broader and more encompassing designation of CSBMs (confidence- and security-building mechanisms). The progressive evolution of CBMs in the European context through a series of increasingly constraining agreements has suggested to many—diplomats and academics alike—that the device might be used in other global trouble spots, including the Taiwan Strait.

However, these efforts to achieve geographic expansion of the concept have prompted another development with regard to CBMs that is particularly relevant for this paper: a phenomenon that might be called "concept creep," whereby efforts to widen the applicability of CBMs have had the effect of reshaping the meaning of such measures. This has been especially striking in two respects: the nature of what is included under the rubric of CBMs and the expectations that are held for them.

With regard to the former issue, one analyst has noted the post–Cold War development of a "more expansive definition of confidence building, according to which economic, political, and cultural tools are viewed as CBMs."[3] With respect to the latter issue, Marie-France Desjardins has cautioned that the concept of CBMs has been "overburdened with promises." She maintains that not only has the scope of these measures been expanded beyond the emphasis on military security, but there has also been a "shift in emphasis" and an expansion with respect to their goals, "from enhancing military security to enhancing cooperation" or building "understanding between states."[4]

She notes that, as a result of these shifts, confidence building has come to be viewed as a "process" in the sense that CBMs are expected not only to evolve from a focus on relatively minor security issues to those of greater import (a "vertical impact"), but also to have a "spillover" effect (or "horizontal impact"), enhancing cooperation in

---

[3] Cathleen S. Fisher, "The Preconditions of Confidence Building: Lessons from the European Experience," in Michael Krepon, Michael Newbill, Khurshid Khoja, and Jenny S. Drezin, eds., *Global Confidence Building: New Tools for Troubled Regions,* New York: St. Martin's Press, 1999, p. 292. For an example of such an approach see A. Z. Hiali, "Confidence- and Security-Building Measures for India and Pakistan," *Alternatives,* Vol. 30, 2005.

[4] Marie-France Desjardins, *Rethinking Confidence Building Measures,* Adelphi Paper No. 307, Oxford: Oxford University Pres, December 1, 1996, pp. 6, 18–19.

other areas of common interest. In short, rather than CBMs being seen as a limited tool for minimizing the risk of unintentional conflict among adversaries, they have been elevated to the status of a process that can build trust in other areas and that can be expected to evolve to the point that they actually resolve militarized conflicts, rather than simply preventing them.

As noted above, discussions of cross-Strait confidence building have often reflected the influence of these trends toward "concept creep." In this paper, I restrict my use the term to its earlier and narrower sense.[5] I focus on "initiatives addressing military planning and operational activity," which have as their "major objective" the provision of "reassurance by reducing uncertainties and constraining opportunities for exerting pressure through military activity."[6]

Such initiatives may be unilateral, bilateral, or multilateral and usually cover "four main areas: communication, constraint, transparency, and verification."[7] However, underpinning all of these is the premise that there is no present intent to use force and that the more immediate danger is misperception or misunderstanding that can be ameliorated by these means.[8]

Along with the enormous attention that CBMs have been given in the post–Cold War era have come numerous attempts to assess the conditions under which such measures might be successfully employed. Drawing lessons from the European experience, but remaining sensitive to the diverse conditions under which such measures might be applied, commentators have sought to guide future implementation by identifying some of the underlying fundamental requirements for success in other geographic areas as well as the pitfalls that await potential CBM negotiators.

There seems to be general agreement that for CBMs to be successfully negotiated they should be seen as increasing the security of both sides. As one Council for Security Cooperation in the Asia-Pacific memo has put it, both sides must see such agreements "in 'win-win' not 'win-lose' terms."[9] The process is considered more difficult when the actors taking part do not have roughly equal military capabilities and the structural context (i.e., borders) is not settled—both of which hold in the case of the Taiwan Strait.[10]

---

[5] By "earlier" I mean first-generation CBMs as they were negotiated during the Cold War.

[6] M. Susan Pederson and Stanley Weeks, "A Survey of Confidence and Security Building Measures," in Ralph A. Cossa, ed., *Asia Pacific Confidence and Security Building Measures*, Washington, D.C.: Center for Strategic and International Studies, 1995, p. 82.

[7] Cited in Holly Higgins, "Applying Confidence-Building Measures in a Regional Context," in Holly Higgins, ed., *Building Nuclear Confidence on the Korean Peninsula: Proceedings of the July 23–24, 2001 Workshop*, Washington, D.C.: Institute for Science and International Security, 2001.

[8] Desjardins, 1996, p. 22.

[9] Council for Security Cooperation in the Asia-Pacific, "Asia Pacific Confidence and Security Building Measures," Memorandum 2, undated.

[10] Francois Godement, "Confidence Building Measures: Can Taiwan Learn from European Experiences," draft manuscript, 2006.

Moreover, as William Zartman has argued, there must be a moment of "ripeness" characterized by a "mutually hurting stalemate." He argues,

> Parties resolve their conflict only when they are ready to do so—when alternative, usually unilateral, means of achieving a satisfactory result are blocked and the parties feel that they are in an uncomfortable and costly predicament. At that "ripe" moment, they seek or are amenable to proposals that offer a way out.[11]

It is this sense of an *immediate* need to act that underpins what Ingolf Kiesow has called "the political will to make it happen," which moves potential opponents to act despite the existence of mutual mistrust.[12] This political will might mean, as was the case with the first-generation European CBMs, maintaining the status quo while lessening the danger of conflict, or, as with the proposals of Mikhail Gorbachev, it may be intended to serve domestic political goals. As Mason has put it,

> confidence building measures simply cannot work to build confidence in the absence of a political decision to attempt to fundamentally alter the current (negative) security relationship between the relevant parties.[13]

As Mason notes, perhaps the clearest example of this dynamic in operation has been the India-Pakistan CBMs which, because of weak political will and the fragile political basis for the agreements that have been reached, have likely worsened the relationship between the two countries rather than improving it.[14] A minimum of will and an adequate political basis are required for such agreements; as the Indo-Pakistani case and the experience of the Koreas both show, "measures that overreach the political willingness of states to implement them can become sources of contention" rather than a means to resolve differences.[15]

Indeed, as Desjardins has pointed out, not only must care be taken to agree strictly to those conditions consistent with each side's political interest, but actors must also avoid overly optimistic assumptions that the "process" of negotiation, or agreement to initial steps on the CBM ladder, will necessarily have beneficial results. CBMs may produce benefits by contributing to a spirit of cooperation that will, in turn, enhance the likelihood of further agreements and cooperation in other areas. However, they may just as easily not; the simple act of negotiating may highlight and intensify mutual distrust as underlying issues and differing objectives are revealed. As

---

[11] I. William Zartman, "Ripeness," *Beyond Intractability*, August 2003.

[12] Ingolf Kiesow, "Confidence Building Measures in Europe During the Cold War: Possible Relevance for Asia Today," Beijing: Institute for American Studies, China Institutes of Contemporary International Relations, 2005.

[13] Margaret Mason, "Confidence Building in the Asia Pacific Region: Prospects and Problems," in Ralph A. Cossa, ed., *Asia Pacific Confidence and Security Building Measures*, Washington, D.C.: Center for Strategic and International Studies, 1995, p. 103.

[14] Mason, 1995, p. 103.

[15] Pederson and Weeks, 1995, p. 95. Desjardins, 1996, makes similar points.

Desjardins notes, negotiations "can actually damage international security" and prove to be part of a "détente consuming" process.[16]

Mainland Attitudes Toward CBMs

China's acceptance, in principle, of CBMs clearly has been tied to the post-Mao effort to seek a peaceful international environment in order to promote the nation's economic development. By the end of the 1990s such agreements were being touted as part of the "new kind of security concept vigorously advocated by China" that would reduce reliance on arms and allies for national security.[17] Chinese discussions affirmed the use of confidence-building methods for the purposes of

> preventing military forces from threatening or harming other countries' security and stability; implementing and sticking to a national defense policy that is defensive in nature; adopting suitable confidence-building measures in border and disputed areas on a bilateral basis; and engaging in friendly contacts between military forces.[18]

During the 1990s, agreements along these lines were signed with India, as well as with Russia and the Central Asian states that would eventually become the core of the Shanghai Cooperation Organization. Elsewhere in Asia, the PRC has participated in multilateral organizations, such as the Conference on Interaction and Confidence Building and, most prominently, in Association of Southeast Asian Nations (ASEAN)–related initiatives. Indeed, CBMs are depicted as the "core" of the nation's security cooperation policy in its relations with the ASEAN states.[19] They are presented as not only promoting a less threatening environment but also assuaging concerns about the rise of China, so much so that some Chinese analysts have argued that the "theory of the China

---

[16] Desjardins, 1996, p. 5.

[17] For early discussions of the Chinese view, see Kenneth W. Allen, "China's Approach to Confidence-Building Measures," in Krepon, Khurshid Khoja, Michael Newbill, and Jenny Drezin, eds., *Global Confidence Building: New Tools for Troubled Regions*, New York: St. Martin's Press, 1999. See also Liu Huaqiu, "Step by Step Confidence and Security Building for the Asian Region," in Ralph A. Cossa, ed., *Asia Pacific Confidence and Security Building Measures*, Washington, D.C.: Center for Strategic and International Studies, 1995, and Michael Krepon, ed., 1997. For early expressions of Chinese policy, see Information Office of the State Council, People's Republic of China, *China's National Defense*, Beijing, July 1998, and Permanent Mission of the People's Republic of China to the United Nations, "Practical Confidence-Building Measures in the Field of Conventional Arms," October 15, 2003.

[18] See Permanent Mission of the People's Republic of China to the United Nations, 2003.

[19] Two very useful recent Chinese discussions of the concept are Teng Jianqun, "Zhongguo jianli xinren cuoshi shijian yu zhanwang" ("The Practice and Promise of Chinese Confidence Building Measures"), *Guoji guanxi yanjiu*, No. 3, 2008, and Chen Hanxi, "Xin anquan jian shijian: Zhongguo di jianli xinren cuoshi zhengce jiqi yingxiang" ("The New Security View: China's Policy of Confidence Building Measures and its Influence"), *Guoji guanxi xueyuan xuebao*, No. 5, 2005. Unless otherwise indicated, the next two paragraphs are based on these sources. For a sampling of more recent activities, see Ministry of National Defense, People's Republic of China, "Regional Cooperation," web page, undated.

opportunity" (*Zhongguo jiyu lun*) has taken the place of the "theory of the China threat" (*Zhongguo weixie lun*) in Southeast Asia.[20]

Other elements have emerged in more recent Chinese discussions of CBMs. The first is a heavy emphasis on the fact that advancement of the national interest lies at the foundation of any successful CBMs (as in the case of China's pursuit of economic development) and that agreement among the relevant parties requires a confluence of such national interests.[21] The second is that the issue of sovereignty and equality must be respected and affirmed. Thus, it is said to be important that agreements reflect equality among the parties and that caution be exercised in developing binding measures that might interfere in the domestic affairs of either party.[22] Indeed, some Chinese commentators have suggested that third-party mediation is a form of such interference, noting that ASEAN states had specifically framed their agreements so as to make it difficult for the United States to intervene in their affairs. This is related to a third point that Chinese authors make: Any CBMs should be consistent with the distinctive conditions of Asia in general and China in particular. Finally, although most Chinese discussions of CBMs focus on agreements between states, it is acknowledged that CBMs can be explored through track II, nongovernmental organizations (such as the ASEAN Regional Forum)—perhaps an indication of adaption to Asian conditions.

Mainland Perspectives on Cross-Strait Confidence Building

The current flurry of interest in cross-Strait confidence building was prompted by a December 31, 2008, speech by Hu Jintao on the occasion of the 30th anniversary of the "Message to Compatriots in Taiwan." Among what would become known as his "Six Points," he offered,

> To help stabilize the situation across the Taiwan Strait and reduce military and security concerns, the two sides of the Taiwan Strait may have contacts and exchanges on military issues at an appropriate time to explore the issue of creating a mechanism of military security and mutual trust (*tantao jianli junshi anquan huxin jizhi wenti*).[23]

This was the most dramatic broaching of the topic of confidence measures ever issued by the mainland, but it was not the first. According to one mainland source, the origin of this effort could be found in Jiang Zemin's "Eight Points," when, in January 1995, he proposed talks "under the principle of one China . . . to end the

---

20 Shi Jiazhu, "Nanhai jianli xinren cuoshi yu quyu anquan" ["South Seas CBMs and Regional Security"], *Guoji guancha*, January 2004. See also, Li Li, "Dongmeng diqu luntan yu yufang xin waijiao" ["The ASEAN Forum and the Foreign Policy of Preventing War"], *Jiangnan shehui xueyuan xuebao*, Vol. 3, No. 4, 2001.

21 This is a central theme in a discussion of the difficulties in Soviet-Japanese relations. See Li Yonghui, "Shuyuan di linju" ["Alienated Neighbors"], *Eluosi zhonyga dongou yanjiu*, No. 2, 2005.

22 Chen Hanxi, 2005, p. 32.

23 Cited in "PRC Pundit Views Cross-Strait Military Trust, Rebuffs Calls to Redeploy Troops," *Zhongguo Qingnian*, 2009. For the text of Hu's speech, see "Hu Puts Forward Six Points to Further the Development of Cross-Strait Relations" (in Chinese), SINA, December 31, 2008.

condition of cross-Strait antagonism."[24] In 2005, in his "Four-Point Guidelines" on Taiwan, Hu Jintao specifically identified the possibility of trust building in his elaboration of his first point that the mainland "would never sway in adhering to the one China principle"

> as long as the Taiwan authorities acknowledge the "1992 Consensus." The two sides can not only talk about the official conclusion of the state of hostility, the establishment of military mutual trust (*junshi huxin*), the Taiwan region's room of international operation compatible with its status, the political status of the Taiwan authorities, and the framework for peaceful and stable development of cross-Strait relations, which we have proposed, but also talk about all the issues that need to be resolved in the process of realizing peaceful reunification.[25]

It is significant that this statement, as well as the one in December 2008 did not use the term *jianli xinren cuoshi*, which is the standard PRC government translation for CBMs. This term is reserved for international agreements. As Major General Luo Yuan, one of the more prominent mainland commentators on cross-Strait relations, reminded readers in one of the earliest articles on the "Hu Six Points" of 2008, "'CBMs' [are] a kind of trust measure between countries, while the 'military security and mutual trust mechanism' put forth by Hu Jintao is a special arrangement according to the special cross-Strait situation."[26] In what ways does this "special arrangement," determined by the domestic nature of the cross-Strait relationship, differ from international CBMs? What are the challenges perceived by mainland writers in negotiating CBMs in the cross-Strait context?

The most important of the special arrangements is obvious, and that is the requirement that both sides acknowledge that they are not negotiating an international issue. The manner of acknowledgement is for both sides to adhere to the "one China principle." As one commentary from August of 2009 put it,

> talks and the resolution of relevant questions must be under the one China principle. The goal of these talks is not only to end the antagonistic state of affairs across the Strait, but even more necessary (*geng xuyao de*) is that both sides must join to uphold China's sovereignty and territorial integrity and henceforth make this the plan of conduct for the development of cross-Strait relations.[27]

The demand that any CBMs be negotiated under the "one China principle" runs through all mainland discussions of the issue (how that principle is defined is discussed below). This demand, in the first instance, represents primacy of the value of sovereignty and resistance to foreign interference in PRC considerations of trust mechanisms.

---

[24] "Jiefangjun wei liang'an huxin weitiao lu duanni" ["A Clue to PLA Fine-Tuning of Cross-Strait Mutual Confidence"], *Xinhua Aobao*, August 3, 2009.

[25] "Four-Point Guideline on Cross-Strait Relations Set Forth by President Hu Jintao," March 14, 2005 (also available in Chinese). This was not the first time a "mechanism of mutual trust in military field" had been mentioned; it had been included in a statement on May 17, 2004. See "Curbing 'Taiwan Independence' Most Urgent Task," *People's Daily Online*, May 17, 2004.

[26] "PRC Scholar Urges Confidence Building with Taiwan Military" (in Chinese), *Guoji Xianqu Daobao*, January 5, 2009.

[27] "A Clue to PLA Fine-Tuning of Cross-Strait Mutual Confidence," *Xinhua Aobao*, August 3, 2009.

Although national sovereignty and security are both vital concerns, the former is even more fundamental. In fact, violations of China's sovereignty and interference with China's internal affairs are often regarded as more serious than a military threat. Issues concerning China's national unity, especially with regard to Taiwan, are China's most sensitive security issues.[28]

This is a non-negotiable issue for PRC analysts. In a later interview with Phoenix Television, Luo Yuan cited Deng Xiaoping in making the case that issues related to sovereignty would not be negotiated: "Sovereignty cannot be discussed. From beginning to end, the country's security and sovereignty should always be in first place."[29]

But adherence to the one China principle is also the litmus test of Taiwan's future intentions. Since the Chen Shui-bian administration, mainland commentators have emphasized that political trust is an important foundation for any cross-Strait military trust mechanism (more on this point below). As one China Institutes for Contemporary International Relations researcher put it in 2006, without mutual political trust, mutual military trust is like building "castles in the air" (*kongzhong louge*).[30] Of course, during the Chen administration, the need to acknowledge one China as a symbol of political trust was related to his perceived aspirations for independence. Yet even since the election of Ma Ying-jeou, this correlation between accepting the one China principle and establishing the political trust necessary for negotiating military trust mechanisms has remained, not only because the DPP is still seen as having considerable political influence but also because of doubts regarding the goals of the new Ma administration.[31]

In this latter case, the issue is identified not as independence but as perpetuation of the "status quo" of separation. In a January 2009 article in *Taiwan Research Quarterly*, even as the author noted that a dramatic change had taken place in cross-Strait relations that enhanced the political foundation for military trust mechanisms, he warned,

> The goal and intention of the two sides in establishing military mutual trust mechanisms is different. . . . [The Taiwan authorities] hope that by reaching an agreement they can achieve a guarantee of their security and a mechanism to avoid the risk of a Mainland attack on Taiwan. Taiwan authorities do not want to push ahead with the close linking of military mutual trust and political mutual trust. Because of this, to a certain degree, the Taiwan authorities' intent has an

---

[28] Liu Huaqiu and Zhang Hua, "Confidence Building in Asia," in Michael Krepon, ed., *Chinese Perspectives on Confidence Building Measures*, Washington, D.C.: Stimson Center, Report No. 23, May 1997, p. 3.

[29] "Liang'an junshi huanxin Taiwan fangnian yu san da misi" ["The Taiwan Side Has Three Big Myths in Regard to Cross-Strait Military Trust"], PhoenixNews.com, September 3, 2009.

[30] Zhai Kun, "Junshi huanxin jizhi yu liang'an de heping fazhan" ["Military Confidence Building Mechanisms and the Peaceful Development of Cross-Strait Relations"], China Internet Information Center, October 1, 2006.

[31] Soon after Hu's "Six Points" were announced, a February 12, 2009, editorial in the Hong Kong newspaper *Wen Wei Po* [*Wenhui Bao*] suggested that a military mutual trust mechanism would "contain the fury of the Taiwan independence forces."

> instrumental quality (*gongjuhua de secai*); they seek to use military mutual trust mechanisms to achieve their security.[32]

Indeed, not only have mainland commentaries insisted on acceptance of the one China principle as a precondition for talks on military trust mechanisms, but some analysts have even depicted its realization as a justification for, and expected result of, such talks. This was apparent soon after Hu's "Six Points," when Luo Yuan described the goal of this initiative as "the realization of the great cause of peaceful unification," and it has remained a theme in discussions of the issue ever since.[33] As one researcher from the National Defense University put it recently, although there have been economic and cultural exchanges, "Only when we have established military security [and] military trust mechanisms can this be counted as a real step forward on the road to peaceful reunification."[34]

The Taiwan side's acceptance of the one China principle is also seen by mainland commentators as addressing another continuing concern, namely the "internationalization" of cross-Strait relations and the roles of the United States and Japan. Exemplary of this line of thinking, one commentator has argued that included in the one China principle is the demand that no foreign power damage China's sovereignty. The identity of that power is obvious from the assertion by the author that Washington is ambivalent about the prospects of a cross-Strait trust mechanism. While on the one hand, many Chinese analysts believe, the United States would like to see tensions between the mainland and Taiwan lessened, on the other, it continues its policy of using Taiwan to contain the mainland. Thus, mainland observers assert, along with Japan, the United States seeks to maintain the lack of predictability in the Taiwan Strait through its arms sales to Taiwan.[35]

The result of this view is not only Beijing's apparent rejection of an American role in negotiating any future agreement (as evinced by the reaction to the rumor regarding Admiral Keating's invitation to talks in Hawaii), but a demand that any agreement

> must eliminate the intervention and influence of foreign forces and blocs. It must eliminate and be on guard for the possibility that military mutual trust mechanisms could take on a 'state to state' flavor. We must especially guard against using international military trust mechanisms and applying them to cross-Strait relations, resulting in the interference of foreign powers and foreign blocs. Because of this, neither side of the Strait may have an alliance in fact with any foreign country.[36]

---

32 Chen Xiancai, "Liang'an junshi huanxin jizhu: lilun jian'gou yu shixian lujing" ["Cross-Strait Military Mutual Trust Mechanisms: Theoretical Design and Path of Realization], *Taiwan yanjiu jigan*, No. 103, January 2009, p. 24. For a similar argument, see Li Jianzhong, "Jiajin cuohao jianli liang'an junshi huanxin jizhu" ["Speed Up the Establishment of Cross-Strait Military Trust Mechanisms"], *Fazhi yu shehui*, No. 13, 2009, pp. 201–202.

33 See "PRC Scholar Urges Confidence Building with Taiwan Military," 2009.

34 Li Jianzhong, 2009, p. 201.

35 Chen Xiancai, 2006, p. 25.

36 Chen Xiancai, 2009, p. 26.

Moreover, the American connection would likely intrude into the negotiation process itself. If, as seems inevitable from its public positions, the Taiwan side raises the issue of drawing down mainland missiles opposite the island as a precondition for talks, the mainland would not only refuse but also likely counter by calling for a reciprocal suspension of American arms sales—including, in the view of one prominent commentator, the sale of F-16C/Ds.[37] The questions of the American connection and the missiles facing Taiwan represent for each side the two most sensitive issues with regard to any negotiations on military trust mechanisms. For Taiwan, the American connection is the indispensible element in its defense against mainland coercion; for the mainland, the missiles are the core of its anti-independence deterrent.

It seems clear that the insistence on operating under the one China principle as the precondition for talks is symbolic of what mainland commentators see as a bundle of elements that set cross-Strait confidence building apart from its international counterpart. Consistent with discussions of this latter type, mainland analysts see the pursuit of national interest as the fundamental force driving Beijing's willingness to consider cross-Strait confidence measures. In this case, a CBM structured as an agreement among "domestic" political actors serves the mainland's clear interest in settling the sovereignty issue in its favor while excluding an international role in the process, weakening defense ties with the United States, and isolating independence forces in Taiwan. Indeed, occasional suggestions that CBMs might be negotiated in a KMT-CCP (Kuomintang–Chinese Communist Party) context represent the logical extension of such reasoning.[38]

When it comes to the actual content of CBMs that might be negotiated between the two sides should these basic requirements be met, mainland authors tend to suggest the usual prescriptions intended to lessen mistrust and increase transparency through joint action, reciprocal visits, etc. For the most part, these conform to the categories and specific actions that are typical of international CBMs. Additionally, there have been suggestions that a staged process might be useful, given the lack of mutual trust between the two sides, conforming to what Desjardins calls "vertical expansion."[39] In short, there is no shortage of proposals from both sides of the Strait as to content and process.

With respect to timing, some of the loudest calls for getting on with the process have come from Major General Luo Yuan. In an article published in August 2009, he was clearly impatient to begin negotiations ("one keeps hearing noises on the stairs but sees no one coming down"), arguing that the Ma Ying-jeou government

---

37 See, for example, "Jianli liang'an junshi huanxin shuangfang dou you qianglie yiyuan," *Aomen Bao*, January 3, 2009. For the specification of F-16C/Ds, see Luo Yuan on Phoenix Television, "Liang'an Junshi Huanxin."

38 "Establishing Military Mutual Trust Mechanisms for Cross-Strait Consultations" (in Chinese), *Xinhua Aobao*, August 2, 2009.

39 See Li Jianzhong, 2009.

should get over its fear of being labeled as pro-mainland, cease making the withdrawal of missiles a precondition, and get on with the talks. It was time for Taipei to show its "governing ability" (*zhizheng nengli*).[40]

Less than a month later, still impatient to get on with the talks, Luo seemed to have grown more conscious of the sensitivity of the issue. In a September 2, 2009, interview with Phoenix Television, he recognized the difficulties involved in negotiating such an agreement due to the absence of political trust and suggested what he called the "four firsts and four laters" (*si xian, si hou*): "first discuss, later negotiate" (*xian lun, hou tan*); "first easy, later hard" (*xian yi, hou nan*); "first peripheral, later core" (*xian waiwei, hou hexin*); and "first second track, later first track" (*xian ergui, hou yigui*).[41]

With this approach, Luo was more in step with both the official and unofficial mainland commentaries of the past six months, which have seemed more cautious about negotiating CBMs in the present environment. As I argue in the next section, this seems appropriate given the given the likely outcome of any near-term efforts to do so in official cross-Strait negotiations.

If It Ain't Broke, Don't Fix It

The ironic lyric that began this paper was meant to convey three meanings: that cross-Strait CBMs were not only unlikely at this point but were not also unnecessary and probably unhelpful for promoting or perhaps even sustaining the cross-Strait détente that has developed since Ma Ying-jeou's election.

Let me take the last point first. It seems clear from what has been published in China thus far is that Beijing will bring two non-negotiable issues to the table that would immediately divide the two sides: the one China principle and arms sales from the United States. As Luo Yuan makes very clear, at the present moment, both of these issues are non-negotiable because they touch on the issue of sovereignty.

In his December 2008 speech, Hu Jintao noted that negotiations could only proceed "on the basis of the one China principle" (*yige Zhongguo yuanze de jichu shang*). Some commentators have suggested the possibility that the 1992 consensus, which facilitated the reopening of cross-Strait talks in 2008, might also be acceptable to the mainland as a stand-in for the one China principle as required by Hu and echoed by other mainland figures. As yet, however, there has been no clear signal from Beijing that this is the case.

This is not surprising. My own sense is that, given the repeated insistence on depicting the achievement of such an agreement as an internal matter as well as a political step toward unification, combined with the continued concerns about independence sentiment in Taiwan and the apparent determination to use CBMs to loosen security ties with the United States, it is likely that the mainland is looking for a deeper commitment from Taiwan on the sovereignty question than is implicit in the ambiguous 1992 consensus which, from the perspective of

---

40 "PRC Pundit Views Cross Military Trust," 2009.

41 "There Are Three Myths in Taiwan Cross-Strait Military Trust," Phoenix News, September 3, 2009.

Taiwan at least, affirms the island's separate sovereignty as the Republic of China. While the consensus might be good enough for economic or cultural agreements, it seems likely that Beijing would demand more before agreeing to negotiate such mechanisms.

From the perspective of Taiwan, setting agreement on the "one China principle" as the precondition for negotiating CBMs in the current environment would likely not only disrupt the current truce based on "mutual non-denial" but also endanger the tenuous status of the 1992 consensus as the implicit basis for the present semiofficial (really official) talks. Additionally, it would threaten to undermine defense relations with the United States, the foundation of the island's security at what is perceived to be a crucial juncture.

Thus, given the current political balance in Taiwan, Beijing's public position on CBMs as described in this paper would likely be a deal-killer. It is extremely unlikely that the Ma administration could do anything more than insist on its current stance of mutual non-denial and affirm the connection with the United States. Indeed, the very public and repeated statements in the mainland commentaries that the goals of CBMs are to achieve reunification, weaken the independence movement, and separate Taiwan from the United States can only increase the suspicions of the KMT's critics and complicate Ma's position.

In short, the central paradox that comes out of this discussion is that Beijing's apparent present stance on negotiating CBMs puts the most intractable issues in cross-Strait relations at the *beginning* of a trust-building process rather at the end, where they belong. Because formal negotiations over CBMs are likely to touch on the issues of greatest sensitivity to both sides, Desjardins's warning about the "détente-consuming" nature of premature negotiations should be taken seriously, as should the example of Pakistan and India, which established CBMs in the absence of significant mutual trust.

I say "apparent" because it is, of course, impossible to know with certainty what the top leadership group in Beijing might have in mind should a decision be made to press on with trust-building measures across the Strait. All that one can say is that the present public record can only serve to increase caution on the part of Taiwan authorities, raise suspicions among independence advocates on the island, and do little to prepare attentive publics on the mainland for any reverse in policy.

Moreover, other than pursuing the largely political goals of reunification and weakening the security relationship between Taiwan and the United States, there doesn't seem to be any compelling military need for such measures (which is, after all, the essence of CBMs). To be sure, there is always a risk of conflict when two militaries face each other, and more, rather than less, certainty never hurts. However, there seems to be little reason to be concerned over accidental conflict or misperception. There are informal understandings (the centerline being the prime example): There is already some cooperation in rescue at sea, many (probably too many) channels of communication exist, and even some unilateral statements of intent have been made. Moreover, and very importantly, viewing the question from the mainland's side, the frequent statements cited above regarding Taiwan's desire to use CBMs to freeze the status quo suggest that it is questionable whether Beijing really wants to reinforce certainty regarding its intent and thus weaken its deterrent to the independence forces, which is still considered to be so essential.[42]

In short, the time is not yet "ripe" (in the sense that Zartman uses it) for military CBMs. Indeed, I have argued above that it is quite possible that efforts to negotiate such measures to create the basis for increased cross-Strait confidence could very well have the opposite effect. However, it should not be forgotten that there are other ways to build confidence that are not fraught with the dangers of negotiation discussed above. If one were to use the broadest definition of CBMs to include economic and cultural measures, then it is obvious that the extent of cross-Strait contacts as reflected in trade, transportation, tourism, cultural exchanges, etc., far surpasses anything that existed in Cold War Europe or the Indian subcontinent. Although commentators on both sides of the Strait have expressed reservations regarding the spillover from these agreements, the fact is that they have taken on new momentum since the 2008 elections, as have some of the more informal mechanisms developed to avoid cross-Strait conflict.

As Inglof Kiesow has argued, negotiating CBMs is a difficult process, the failure of which can have "disastrous results." At this point, it would seem safer to build on—and expand—the process that exists rather than start a risky, and probably unnecessary, new one. In other words, to borrow a useful 成语: "If it ain't broke, don't fix it."

[42] As Glaser and Glosserman, 2008, note, this comes out in discussions with mainland officials.

6. Limits of Coercion: Compellence, Deterrence, and Cross-Strait Political-Military Affairs

Christopher P. Twomey[1]

Introduction

China's rise has manifested in many ways across the globe. No one is affected more than its immediate neighbors, and Taiwan, among the smaller and more geostrategically contested, feels these changes the most. This paper looks to assess the impact on Taiwan, and secondarily the United States, of China's increased military capabilities as they pertain to the Strait.

This is a critical issue. One of the most fundamental lessons to learn about Chinese foreign policy is the importance of the Taiwan lens.[2] Until very recently, Taiwan was the primary driver of China's naval and air force modernization, and today it remains central. Due to historical legacies, national interests, and deep social and political ties, the United States has significant security ties to Taiwan. Understanding how the dramatic rise in Chinese military power affects those ties helps analysts to understand one of the most important security dynamics in Asia today.

Through analysis of the triangular relations, this paper concludes that the substantial military capability enhancements by the People's Republic of China (PRC) have not led to commensurate gains in coercive outcomes. There appears to be some degree of deterrence success in stemming a further move toward independence within the Taiwanese body politic. However, there is no sign of significant compellent success in pushing it toward reunification. The U.S. role in this is central, as it too is affected by that balance and it too can influence policy in Taiwan.

Before turning to that analysis, it is worth emphasizing that power does not need to be wielded overtly to affect outcomes. Tacit or implicit threats can shape real outcomes. This greatly complicates analysis, but to ignore such effects in an effort to obtain some methodological purity would condemn this important line of questioning to irrelevance. Similarly, perceptions matter more than the real power balance. Absent conflict, it is the perception of the balance that affects the likelihood of coercive success, whether that coercion is overt or tacit. A final important complication is the multiple sources of strategic influence and determinants of strategic policy. The balance of power, the focus of this study, is only one of these. As will be clear, however, domestic politics, the efficacy of strategies, perceptual biases, and individual leaders all shape the conduct of international politics in this triangle.

---

[1] The opinions and conclusions in this paper are the author's alone and do not necessarily represent those of the U.S. Department of Defense. The author would like to express appreciation to Scott Harold, Phillip Saunders, and Andrew Scobell for their comments on previous versions of this paper.

[2] Susan L. Shirk, *China: Fragile Superpower*, New York: Oxford University Press, 2007.

With those complications acknowledged at the outset, the paper now turns to a quick assessment of the balance of power among China, Taiwan, and the United States in the strategic geography of the Taiwan Strait. A notional sketch of this author's views is laid out explicitly, and it shapes the bulk of the analysis and conclusions drawn below. Then, a set of stylized goals is laid out for China and Taiwan with regard to future development on the unification/independence issue. (U.S. goals are also briefly discussed.) The bulk of the paper looks at how successful each of the three has been in achieving those goals in the context of the evolving military balance. While the types of data used vary substantially across the three, the conclusions all emphasize the challenges in relying primarily on power to assess the development of politics in the region.

The Evolving Military Balance Across the Taiwan Strait

This chapter will not repeat the detailed analysis on the recent evolution of the military balance provided by Cole and Shlapak's contributions to this volume.[3] Still, it is worthwhile to consider the range of strategies that have become realistic for China today and those that Beijing might soon obtain. Detailed discussions are likely superfluous for the purposes here: Changes in specific capabilities and even how operational options change with the incorporation of new weapons into the Chinese (and Taiwanese and U.S.) military would not correlate highly to any political outcome. Perceptions, held by a wide range of actors, are unlikely to revisit detailed net assessments on a month-by-month basis. Rather, an overall sense of viable military strategies as they evolve over several years is likely to be the appropriate scale of resolution for determining the political effects of these military changes.

A rough chronological look at that level of assessment over the past 20 years might be as laid out in the following way (see Table 6.1), in terms of describing the maturation of what China might be able to achieve militarily. At this level of resolution, one might confidently predict a few trends as well. These are all notional, based on the author's impressions after watching this area for several decades. That said, as noted, it is in line with the sources cited above.

Of course, all these future estimates depend on actions taken by Taiwan and the United States. Adoption of a porcupine strategy by Taiwan would go a long way to forestall these outcomes.[4] Changes in U.S. naval strategy

---

[3] See also Robert S. Ross, "Taiwan's Fading Independence Movement," *Foreign Affairs*, Vol. 85, No. 2, March–April 2006a. For an evaluation of the military balance in one specific arena and consideration of the political implications of that balance, see Michael A. Glosny, "Strangulation from the Sea? A PRC Submarine Blockade of Taiwan," *International Security*, Vol. 28, No. 4, Spring 2004.

[4] William S. Murray, "Revisiting Taiwan's Defense Strategy," *Naval War College Review*, Vol. 61, No. 3, 2008. Even aside from this approach, this author would not go as far as to say that ongoing military modernization will not materially affect the balance, contra Robert S. Ross, "Explaining Taiwan's Revisionist Diplomacy," *Journal of Contemporary China*, Vol. 15, No. 48, August 2006b.

would have a similar effect.[5] Still, those changes would require rather substantial political will in either country and should not be treated as a baseline.

Table 6.1: Operational Strategies Enabled by Chinese Military Modernization

Period	Strategy
Early 1990s	Missile barrages against soft targets and cities in Taiwan
Late 1990s	Submarine warfare against Taiwanese shipping (including use of mines)
Early 2000s	Accurate missile attacks on military targets
	Sea denial to Taiwanese naval forces
Late 2000s	Air control over Taiwan Strait and ability to conduct sustained offensive air operations against Taiwan itself, except against substantial American intervention
	Sea denial against Taiwanese and American naval forces in waters near Taiwan
Late 2010s?	China will have solidified its ability to conduct sustained offensive air operations over Taiwan even if the United States becomes heavily involved[a]
Early 2020s?	A robust sea denial might to reach a few hundred miles beyond Taiwan proper[b]
Thereafter?	A viable amphibious invasion would seem plausible

[a] A DF-21 buildup and willingness to hit Japan and Guam would achieve this.
[b] Key capabilities here would be continued conventional attack submarine development and an operational anti-ship ballistic missile (ASBM).

Thus, we might view the late 1990s as a period that allowed China to impose fairly blunt costs on Taiwan. Over time, this capability has been bolstered, to be sure, but through the 2000s, China has layered on top of that the ability to more selectively target the Taiwanese military without wreaking havoc on civilian centers. Most recently, and heading into the future, China will have the ability to do that even in the context of substantial U.S. involvement.

If any of these strategies were implemented, China too would bear costs, of course. However, the military costs decline over time. The political costs also vary: The blunt punishment strategies that would have been the only ones available in the (early and mid-) 1990s would have had high costs in terms of international reputation and a

[5] Wayne P. Hughes, *The New Navy Fighting Machine: A Study of the Connections Between Contemporary Policy, Strategy, Sea Power, Naval Operations, and the Composition of the United States Fleet*, Monterey, Calif.: Naval Postgraduate School, NPS-OR-09-002-PR, August 2009.

virulent backlash from the Taiwanese population.[6] More selective targeting, available more recently, lowers these costs beginning in the 2000s. Implementing future strategies, if they required the full use of force to coerce outcomes, would likely bring a return to a period characterized by higher political costs for Beijing.

One way to conceive of this is to highlight that China now has at its fingertips better-quality punishment strategies—ones less likely to alienate the Taiwanese population and foment strong international condemnation. That is, China has increasingly viable deter-by-punishment strategies.[7] It could also attempt to use the same force to "coerce by punishment." That is, it might attempt to force concessions on the Taiwanese through the threat of punishment (or the threat of increased or continued punishment once a war has started).

Still, Beijing continues to lack the ability impose its will on Taiwan through the use of blunt force. Beijing cannot defeat all military opposition by Taiwan through an invasion and occupation of the island. Instead, victory for Beijing today requires winning a competition of willpower. Beijing must be more willing to accept military costs (from Taiwanese and, likely, U.S. forces) and international pressure than Taiwan is willing to accept the military costs that Beijing can impose on it from afar and in the air above the island.

Even considering that last caveat, if the military balance plays a central role in achieving political ends, we should expect some progress for the PRC over this entire period and erosion for the United States and Taiwan. With that overview of the evolving balance, the paper now turns to the goals that such military strategies might serve or assail.

Potential Goals for Each Side

For both China and Taiwan, there is a straightforward range views regarding plausible outcomes. A notional list appears in Table 6.2, in order of likely PRC preferences (with those toward the bottom opposed with increasing vigor).[8]

Taiwan's preferences are similar to the converse of the list presented in Table 6.2. But—and to some extent, the same could be said for China—there is variation within Taiwan to the point where it does not make sense to describe it as a unitary actor, certainly with regard to the final point on the list in Table 6.2.

---

[6] Such reputation matters not because China fears the scolding of human rights groups, but because grave civilian costs of conflict can lead to national reactions by third parties, as happened in the wake of the Tiananmen Massacre in 1989 as well as the Taiwan Strait Crisis of 1995–1996. On the typical reaction of target countries to such coercive campaigns against societal targets, see Robert Pape, *Bombing to Win: Air Power and Coercion in War*, Ithaca, N.Y.: Cornell University Press, 1996.

[7] Deter by denial lacks relevance here in the Sino-Taiwan dyad, since Taiwan's actions (further declarations of independence) are hard to "deny" militarily. Further in the future, China can deny the United States the ability to enter the conflict, but that shifts the focus.

[8] The author would like to thank Phil Saunders for sketching out this list.

Table 6.2: Beijing's Notional Preferences Regarding the Taiwan Strait

Preference	Outcome
Most Opposed—Most Preferred	1. Formal unification with unchanged PRC regime
	2. Confederation that permits some Taiwanese autonomy
	3. Ambiguous political association with mainland that preserves high degree of autonomy
	4. *De facto* sovereignty with limited international space (e.g., the status quo)
	5. *De facto* sovereignty and robust assertion of Taiwan's international space
	6. *De facto* sovereignty, robust assertion of international space, and formal alliance with the United States
	7. *De jure* Taiwanese independence

More generally, several of these options are closely related (e.g., 1 and 2, as well as 4 through 6). Obviously, one could continue to further parse the options. One interesting option that is hard to place on this sort of list would be "confederation in the context of dramatic political reform in the PRC." Where exactly such an option would fall on the list would depend on the details of political reform, the nature of confederation, and whose views in Zhongnanhai were making the ranking.

Item 4 on the list is particularly important as the locus of the status quo. Beijing wants to *deter* movement higher in the list and *compel* progress toward the lower numbers. International relations theory is quite clear that compelling concessions (i.e., moving Taiwan toward 3 or lower) is very challenging, while deterring new provocations is somewhat less difficult.[9]

On the other side, Taiwan's preferences might simplistically be viewed as the inverse of that ranking. There are certainly some Taiwanese constituencies who value the concept of reunification—with various political preconditions, to be sure—more than the inverse of the above would reflect. Still, even if we allow that the real world is more complex, and particularly that neither Taiwan nor China is a "unitary actor" easily represented by any "median-voter" concept, this list allows some discussion of the interaction between the evolving military balance as discussed in the previous section and these political outcomes.

For the United States, the picture is rather different. Perhaps the most important goal might be to serve as a reliable friend to a longtime partner that shares many American values and is acting responsibly in international

[9] Thomas C. Schelling, *Arms and Influence*, New Haven, Conn.: Yale University Press, 1966; Jack S. Levy, "Loss Aversion, Framing Effects, and International Conflict," in Manus I. Midlarsky, ed., *Handbook of War Studies II*, Ann Arbor, Mich.: University of Michigan Press, 2000; Gary Schaub, Jr., "Deterrence, Compellence, and Prospect Theory," *Political Psychology*, Vol. 25, No. 3, 2004.

politics.[10] Obviously, the precise definition of "acting responsibly" is a challenge, but recent characterizations of what that might mean capture the core as avoiding unilateral challenges to the status quo.[11] An important second goal would be avoiding war, particularly large-scale war.

Again, there are constituencies within the United States who might switch the order of these, or who have views that might be orthogonal to these issues. Most important among the latter would be a hardened offensive realist view that would suggest that, by complicating China's ability to project power, a Taiwan that remains militarily separate from China is in the U.S. national interest, *ceteris paribus*.[12] Nevertheless, with that one (not widely held, particularly within official circles) exception, most American views would then cede the initiative to Taiwan and China. That is, American interests are fundamentally about the nature of the interaction between those two players rather than the outcome that comes out of that interaction. Thus, U.S. interests are served, to a significant extent, by either a stable status quo or peaceful resolution toward a number of final dispositions.

Political Impact of the Evolving Military Balance

Measuring the effect of overt coercive attempts is challenging. Arguments continue to this day regarding the causes and outcomes of the resolution of the Cuban Missile Crisis, a case about which we know a stunning amount of detail.[13] Trying to determine the effect of tacit coercion in contemporary cases is much more challenging.

Given the range of different goals as discussed in the previous section, it is worth considering the effects of the military changes on each of the three participants in cross-Strait politics. Also, due to the nature of the domestic politics in each country, the data available differ. The best data are available for Taiwan, where extensive polling on closely related issues provides some grounds to draw robust conclusions. This is a direct measure of the impact of the shifting military balance: What changes does it lead to in Taiwanese voters' minds? Given the issue's lower salience in the United States, such polling is not available, but senior leaders are willing to discuss the issue on the record, both while in office and after. In China, while there is certainly a record of statements, these are less reliable indicators, and tenuous inferences must also be drawn from behavior.

Taiwan

If the shift in the military balance has had a political effect, it should be visible first and foremost in Taiwan. It should manifest there in public opinion, leadership statements, partisan shifts, and actual policy. This section

---

[10] This might be a useful time to reiterate that this paper represents the author's views and not official policy.

[11] Thomas J. Christensen, U.S. Deputy Assistant Secretary for East Asian and Pacific Affairs, "A Strong and Moderate Taiwan," speech to the U.S.-Taiwan Business Council, September 11, 2007.

[12] Such a view would be entirely consistent with John J. Mearsheimer, *The Tragedy of Great Power Politics*, New York: W. W. Norton & Company, 2001.

[13] Was the Soviet Union coerced into backing down, or did the offer of withdrawal of Turkish missiles and guaranteeing the security of Cuba serve as the key carrots? See, for instance, Graham Allison and Philip Zelikow, *Essence of Decision: Explaining the Cuban Missile Crisis*, New York: Addison-Wesley Longman Publishers, 1999.

evaluates the evidence in each of these areas, with an emphasis on public opinion as the key driver of those other factors in a democracy.

The cross-Strait issue is one of the most important in shaping voting preferences of the Taiwanese electorate.[14] Thus, the data available are substantial and important. The starting point for discussing Taiwan in terms of this issue should be Figure 6.1, which shows expressed preferences on some of the goals that were discussed above.

Figure 6.1: Preferences in Taiwan on Political Status

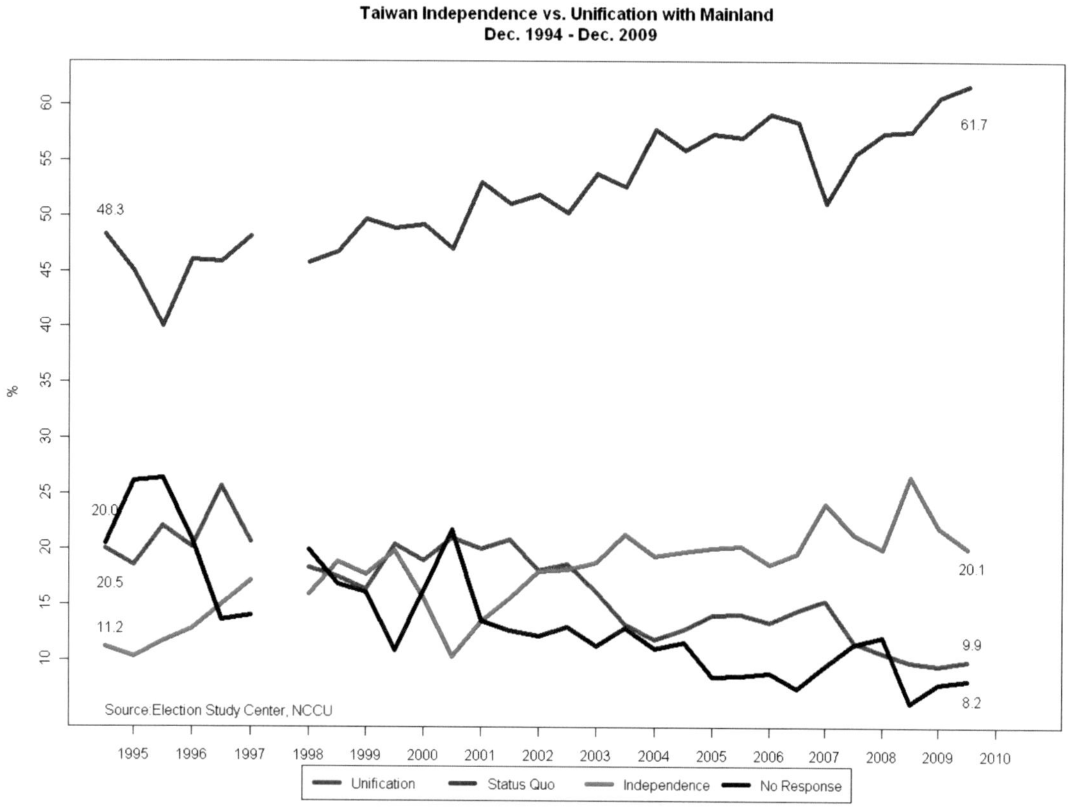

SOURCE: Adapted from Election Study Center, National Chengchi University, "Changes in the Unification-Independence Stances of Taiwanese as Tracked in Surveys by Election Study Center," undated.

Interestingly, the development of blunt punishment–based strategies in the 1990s by China had no clear effect on Taiwanese preferences. Were the population "compelled," the preference for "unification" should have risen in that period. While there is certainly some variation, if anything, from 1995 to the middle of 1999, it fell, and extending the comparison into 2001 or 2002 only allows a conclusion of "no change." The flip side of

---

[14] Chiung-chu Lin, "The Role of Issue in Taiwan's Politics, 1996–2004," *Issues and Studies*, Vol. 44, No. 1, 2008.

compellence is deterrence: Was the Taiwanese population increasingly deterred from supporting independence in that period? From 1995 to 1999, support doubled. After a volatile two years from 1999 to 2001, it remained at that higher level. Plausibly, some in Taiwan have been deterred from shifting to support independence; it might have been reasonable to expect a continuation of the growth in support after 1999. Thus, there may have been some deterrence of further pro-independence views.

Similarly, the development of more selective punishment capabilities that could target the military only in the early 2000s has a paradoxical effect on Taiwan's population: a 5-percent decline in support for unification and a slight increase in support for independence. Those trends continue to the end of the decade as well, while China is increasingly deploying capabilities that expand its military advantages to challenge even the United States in a role supporting Taiwan. These trends should increase the credibility of Chinese threats to use force, since Beijing could chose to avoid massive civilian causalities and the associated international approbation (if it chose; it certainly has the ability to pursue a less discriminate strategy if it chose to do so). That this increase in qualitative capabilities has not led to increased coercion of Taiwanese opinion is surprising.

Indeed, the dominant trend in Figure 6.1 is a steadily rising preference for the status quo over a 15-year period; all the while, the military balance was tilting against Taiwan. As noted above, there are some qualifications that one might make. Beijing may have prevented things from getting worse. Still, the overall picture is one of very limited value for the military tools Beijing has developed.

Still, correlation analysis is an imperfect measure to be sure. Many other factors would affect this expressed preference. For instance, the nature of politics at home and abroad could shape the relative attractiveness of such options. Similarly, economic factors could play a role, as could changes in the salience of ethnic identity. The "identity variable" also plays an important role as a distinctly Taiwanese political identity rises.[15] These factors all have effects independent from the military balance. However, more sophisticated multivariate analyses of Taiwanese voters' preferences can help isolate the factor of interest here: the effect of the perceived change in military balance. These provide a similar, if nuanced, rejection of a hypothesis emphasizing rising coercive power in China's military capabilities.

One particular study is highly valuable for our purpose here. It looked at Taiwanese preferences regarding independence, the status quo, and reunification, but also made use of control variables such as assessment of the military balance and expectations regarding U.S. entry into any potential conflict. Additionally, instead of relying on an outsider's assessment of the military balance, the respondents' own views are captured, thus controlling for any large difference between this author's assessment of the military balance and that of the Taiwanese population. This study found the following:

---

[15] Carol Lee Hamrin and Zheng Wang, "The Floating Island: Change of Paradigm on the Taiwan Question," *Journal of Contemporary China*, Vol. 13, No. 39, 2004; T. Y. Wang, "National Identity and Democratization in Taiwan: An Introduction," *Journal of Asian and African Studies*, Nos. 1–2, April 2005b.

> While the perceived military threat from China succeeds in preventing Taiwan residents from pursuing de jure independence, it does not gain their compliance to Beijing's demands. Consistent with the previous findings, threats do not lead to submission. The perceived military threat from China merely prolongs Taiwan's de facto independence.[16]

An increased in perceived military threat did not lead to greater support for unification, although it did shift support from independence to the status quo.[17] (Ross finds a similar effect on elites he has interviewed.[18]) Again, this is pointing out that there has been some deterrent effect on preventing further shifts toward a pro-independence line, but no compellent success in increasing the size of the pro-unification movement.

The same study, however, emphasizes the importance of Washington's expected role:

> While the belief that the United States will not intervene if Taiwan is attacked by China shows no statistically significant effect on the pro-unification and pro-status-quo positions, it has negative effects on the pro-independence stand. Specifically, the odds of supporting an independence position relative to an undetermined stand are 61 percent smaller for those who believe that the United States will not intervene in a cross-Strait military conflict due to Taiwan's pursuit of independence. This finding suggests that the United States plays a crucial role in Taiwan citizens' decision to pursue formal independence.[19]

All this suggests that Beijing is getting limited, although discernable, direct political influence out of its increasingly robust ability to coerce Taiwan: Potential strengthening of the pro-independence movement has been deterred, but that movement has not weakened, nor has there been compellent success in creating a stronger pro-unification movement. More important is Taiwan's perception of U.S. policy. It cannot be assessed from these data, however, whether the Taiwanese voters are assessing the Sino-U.S. military balance as part of that assessment (rather than focusing solely on willpower).

Moving beyond public opinion to the position of Taiwan's political parties provides another window onto this issue. One analysis of party positions on the unification-independence issue rates perceptions of each party on a 0–10 scale ranging from 0 (independence) to 10 (reunification). The Kuomintang (KMT) was seen to have shifted from 6.1 to 7.4 from 1996 to 2004, as one would expect given the shift in the military balance. However, the Democratic Progressive Party (DPP) moved from 2.0 in 1996 to a high of 3.1 in 2000 before falling back to 2.2 in 2004.[20] (Note that the same survey echoed the conclusion above about the overall electorate moving toward independence, dropping from 5.1 to 4.7.) While the KMT's shift accords with the increase in Chinese

---

[16] T. Y. Wang, "The Perception of Threats and Pragmatic Policy Choice: A Survey of Public Opinion in Taiwan," *Issues and Studies*, Vol. 41, No. 1, March 2005a.

[17] Similar conclusions are drawn in Ross, 2006b, p. 452.

[18] Ross, 2006a.

[19] Wang, 2005a, pp. 100–102.

[20] Chiung-chu Lin, 2008, pp. 86–87.

military power, the DPP's works in the opposite direction for at least the latter half of the period of study. Furthermore, these changes were relatively small in scale (other issues saw 2-point swings in the same period).

A final window onto the political effect of the changing military balance looks to actual policy. The history of Taiwan's policy under presidents Lee Teng-hui and Chen Shui-bian is well known and cannot be characterized as having been meaningfully compelled by the mainland. Nor can it be said that either was *increasingly* deterred as China's power increased. That said, the problem of multiple influences on policy is substantial. Many authors emphasize the role of domestic politics in shaping particular initiatives of former President Chen Shui-bian.[21] U.S. policy has clearly aimed to influence Taiwanese policy as well (as discussed later). These concerns notwithstanding, clearly, the trend has been for increases in provocation through the Lee Teng-hui and Chen administrations, again, precisely as the military balance tilted increasingly toward the PRC. It is only with the election of President Ma Ying-jeou in 2008 that Taiwanese policy shifted in the direction predicted by the evolving military balance. Certainly, in that case, Ma promised a less confrontational policy with the mainland, avoiding referenda and provocative moves, such as the abolition of the National Unification Council. Ross makes a strong case for the death of the Taiwanese independence movement.[22] This suggests that at least one outcome has moved off the table, and deterrence can account for this.

Nevertheless, more broadly, it seems plausible to conclude from *all* these categories of data that China's ability to coerce Taiwan has not been as sensitive to the bilateral military balance as one might have expected, focusing narrowly on the military power itself. Consistent with work on strategic bombing, threatened violence seems to deepen enmity and willpower on the part of one's adversary.[23] The KMT's shift is the main exception to this, and its electoral victory is an important piece of data, as is the shift in KMT policy as Ma consolidated power in the lead-up to the election. Still, after 2008, it is unclear if an objective look at the KMT's positions would suggest that it is continuing to move toward a pro-independence position, as it should if the continually deteriorating military balance were the primary determinant of policy.

Thus far, the analysis has been narrowly confined to the effects of the shifting military balance on Taiwan. Of course, this is an oversimplification. Taiwan's policy is a product of the military balance, but also of Beijing and Washington's policies (to say nothing of the evolving domestic political situation, which was discussed in passing above). The next two sections highlight those other effects, recognizing that they cannot be artificially separated from Taiwan's policy.

---

21 See, e.g., Shih-chung Liu, "Convergence and Divergence in Taiwan's U.S. Policy, 2004–2008," Washington, D.C.: Brookings Institution, CNAPS Visiting Fellow Working Paper, November 2009.

22 Ross, 2006a.

23 Pape, 1996.

China

Assessing the impact of the changing military balance on Chinese behavior is the most challenging given the opacity of that system. No polls of senior Chinese leaders allow for standardizing their understanding of the level of threat and then assessing their policy preferences. However, we can assess the shifting nature of Chinese policy over time. While drawing conclusions from that is problematic—behavior depends on a variety of inputs—it at least allows some notional conclusions. In particular, it is clear that China's strategy has been to move away from the use of military tools to compel Taiwanese concessions. This choice of policy likely rests on more than just an evaluation of the effectiveness of its military toolkit. Still, one would expect that to have played some role in such a determination.

One plausible expectation derived from the shifting balance would be an increase in overt coercive diplomacy efforts by China if Taiwan were not moving in the appropriate direction. This has not occurred, at least after the turn of the century. Indeed, the opposite has occurred: One no longer hears discussions of deadlines for progress as was common under Jiang Zemin. Further, after the high point of the 2000 white paper on Taiwan, China abandoned the *sine die* provision in its policy toward Taiwan. That language was lacking in the Anti-Secession Law passed a few years later in 2005, which emphasized the carrots in Beijing's policy (while certainly restating long-standing elements in the "stick" side of its policy).[24] It has abided by an informal truce with regard to competition over diplomatic recognition with small states. Arguably, the Chinese leadership recognized that the 1995–1996 Taiwan Strait Crisis—the high point of coercive statecraft—had important costs throughout the region for China.[25] In the wake of that militarized event, a wave of counterbalancing against China occurred (Japan, Singapore, the Philippines, etc., all reinvigorated their security relationship with the United States). Furthermore, such activity received much international approbation. In response, China engaged in a very public campaign aimed to refurbish its image internationally: the New Security Concept and associated smile diplomacy by the PRC. Today, China's policy toward Taiwan is characterized by a "de-emphasis on the use and show of military force in cross-Strait relations."[26]

Beyond that, China does not appear to be demanding more from Taiwan as its power position improves. Most observers of China's policy over the past decade would characterize Hu Jintao as having moderated Beijing's demands. While the shift in leadership in Taipei has centrally affected relations across the Strait, China's policy has permitted Taiwan a wide range of behavior that would not have been possible in around the year 2000. Not all of these can be attributed to President Ma's election. These shifts have been precisely along the dimensions

---

[24] For similar views emphasizing the restraint in the Anti-Secession Law, see Chong-pin Lin, "More Carrot Than Stick: Beijing's Emerging Taiwan Policy," *China Security*, Vol. 4, No. 1, Winter 2008, p. 5.

[25] David Shambaugh, "China Engages Asia: Reshaping the Regional Order," *International Security*, Vol. 29, No. 3, 2004.

[26] Chong-pin Lin, 2008, p. 3.

laid out above with regard to the timing of the final status of the reunification and—quite markedly—a tolerance for international space:

- a notable softening of the *sine die* proviso that explicitly ruled out the status quo in perpetuity
- a truce on competition for diplomatic recognition among small Latin American, Pacific Island, or other states
- permitting Taiwan to have observer status in the World Health Assembly (WHA)[27]
- permitting Lien Chan, former chairman of the KMT, to participate in the Asia-Pacific Economic Cooperation (APEC) on behalf of Taiwan
- support for the Economic Cooperation Framework Agreement process, which Taiwan explicitly views as a foundation for free-trade agreements with third parties
- essentially returning to an acceptance of the 1992 consensus.[28]

The key challenge here is that China is not facing a static situation in Taiwan. Recognizing that its bluster backfired in the 1996 and 2004 elections, it would be quite reasonable to expect China to shift strategies. Interlocutors on the mainland readily acknowledge this. All these concessions occurred in the wake of Ma's election there and his commitment to reduce provocations on independence issues. It is certainly plausible to argue, in fact, that these moderations in policy would have been less likely under a less advantageous military situation (from Beijing's perspective).

Returning to the compellence-deterrence dichotomy, one reasonable interpretation is that Beijing is comfortable with having achieved successful deterrence and recognizes the challenges of striving for compellence. Deterring moves further away from Beijing is not the same as compelling movement toward reunification. The latter has much more stringent requirements in terms of capabilities, willpower, and permissive conditions in other areas (in particular, the role of the United States has to be managed successfully). In part, the success of deterrence has come about as a result of Taiwanese shifts in domestic politics (both in party platforms and in the electoral success of each party), although as noted above, these are not entirely separate from the role of Chinese military capabilities. Furthermore, part of the reluctance to attempt compellence likely comes from the recognition that such belligerence will only further engender Taiwanese political nationalism, already on the rise.[29] Nevertheless, one reasonable conclusion would be to emphasize the limitations of the utility of military power for compellence. This is particularly the case, one imagines, when the military balance provides a wide range of punishment options but lacks the ability for one side to impose its will on the other. Were that to change, compellence might look more plausible.

---

[27] Jacques deLisle, "Taiwan in the World Health Assembly: A Victory, With Limits," Washington, D.C.: Brookings Institution, Brookings Northeast Asia Commentary No. 29, May 2009.

[28] This author's read is that if one characterizes the 1992 consensus as "one China, different interpretations," what Beijing is now accepting is "1992 consensus, different interpretations." A 1992 consensus prime, if you will.

[29] Wang, 2005b.

However, another important shift in Chinese behavior since about 2004 (some see the Anti-Secession Law as the turning point on this and several issues) has been to influence Taiwan through the United States. This paper now turns to that relationship.

United States

Several of the emerging military capabilities possessed by the People's Liberation Army (PLA) directly affect the U.S. military. The emerging anti-access/area-denial capabilities call into question the ability of the United States to operate freely in waters even to the east of Taiwan. Furthermore, clearly, China has aspired to use its military leverage on the Taiwan issue in exactly this fashion: "Beijing has shifted its strategy vis-à-vis Taiwan from acting directly across the Strait to indirect pressure through Washington and elsewhere."[30] What have been the political effects in the United States?

At the simplest level, if the effect of military shift was straightforward, one would expect to see a distancing from the implicit security commitment that Washington has made to Taiwan. This is clearly not happening. The steady flow of arms sales to Taiwan has continued over a period of decades. The most significant impediments have been domestic politics in Taiwan rather than U.S. reluctance. Furthermore, the United States remains heavily involved in alliance diplomacy in the region, demonstrated by the statement at the 2005 "two-plus-two" meeting between U.S. and Japanese defense and foreign affairs officials that noted that peace in the Taiwan Strait was an interest of the alliance. Furthermore, the United State continues to build up its forces in the region, with a notable enhancement of capabilities in Guam, optimized to face any potential challenge from China.

That said, a few categories of U.S. policy in this area push in a different direction. A sharp line was taken against a series of statements, policies, and referenda pushed by Chen Shui-bian's government over the course of the mid-2000s aimed at promoting independence and carving out international space. These critiques were frequent and increasingly sharp through 2007,[31] culminating in a statement by Deputy Assistant Secretary of State Thomas Christensen that complained publicly of the government's recalcitrance in the face of repeated appeals made privately.[32] Might this constitute a success of coercion by the PRC? This series of critiques was unprecedented in the history of post-1979 U.S.-Taiwan relations and went far beyond any reprimands made against President Lee during his term in office from 1992 to 2000. Lee himself was not beyond engaging in provocation with the mainland over similar issues germane to Taiwan's status and sovereignty. That said, President Chen's actions went well beyond those earlier statements and actions. Lee's "vacation diplomacy" and

---

[30] Chong-pin Lin, 2008, p. 6.

[31] See Appendix 5 in Chong-pin Lin, 2008.

[32] Christensen, 2007.

statements such as "special state to state relationship"[33] pale in comparison to referenda on provisions for United Nations entry, abolishing offices within Taiwan's government responsible for reunification, and routine statements asserting Taiwan's independence.

Since the goal here is to isolate the impact of the changing military balance on U.S. policy concerning the Taiwan Strait, one must attempt to isolate other factors, such as the nature of Taiwan's policy. On this issue, the severity of reprimands against provocative behavior from Taiwan in the 2000s and other factors seem sufficient to explain the shift in U.S. policy—the intensity of those provocations themselves.

That said, one final area of U.S. policy does seem to have shifted, and it lacks other equally plausible explanations. Clearly, the nuance of U.S. declaratory policy on Taiwan's status is subtle and opaque. Douglas Paal, former director of the American Institute in Taiwan, refers to it as "the catechism of the triangular relationship."[34] Still, close analysis of it over the past 15 years charts a gradual change. In the early days of the post-normalization period, the United States did not take a stand on Taiwan's international status. Instead, it pointedly "acknowledged" that all Chinese on both sides of the Taiwan Strait believed there was "one China." This did not suggest that all or even most people had such beliefs (Were all people living in Taiwan at the time "Chinese"?) and certainly did not commit the United States to sharing such a view. The U.S. view was unstated. This was the basis for the United States' "one China" policy.

Beginning in the late 1990s, the Clinton administration conceded publicly to present the "three no's," which stated that the United States

- did not have a "one China, one Taiwan" policy nor a "two China policy"
- did not support Taiwanese independence
- did not support Taiwanese membership in the United Nations or other international institutions for which statehood is a prerequisite.

These commitments had been made privately before, but to make them publicly (and to do so in China, as Clinton did) was an important shift.[35] Still, to take a position that the United States "did not support" Taiwanese independence was not the same as "opposing" it or characterizing what the contemporary status of Taiwan actually was. The next step in the evolution of U.S. policy moved closer to doing exactly that. Over the course of the Bush administration, a series of statements by Secretary of State Colin Powell, National

---

33 On the less provocative nature of Lee's vision, see J. Bruce Jacobs and I-hao Ben Liu, "Lee Teng-Hui and the Idea of 'Taiwan,'" *China Quarterly*, Vol. 190, 2007, p. 375.

34 Douglas Paal, remarks prepared for the Carnegie Congressional Series on China: Taiwan Policy, Washington, D.C., March 26, 2008, p. 2.

35 Nancy Bernkopf Tucker, "China-Taiwan: US Debates and Policy Choices," *Survival*, Vol. 40, No. 4, January 1998.

Security Council Senior Director Dennis Wilder, and Deputy Assistant Secretary of State Thomas Christensen explicitly stated the view that Taiwan was not independent.[36]

Thus, there is some evidence that U.S. policy on Taiwan's actual status has shifted over time, subtly. Returning to the point at the outset of this section, this was precisely the goal of Beijing's policy. Wachman sees this as a success for Beijing: "Washington seems to have slipped into a pattern of reacting to these diplomatic dilemmas by carrying water for Beijing."[37] To be sure, that policy from China depended on more than just military levers, and Taiwan too was involved in provocative diplomacy that likely played an important role in influencing U.S. policy. But the increase in Chinese power in the 2000s that pertains most directly to U.S. capabilities certainly provides a backdrop for this subtle shift in U.S. policy to actively characterize Taiwan as "not independent."

The Obama administration has not been forced by events to delve into responding to provocations on Taiwan's status in the way that the Bush administration was. Nevertheless, the U.S. policy maintains precisely the same declaratory language[38] while also continuing the practice of engaging in arms sales aimed at ensuring that Taiwan's legitimate defensive needs are adequately maintained.

Conclusions

Beijing has created a variety of formidable capabilities over the past few decades, a trend likely to continue. And yet, the evidence above shows that this has led to only a moderate increase in Chinese influence over issues it cares about across the Taiwan Strait. To be sure, there has been some influence, particularly through the shifting Sino-U.S. balance, but even there, the change has not been dramatic. There has been no success in compelling the outcomes that Beijing desires and only limited, ambiguous success in deterring a further deterioration of the situation.

There are likely several reasons for this. First and foremost, Hu Jintao chose to pursue a more moderate Taiwan policy.[39] As noted above, it would be reasonable to believe that this was shaped by greater confidence that China's ability to deter the worst outcomes had increased to the point where a more

---

[36] See the Appendix 5 in Chong-pin Lin, 2008. Wachman also emphasizes this point. See Alan Wachman, "Ensnared by Beijing: Washington Succumbs to the PRC's Diplomacy of Panic," *China Security*, Vol. 4, No. 1, Winter 2008.

[37] That said, he views it as a failure of U.S. policy rather than a function of the military balance. See Wachman, 2008, p. 78.

[38] See, for instance, David B. Shear, Deputy Assistant Secretary, Bureau of East Asian and Pacific Affairs, "China-Taiwan: Recent Economic, Political and Military Developments Across the Strait and Implications for the United States," testimony before the U.S.-China Economic and Security Review Commission, Washington, D.C., March 18, 2010.

[39] For the key elements in that, see Bonnie S. Glaser, *Building Trust Across the Taiwan Strait: A Role for Military Confidence-Building Measures*, Washington, D.C.: Center for Strategic and International Studies, January 2010, 2ff.; Shu Keng and Gunter Schubert, "Agents of Taiwan-China Unification? The Political Roles of Taiwanese Business People in the Process of Cross-Strait Integration," *Asian Survey*, Vol. 50, No. 2, 2010.

cooperative policy might be expected to be lower risk. Ma's election would have been an important signal that such deterrence had succeeded, but as noted, Beijing's policy began to shift before then. Thus, that is unlikely to be the whole story.

In general, projecting influence from power is not straightforward. In part, this argument is linked to broader social science debates about coercive power in many arenas.[40] However, even in this particular case, it is clear that many intervening variables and countercurrents that are endogenous to the change in power itself affect actual political outcomes. Third parties are energized to get involved; the United States becomes increasingly involved. Domestic politics are aroused; both parties moderate their provocations and Ma is elected.

Indeed, perhaps the critically important element is that military coercive power has complex effects on a democracy. When military power lies in the background—when threats are only tacit—there is much noise in the political sphere and such issues do not seem to dominate debates. However, if military power is wielded overtly, it tends to provoke a backlash. This is certainly the story of several rounds of overt coercive attempts by China: A more resolute Taiwanese population moved counter to Beijing's wishes. The more conciliatory policy under President Hu has forestalled that,[41] but only at the cost of allowing the question of reunification to drift out of contemporary debates.

Since the strategies for which Beijing has been able to develop capabilities to date all involve threatening punishment in the event of actions taken or untaken, they fall in the realm of strategic coercion. Were Beijing to develop an amphibious assault capability, giving it the option of imposing its will through brute force regardless of the tenacity of Taiwan's willpower under attack, the outcomes could be quite different, and the past may provide little insight into such a radically different situation. To date, the military balance has been relevant for providing the context for a contest of willpower: How much pain could Beijing impose on Taiwan, and how long would Taiwan suffer it before conceding? Were the military balance to shift further, entirely different dynamics would come into play. China would not have to worry about the complex determinants of Taiwanese willpower if it could (fairly rapidly) conquer the island.

The most promising area for Beijing has been in its interaction with the United States. There, a narrowing of the military advantages once held by Washington has pushed the United States into a more active involvement in managing problems across the Taiwan Strait than it has had in decades. The cost here for Beijing is analogous to that it faced with Taiwan in the 1995–early 2000s period: Increasing military coercive leverage, and engaging in occasional bluster, tends to provoke counter-reactions in those on the other side.

---

[40] Robert O. Keohane and Joseph S. Nye, *Power and Interdependence*, New York: Longman Publishers, 2001. For a study that finds limited influence from Beijing's dominance of the economic relationship, see Keng and Schubert, 2010.

[41] He has done so to some extent, in any event. The political identity in Taiwan continues to develop in ways that undermine eventual prospects for reunification.

Increasingly, the United States is viewing Beijing's military buildup as threatening. This is likely to shift the focus for the development of future U.S. military capabilities toward China.

If Beijing has traded its "Taiwan" problem for a "United States" problem, that will not be viewed as a Chinese success in the long term.

7. Implications of Improvements in PRC Naval Capabilities: 2000–2010

Bernard D. Cole

Introduction

The People's Liberation Army Navy (PLAN) of the People's Republic of China (PRC) launched a significant modernization program in the mid-1990s, spurred by factors including the Taiwan Strait Crisis of 1995–1996. That event brought sharply home to China's military leaders that their navy was inadequate for its primary mission: applying decisive maritime power in a Taiwan scenario.

Beijing's naval modernization program has progressed impressively and has altered the balance of military power across the Taiwan Strait. That balance, of course, is a function not just of China's military capabilities but also those of Taiwan and of U.S. Pacific forces. All three countries' naval capabilities are continuing to evolve. China's maritime power continues to grow and modernize. By contrast, Taiwan's military capabilities have been improving only marginally—and have lost ground in comparison to the mainland. Finally, while U.S. military power continues to lead the world in terms of technological sophistication, in terms of numbers, its Pacific maritime forces are at their lowest point since the late 1940s.

China's increasing naval power is being demonstrated daily, in the Gulf of Aden, where the PLAN's counterpiracy operations are now almost 18 months old and have become almost routine for the PLAN, a factor of great significance in the maturing capability of that navy.

As China's naval abilities improve, the reduction in the U.S. Navy's on-station capability changes the maritime environment confronting the Chinese navy. PLAN planners no doubt have a list of likely conflict scenarios. These would include, in order of importance to Beijing, Taiwan, the disputes with Japan in the East China Sea, and the South China Sea. Taiwan's importance is obvious: Reunification with the mainland is required, in Beijing's eyes, to complete the Chinese revolution.

In the East China Sea, China confronts its age-old adversary, Japan. In addition to this historic enmity, Beijing is concerned about securing sea-bottom energy resources and two sovereignty issues in the East China Sea: first, the disputed location of the continental shelf and second, ownership of the disputed Diaoyu/Senkaku Islands. The South China Sea is important to Beijing primarily for its potential: Should significant energy resources be discovered in the central part of the sea, then its importance to China will immediately and significantly increase.

Shipbuilding

During the past 20 years, the PLAN has added to its ranks approximately 38 conventionally powered and five nuclear-powered submarines—two or three of them ballistic missile submarines (SSBNs). Additionally, China has added 15 guided-missile destroyers (DDGs), 16 guided-missile frigates (FFGs), almost three dozen modern patrol craft capable of firing cruise missiles, one or two *Yuzhao*-class landing platform docks (LPDs), 24 landing ship tanks (LSTs), and two replenishment-at-sea (RAS) ships to its naval fleet.[1]

Beijing's steady, moderate program of naval modernization has accelerated since 2000. All five of the nuclear-powered and 22 of the PLAN's conventionally powered submarines have been commissioned in the last nine years, as have ten DDGs and six FFGs, all of the 26 amphibious ships, and at least 40 *Houbei*-class missile patrol boats. In the first decade of this century, China has led the world in submarine construction, building almost three boats per year.

Except for submarines, however, China remains far behind the United States in terms of fleet expansion. During the century's first decade, the United States has built seven nuclear-powered submarines, two nuclear-powered aircraft carriers, 33 DDGs, two FFGs, two amphibious assault ships (LHDs), eight LPDs, and nine RAS ships. More important than these numbers, however, is China's focus on modernizing its navy with specific scenarios in view; for the past 20 years, this focus has been Taiwan. Hence the PLAN's concentration on increasing and improving its submarine fleet, rightly viewed as the efficacious means of preventing the U.S. Navy from intervening effectively in a scenario in Taiwan's waters.

More broadly, Chinese naval analysts have recently emphasized the value of technological advances, which have enabled a shift "from platform-centric to network-centric . . . strategy based on the speed of command."[2] This refers to the U.S. Navy doctrine that fleet operations are most effectively conducted not by individual ships acting on the basis of their own sensors, weapons, and communications, command, and control systems but by groups of ships operating as members of a cooperative network. The ships, aircraft, and even shore stations will be linked by computers and operate in a coherent "network-centric" environment, passing information back and forth and functioning as an integrated entity.

Until early 2008, however, the PLAN was still very much "platform-centric," almost wholly dependent on individual ship and aircraft operations with only rudimentary radio and data-link coordination. As the first decade of the new century comes to an end, China is deploying ships capable of operating as a relatively coherent naval task force able to project power on the seas. These new platforms are the beginning of the first really modern navy that Beijing will deploy as an instrument to deter Taiwan, thwart U.S. intervention, and secure its territorial claims in the East and South China Seas, as well as to carry out other maritime missions characteristic of a world economic power.

They embody significant improvements in several naval warfare areas, all of them crucial to performing effectively at sea in the new century. First among these improved areas are the administrative realms of maintenance

---

[1] Ship information is from Bernard D. Cole, *The Great Wall at Sea: China's Navy in the Twenty-First Century*, Annapolis: U.S. Naval Institute Press, 2010, pp. 92–93.

[2] Chen Wanjun and Cao Junping, "PLA Navy Develops Combat Software for Surface Vessels," Xinhua, November 14, 2005.

procedures and training paradigms. These are not dramatic subjects, but they underlie every facet of operational performance. Significantly improved at-sea capabilities include anti-air warfare, surface warfare, and operations across the electromagnetic spectrum. These improvements have focused on hardware, such as new missiles and sensors, but also reflect maturing doctrinal procedures. Chinese naval modernization goals appear to focus not on attempting to overwhelm or even match the U.S. Navy on a one-for-one basis, but rather on deploying maritime forces capable of helping to achieve specific national security interests.

Of particular significance for either a Taiwan scenario or operations among the disputed land features of the South China Sea is the first large amphibious warfare ship commissioned by Beijing. The nearly 20,000-ton-displacement Type 71 LPD emulates a U.S. design and provides the PLAN with its first modern amphibious warfare vessel. This may be the first of several such ships and would form a formidable task force if accompanied by the new destroyers that have been joining China's fleet since 2005. These ships are the PLAN's first escorts capable of area anti-air warfare defense, crucial to a task force operating in a hostile environment. China's continuing submarine construction program is the largest in the world and is providing the PLAN with the conventional- and nuclear-powered submarines to engage in an area-denial strategy against possible U.S. intervention in a Taiwan scenario.

Much media and analyst attention has been focused on China's possible first aircraft carrier, *Varyag*, a partially completed Russian ship towed to China from the Black Sea in 2002. Since its arrival in China, *Varyag* has apparently been undergoing a slow completion process, although the installation of a propulsion plant has not been reported or observed in open sources. Seagoing air power is not a crucial factor in a Taiwan scenario, given the island's 100-nautical-mile distance from the mainland, but when a large air-capable ship inevitably does join the PLAN, it will significantly improve that service's ability to conduct missions at a greater distance from mainland airfields and to project power in a hostile maritime environment.

Training

Beijing's emphasis on "science and technology" has also been espoused by presidents Jiang Zemin and Hu Jintao as a guidepost for military training and exercises. This not only draws on remnants of classic communism but also recognizes that the PLAN would be at a disadvantage in a current or near-term maritime conflict with technologically advanced navies, such as the U.S. Navy. Revised training regulations were issued in 2002, replacing the 1990 version; the new regulations emphasize standardized training relying on science and technology to prepare for "modern warfare." The current *Outline of Military Training and Evaluation* went into effect in January 2009.[3]

---

[3] Frederic Vellucci, "Recent Trends in PLA Navy Training and Education," testimony before the U.S.-China Economic and Security Review Commission, Washington, D.C., June 11, 2009.

It emphasizes that training must be "scientific" and focuses on developing operational proficiency at the tactical level, on combined-arms tactics, and individual and unit training, before addressing joint training.

Among the 30 or more major exercises conducted by the PLA in the past decade, those most pointedly aimed at Taiwan were the series of "Dongshan" exercises conducted on a large scale each year from 2000 to 2004. The exercise may have been, to a significant degree, a public relations event, and while it demonstrated PLA limitations as well as capability to conduct joint and combined-arms warfare, it was nonetheless a clear signal of China's preparation to follow through on its refusal to renounce the potential use of military force against Taiwan.

The forces most likely tasked with a Taiwan mission include the PLAN's East Sea Fleet, headquartered in Ningbo, as well as two amphibious infantry divisions and an amphibious armored brigade trained specifically in amphibious warfare, present in the Nanjing and Guangzhou military regions. These units would obviously have as their core mission preparing to operate against Taiwan, as might the two brigades of the PLAN Marine Corps, based at Zhanjiang and assigned to the South Sea Fleet.

In sum, China has devoted very significant material and personnel resources to modernizing its navy's platforms and systems and to improving its capability to operate successfully in a 21st-century maritime environment through revisions to its doctrinal and tactical guidelines. These improvements were spurred by several events. These include the 1995–1996 Taiwan Strait Crisis, which pointedly brought home to China's naval leaders their service's inadequacy in a Taiwan scenario; the rapidly expanding Chinese economy, which has enabled continuously increasing annual military budgets; and the fear that the Chen Shui-bian administration (2000–2008) would declare outright independence for Taiwan. This last concern has been lessened since Ma Ying-jeou's inauguration as Taiwan's president. Of equal importance, Beijing's concern about possible U.S. intervention on Taiwan's behalf during an armed confrontation has been eased by the U.S. military's absorption in the Iraq and Afghanistan conflicts and by the decrease in U.S. naval capability. This reduction is reflected both in the number of combatant ships it is able to deploy and, particularly, in the reduced firepower of current aircraft carriers. Carrier capability limitations lie in the lack of a medium- to long-range strike aircraft, the lack of organic tanker aircraft, and the lack of a dedicated fighter aircraft. Current aircraft carrier wing composition includes only the F/A-18 as both strike and fighter aircraft, and that in relatively limited numbers; as a compromise design, the F/A-18 performs neither mission as well as its predecessors, the A-6 and F-14 aircraft.

Scenario Implications

The implications of these elements—improved and improving Chinese naval capabilities, Taiwan's relative quiescence in naval modernization efforts, and relatively decreased U.S. naval capabilities in the Pacific during the past five years—are obvious: The potential naval threat to Taiwan's security has increased significantly during the past decade. In particular, China's ability to seize the small offshore islands of Jinmen and Mazu has increased to a substantial degree due to its improved ability to conduct naval missions across all warfare areas, but especially in amphibious assault; these islands have been relatively easy objectives for the past several years. The PLAN's amphibious capability has been improved by the acquisition of new amphibious shipping, its continuing emphasis on amphibious assault exercises, and its recently developed ability to conduct area air defense of escorted task forces.

More significant than its amphibious capability has been China's ability to impose a blockade of Taiwan and to delay U.S. intervention into a conflict in the area. These objectives would be served by the PLAN's mine warfare capability. While this is not an activity in which the PLAN excels, even the appearance of minefields in Taiwan's near-shore waters would cause maritime insurance rates to increase dramatically and make foreign ship owners hesitant to trade with the island.

Both of these capabilities rely primarily on the area of greatest PLAN improvements during the past decade: the construction and deployment of advanced submarines. An attempt to isolate Taiwan would depend on effective submarine warfare, including emplacing minefields, attacking and penning up Taiwan's naval combatants, preventing the entry and egress of merchant shipping from the island's ports (of which there are relatively few), and delaying the entry of U.S. aircraft carrier task groups into the area by forcing the U.S. Navy to locate and avoid, or potentially sink, Chinese submarines.

More important than these material improvements, however, has been the PLAN's ability to make progress in personnel recruitment, education, training, and retention. Particular objectives have been improvements in the quality of officers and noncommissioned officers. The success in achieving these objectives has yet to be determined, but improvements in personnel capabilities may safely be assumed, given the overhaul of the PLAN's training system and standards following the loss of the *Ming*-class submarine crew in May 2003. This disaster was apparently the consequence of inadequate maintenance and personnel error; it has lent urgency to reorganizing and improving equipment maintenance and repair, especially the higher-level functions located in shore-based shipyards and other facilities. These efforts have included wholesale replacement of personnel connected with the tragedy and the reorganization of navy-wide maintenance and supply procedures.

Future Developments

It is reasonable to assume that China's naval capabilities will continue to improve during the next five years. Current trends in China's military modernization efforts and planning—especially with respect to the air force and navy—imply that most of Beijing's efforts are focused on Taiwan scenarios. The navy continues its expansive submarine construction program, adding nuclear-powered boats to its force. Supporting this key area of modernization is the amphibious ship construction program, led by the Type 71 LPDs. This ship will likely be assigned to the South Sea Fleet, but in addition to amphibious warfare missions in the South China Sea and in a Taiwan scenario, it will be ideal for conducting humanitarian relief operations.

Assumption of significant improvements in naval forces may be safely made in the case of Taiwan, given the Ma administration's obvious priorities. The U.S. Navy's future remains clouded by the continuing, draining commitments in Southwest Asia; it would not be difficult for Beijing to track those commitments, selecting an operational window when no U.S. aircraft carriers are within effective ten-day sailing distance of Taiwan, for instance. This factor certainly is subject to a rapid change of course, if Washington shifts strategic priorities; a reconcentration of U.S. naval effort in the Western Pacific would cause Beijing to reconsider a major employment of maritime force against Taiwan.

There is no indication that China's economy will slow to the extent that would dictate severely reduced budget allocations for the PLAN, nor is there a strong indication that Beijing will ease its position on resorting to military force should it deem it necessary to ensure that Taiwan does not achieve *de jure* independence. Within the PLA, the trend toward the PLAN gaining further prominence as a service branch is enhanced by the near-yearlong successes of its operational deployments to the Horn of Africa. These operations provide the clearest possible proof to China's leadership of the value of a capable, well-equipped navy and provide PLAN planners with valuable arguments to use in bureaucratic struggles within the defense establishment for greater resources and status. Furthermore, if the PLAN makes maximum use of "lessons learned" from these deployments, then its capabilities will be improved, service-wide, as experienced personnel spread throughout the fleet and as the navy's training and exercise regime benefits from the lessons learned across the spectrum of maritime operations, from logistics to performance in the naval warfare areas—particularly surface, air, electromagnetic, and command-and-control operations.

In particular, a large air-capable ship, perhaps the ex-Russian *Varyag*, will probably join the fleet by 2015, if not sooner. China should also be expected to add two additional Type 71 LPDs to bolster its amphibious assault force, and perhaps three additional *Jin*-class SSBNs to extend its nuclear deterrent capability. While the *Shang*-class nuclear-powered attack submarine construction program has apparently been suspended, a follow-on nuclear-powered fast-attack submarine will likely be developed. Additions to the destroyer-frigate force will also join the fleet, perhaps four to five of each. The *Houbei*-class trimaran missile boat force may well number over 100 hulls by 2015.

This construction will significantly strengthen China's naval power in a Taiwan scenario, but it also reflects Beijing's concerns for "after-Taiwan" scenarios, including concerns in the East and South China Seas and possibly in the eastern Indian Ocean.

Conclusion

The PLAN's ability to execute a range of maritime missions against Taiwan, including presence, intelligence gathering, deterrence, isolation, and amphibious assault, has improved significantly during the past ten years. The next five years will very likely witness continued improvements in these areas. China's ability to employ naval power effectively against the interests of both Taiwan and the United States in a scenario centered on the island's future status will increase.

The implications for Taiwan and the United States are clear. Taipei must resume significant improvements to its defensive maritime posture. This includes acquisitions of ships and ordnance, but that is secondary to recruiting, training, and retaining the personnel needed to operate these weapons and platforms. Even more important to the island's defense is continuing to improve its command-and-control infrastructure. The navy by itself cannot defeat a major Chinese military effort against Taiwan, but it can and should possess the capability to so damage any such effort as to give Beijing pause.

By the same token, Washington must reassess its priorities in Asia if it is to ensure the capability to intervene decisively in a Taiwan scenario. The recent reassignment to the Pacific Fleet of additional carrier and submarine forces is notable, and U.S. anti-submarine warfare capabilities must be improved. Most important would be an early end of the commitment of naval platforms and personnel—both at sea and ashore—in Southwest Asia and a refocus on Western Pacific missions, where the United States has treaty allies in South Korea, Japan, the Philippines, Australia, Thailand, and, de facto, Singapore . . . and in Taiwan.

8. The Red Rockets' Glare: Implications of Improvements in PRC Air and Missile Strike Capabilities[1]

David A. Shlapak

Autumn 2009 found relations between China and Taiwan less contentious than they had been in years. The 18 months since Ma Ying-jeou succeeded Chen Shui-bian as president in Taipei saw a welcome thaw in what had been frosty relations between Taipei and Beijing.

These improvements in cross-Strait relations are substantial and have dramatically lowered tensions between Taiwan and China. To date, however, there has been precious little movement on the issue at the crux of friction between Beijing and Taipei (and Washington), which is the ultimate resolution of the dispute regarding sovereignty over the island. On the one hand, Taiwan's population appears to have a strong preference for maintaining the cross-Strait status quo: In one survey conducted almost a year into Ma's term—and the associated relaxation in tensions—nearly 85 percent of those polled favored the existing state of affairs, versus a miniscule 1.2 percent supporting "unification as soon as possible."[2] On the other hand, Beijing has not relaxed its long-standing position that Taiwan is part of China and must be reunited with the mainland, nor has it withdrawn any of the hundreds of short-range ballistic missiles (SRBMs) it has pointed at Taiwan—indeed, these have increased in number since Ma's inauguration.[3]

Warming relations across the Taiwan Strait, then, have had little or no impact to date on the fundamental problem in China-Taiwan relations. The Strait remains a flash point for crisis and conflict, and the state of the military balance between the two sides likewise remains important.

This paper discusses one broad component of that balance: the potential impact of Chinese conventional strike capabilities—as embodied by China's SRBM and land attack cruise missile (LACM) forces and its modernizing air force—in a cross-Strait battle.[4] It concludes that these capabilities pose a serious threat to the

---

[1] This paper draws on analysis undertaken in a RAND Corporation project sponsored by the Smith Richardson Foundation and published as David A. Shlapak, David T. Orletsky, Toy I. Reid, Murray Scot Tanner, and Barry Wilson, *A Question of Balance: Political Context and Military Aspects of the China-Taiwan Dispute*, Santa Monica, Calif.: RAND Corporation, MG-888-SRF, 2009. However, the views expressed in this paper are the author's own; no endorsement by the RAND Corporation or the sponsors of its research is implied.

[2] Mainland Affairs Council, *Liang'an Jingji Tongji Yuebao* [*Cross-Straits Statistics Monthly*], various issues. The number of respondents desiring immediate independence—6.7 percent—can be seen as either another small number or as five times the number of people who want "unification as soon as possible."

[3] See U.S. Department of Defense, *Military Power of the People's Republic of China, 2009*, Washington, D.C.: Office of the Secretary of Defense, 2009, especially p. 48.

[4] This paper does not specifically address the utility of China's LACMs. In general, a cruise missile can carry a similar variety of warheads as a ballistic missile and can be even more accurate. In this way, LACMs can be thought of as broadly interchangeable with China's SRBMs. However, because they don't follow a ballistic trajectory, cruise missiles are not constrained to attacking a target from above. This is a valuable characteristic because the roof of an aircraft shelter is typically the hardest part of the structure to penetrate; the sides are less protected, and the door—which cannot be so heavy that it won't open and close—is weaker still. Approaching in level flight, a LACM can be aimed at the door; even if it fails to penetrate to the interior, it would likely jam the door closed, trapping the aircraft inside the shelter.

Taiwanese and U.S. air bases that are vital to a robust defense of Taiwan. It then considers how this threat might be addressed by Taiwan and the United States and concludes with some broader observations regarding the long-term impact of the changing cross-Strait military balance.

Chinese Conventional Strike Capabilities and the Cross-Strait Military Balance

In 2000, RAND published a report that assessed the evolving balance and made recommendations based on that analysis. It concluded with the observation that

> any near-term Chinese attempt to invade Taiwan would likely be a very bloody affair with a significant probability of failure. Leaving aside potentially crippling shortcomings that we assumed away—such as logistics and [command-and-control] deficiencies that could derail an operation as complex as a "triphibious" (amphibious, airborne, and air assault) attack on Taiwan—the [Chinese military] cannot be confident of its ability to win the air-to-air war, and its ships lack adequate antiair and antimissile defenses. Provided [Taiwan] can keep its air bases operating under attack . . . it stands a relatively good chance of denying Beijing the air and sea superiority needed to transport a significant number of ground troops safely across the strait.[5]

A recent RAND study that I led has described a cross-Strait military balance that has shifted greatly in Beijing's favor over the intervening years since the 2000 study was conducted.

The core of the emerging threat to Taiwan's air bases is the People's Liberation Army's (PLA's) conventionally armed SRBM force. Beijing has deployed over 1,000 of these missiles; newer models offer "greater ranges, improved accuracy, and a wider variety of conventional payloads, including unitary and submunition warheads."[6] These improvements transform China's SRBMs from terror weapons—somewhat updated German V-2s, or Iraqi SCUDs—into operationally useful assets.

In examining how China's new SRBMs could be used against Taiwan's air bases, the 2009 RAND study began by assessing how many missiles of a given accuracy and carrying appropriate submunition warheads—optimized for runway "busting"—would be needed to temporarily close every runway at each of Taiwan's ten primary fighter bases.[7]

---

[5] David A. Shlapak, David T. Orletsky, and Barry Wilson, *Dire Strait? Military Aspects of the China-Taiwan Confrontation and Options for U.S. Policy*, Santa Monica, Calif.: RAND Corporation, MR-1217-SRF, 2000, p. xvi.

[6] U.S. Department of Defense, 2009, p. 48.

[7] The approach used in conducting this analysis—and the assessment of aircraft parked in the open that is described next—is detailed in Shlapak et al., 2009, pp. 37–40, 48. In both cases, we employed statistical models to determine whether a Chinese missile arrived at the target and, if it did, whether it dispensed some or all of its payload on the runway or parking ramp. This involved making assumptions about, e.g., missile reliability and warhead configurations. Clearly, different assumptions—loading only half as many bomblets into each warhead or specifying that the missile was only 50-percent reliable as opposed to 85-percent—would result in different outcomes, perhaps very different ones. We used what we thought to be reasonable values.

A commonly used measure of a missile's accuracy is it circular error probable (CEP), the radius of a circle around the target into which 50 percent of the missiles fired at that target would fall.[8] Missiles with CEPs of 700–1,000 ft (200–300 m), accuracies characteristic of China's older SRBMs, are practically useless for attacking runways (or much of anything else); they simply aren't sufficiently precise. With missiles capable of improved CEPs, an attack aimed at closing Taiwan's air bases starts to look increasingly feasible. If the PLA fields missiles with an accuracy of 130 ft (40 m), 200 SRBMs are needed; if it employs highly accurate missiles—with CEPs of 16 ft (5 m)—only 60 are required.

We performed a similar analysis to estimate how many submunition-equipped SRBMs would be required to have a 90-percent chance of blanketing every parking ramp at the same Taiwanese bases with explosives, thereby destroying or damaging almost every aircraft not already in the air or parked in a hardened aircraft shelter (HAS). With sufficiently accurate missiles and appropriate warheads, only about 30 to 40 additional SRBMs would be needed.[9]

In all, then, between 90 and 240 sufficiently accurate, submunition-equipped SRBMs—less than a quarter of the number of such missiles that Beijing currently has deployed—would give China a better-than-fair shot at shutting down Taiwan's fighter force in a matter of minutes. If Taiwan's surface-to-air defenses can also be suppressed, a window would open through which the PLA Air Force (PLAAF) could fly perhaps hundreds of sorties delivering precision-guided munitions (PGMs) on HASs and other targets too small or hardened to be at risk from SRBMs. Blows like this could essentially knock Taiwan's air force out of the war in the opening hours of a conflict.[10]

With Taiwan's air force burning on the ground or trapped behind cratered runways—and those few jets that manage to get airborne encountering potentially overwhelming numbers of the PLAAF's increasingly capable fighters—China would have laid Taiwan open to follow-up attacks intended to coerce or conquer the island and its people. While doubts may remain about China's ability to plan and execute the scale of air operations needed to successfully implement this concept, Beijing's ability to even temporarily suppress Taiwan's air force with its SRBMs represents a serious threat to Taiwan's ability to defend itself.

Countering this threat appears to be very challenging.

---

[8] CEP is useful shorthand for a weapon's accuracy; a more complete treatment of the topic would include bias, which is the distance between the intended point of impact and the actual one. For the purposes of this analysis, we assumed that the SRBMs' bias was small.

[9] Different types of submunitions would be used to attack runways and parking areas. We assumed that operating surfaces would be struck with relatively heavy (4.5-kg) penetrating munitions designed to slice through the concrete before detonating beneath it. Ramps, on the other hand, would be peppered with much smaller bomblets, configured to maximize fragmentation and incendiary effects versus penetration.

[10] It's worth noting that U.S. bases located relatively close to China, like those on Okinawa, increasingly confront a similar threat from China's latest missile variants.

Options to Shift the Cross-Strait Military Balance

The first option involves existing and planned ballistic missile defense (BMD) systems, which have limited capabilities and are very expensive. The hope that, in the longer run, the SRBM threat can mostly be parried through active defenses requires confidence that it will ultimately prove easier and cheaper to build a missile that can hit another (miniscule and fast-moving) missile than it is one that can hit a relatively large and completely stationary target like a runway or parking apron. Of course, to the extent that the missile defenses themselves rely on vulnerable components—such as radars or even the BMD missile launchers themselves—they would likely number among the first victims of a Chinese missile barrage.

A second option is greater reliance on passive defense. These measures, such as hardening, camouflage, decoys, jamming, and, for air bases, the ability to repair runways and otherwise rapidly recover after an attack, are valuable, especially against smaller attacks. Little, however, can be done to protect operating surfaces, and dozens or even hundreds of craters would likely need to be fixed after a large submunition attack. If, during the interval while Taiwan's fighters are grounded, the PLAAF can hit the bases with modern PGMs, even aircraft parked in hardened shelters would be vulnerable.[11]

A third option would be to disperse Taiwan's fighter force across a large number of smaller air bases and even highway strips. The Swedish air force, among others, has long relied on dispersal to improve its fighters' survivability on the ground. To succeed, however, these operations require preparation—e.g., the prepositioning of munitions, fuel, and other necessities at planned dispersal sites—and practice. Many additional skilled personnel, like mechanics and ordnance handlers, would likely be needed to support the force as it flew out of these widely scattered and most likely rather primitive sites. Dispersed operations would increase the Taiwanese air force's exposure to Chinese special forces and saboteurs, and both command-and-control and logistics support become more complex and more costly with forces scattered across the countryside. Finally, it is very useful to have aircraft that are designed to operate from these less well-endowed "bases." The Swedish Drakken, Viggin, and Gripen fighters, for example, can take off and land on short stretches of pavement and safely operate on surfaces that are not perfectly smooth.[12] The U.S. and French fighters fielded by Taiwan, on the other hand, generally require at least 5,000 feet of smooth runway for safe operation.[13]

---

[11] Even if shelters prove vulnerable, they are valuable if for no other reason than that they force the PLA to do several complex things in proper sequence with proper timing. The launches and times-on-target of hundreds of SRBMs, LACMs, and manned aircraft would need to be coordinated with fair precision. Since the PLA would probably never have rehearsed the operation at any comparable scale—except perhaps in command post exercises or computer simulations—any number of things could go wrong. Taiwan has also reportedly built underground hangers on at least two bases. These shelters could prove almost invulnerable to conventional attack (although the doors might be less robust). Preserving a sizable fraction of the Taiwanese air force until China had run out of missiles, and was perhaps running low on other PGMs as well, would once again complicate China's planning and operations.

[12] The ultimate expression of this design philosophy is the Harrier jumpjet of Falkland Islands fame. The Harrier, known as the AV-8 in U.S. Marine Corps, can get airborne in about 1,000 ft or, at some loss in payload capacity, even take off vertically; it routinely lands vertically. These qualities allowed Britain's Royal Air Force to plan for highly dispersed

Fourth, Taiwan and the United States could develop and field the capability to reciprocally threaten the PLAAF's bases inside China. Using open-source lists of Chinese bases and Google Earth imagery of each, we identified about 40 installations in the two Chinese military regions directly across from Taiwan where Chinese fighter or attack aircraft appeared to be based or that looked capable of accommodating fighters.[14] Assuming that Chinese runways and parking ramps are neither less nor more vulnerable than Taiwan's, we estimated that roughly 10–12 sufficiently accurate missiles with the appropriate submunition payloads per base could cut the runways and sweep clean any aircraft parked outside. To allow for missile reliability, about 15 might be allocated to each base, making a total of around 600 missiles. These could be long-range, stealthy cruise missiles—perhaps resembling a much longer-ranged joint air-to-surface standoff missile (JASSM)—or a force of medium- and/or intermediate-range ballistic missiles launched from hardened land installations or ships and submarines.[15]

The goal of the first three of these investments—active and passive defenses and dispersal—would not be as much to protect the air bases as to compel Beijing to initiate any hostilities at a fairly high and unambiguous level of violence. By rendering ineffective small attacks with handfuls of missiles—which could fall in the grey region between "war" and "non-war," clouding the political situation and perhaps limiting the support forthcoming to Taiwan from its friends, including the United States—a more "robust" Taiwan would confront China with the choice of starting a fairly big war, or no war at all.[16] Removing a number of rungs from the bottom of China's perceived escalation ladder should at least modestly enhance deterrence of *any* attack. We similarly would expect that a credible ability to play tit-for-tat against the PLAAF's infrastructure—our fourth option—would likewise enhance deterrence by increasing Beijing's fear of a failed attack. All four options are worth close scrutiny by a Taiwan whose range of choices for protecting itself from Chinese strikes is shrinking.

---

operations in Europe in the event of a NATO-Warsaw Pact war; the U.S. Marine Corps continues to employ a similar concept for expeditionary operations. The three primary Harrier users—the Royal Air Force, the U.S. Marine Corps, and the Royal Navy—plan to replace their jumpjets with the much-delayed and increasingly costly short take-off, vertical landing variant of the U.S. joint strike fighter (which has been designated the F-35B Lightning II).

13 The question of whether Taiwan should seek to acquire new fighters involves many considerations that lie beyond the scope of this paper. However, it should be noted that, left unsheltered, any aircraft, regardless of vintage or type, would be in danger of destruction from attacks on parking ramps. And, with the exceptions of the aforementioned Harrier, Gripen, and F-35B—the last of which is still several years from being operational—all fighters currently available or in development have similar requirements for runway length and quality. Runways damaged as described above would be just as problematic for any of them as for Taiwan's currently deployed fighter fleet. This is not to say that Taiwan should not invest in fighter modernization; the improved performance and enhanced capabilities of newer jets might be useful in scenarios other than the one examined here. However, our work strongly suggests that the acquisition of new fighters would have very little impact on the outcome of a major cross-Strait conflict.

14 The Guangzhou and Nanjing military regions.

15 We did not assess how strikes on PLAAF bases might affect combat outcomes. Given the impact of similar attacks on Taiwan's bases, we would expect the effects to be substantial.

16 Or, if China, despite the low probability of success, nonetheless chose to employ small numbers of missiles, the opportunity to choose between a big war and an ineffectual one.

Implications of a Shift in the Cross-Strait Military Balance—for the United States and Taiwan

This paper closes by expanding on that final point. Our analysis suggests that, as China's ability to deliver accurate fire across the Strait grows, it will be increasingly difficult and soon may be impossible for the United States and Taiwan to protect the island's military and civilian targets from serious damage. While we argued in our 2009 report that Taiwan should still be able to mount a reasonably robust anti-invasion defense without having air superiority, China's ability to neuter Taiwan's air force and then pound the remainder of Taiwan's defense infrastructure would dramatically elevate the defender's degree of difficulty.[17] By giving China's leaders increased confidence that military force could succeed in solving their "Taiwan problem" once and for all, these changes erode deterrence and risk making cross-Strait crisis or conflict more likely.

In the longer term, the United States and Taiwan may confront an even more fundamental strategic dilemma, one inherent in the basic geography of the situation. All of Taiwan lies within a few hundred miles from the Chinese mainland. Taipei, meanwhile, is about 1,500 nm from the nearest U.S. territory (Guam); it is nearly 4,400 nm from Honolulu and about 5,600 nm from the West Coast of the United States. This geographic asymmetry, combined with the limited array of forward basing options for U.S. forces—and China's growing ability to mount sustained and effective attacks on those forward bases—calls into question Washington's ability to credibly serve as guarantor of Taiwan's security in the long run.

Parallels to Western Hemisphere examples may be instructive. Havana is about 205 nm from Miami; it is roughly 5,200 nm from Moscow. During the Cold War, Cuba was thus in a situation broadly analogous to Taiwan's today: It was a long way from its patron and uncomfortably close to its potential adversary. The ramifications of this disparity revealed themselves most dramatically in 1962, when U.S. dominance of the Caribbean posed a conventional threat to Cuba that the Soviet Union could offset only with nuclear threats. Throughout the years of East-West confrontation, West Berlin was in similarly precarious circumstances vis-à-vis the Soviet Union, particularly up to and through the construction of the Berlin Wall in 1961. Crises revolving around actual or feared Soviet threats to the city were a periodic feature of the Cold War in the late 1940s, 1950s, and early 1960s.

In the cases of both Cuba and West Berlin, the defending superpower's ability to mount a credible conventional defense was very limited. Under those circumstances, the security of each side's outpost came to be seen as dependent on its being folded into the broader set of extended deterrent commitments made by Washington and Moscow, which, in turn, ultimately rested on each side's asserted willingness to risk nuclear conflagration in defense of its interests.

---

[17] Regarding the possibilities for invasion defense, see Shlapak et al., 2009, especially Chapter 5.

Is this the future of the U.S.-Taiwan security relationship? If China's military power continues to grow and a permanent solution to the China-Taiwan imbroglio remains elusive, this question could take on increasing salience. Is Taiwan's security of sufficiently great importance that the United States would be willing to rely not on a decreasingly credible conventional deterrent but instead threaten Beijing that any attack on Taiwan would risk a broader, more dangerous—though not necessarily nuclear—conflict between China and the United States? With another decade of improvements in the PLA like what has been seen in the past ten years, these questions may become troubling indeed for U.S. security planners and political leaders.

By raising these questions, we do not mean to endorse one answer or another, nor to imply that Beijing has or will develop any sort of hegemonic appetite regarding East Asia. We do want to suggest, however, that a China that is conventionally predominant along the East Asian littoral could pose a direct, difficult, broad, and enduring challenge to the U.S. position as guarantor of regional stability and security, a challenge that could extend well beyond Taiwan.

9. Implications of Recent and Planned Changes in Taiwan's Defense Posture

Albert S. Willner

With the publication of two key documents in 2009, the Taiwan Quadrennial Defense Review (QDR) and the National Defense Report (NDR), Taiwan has formally laid out an ambitious agenda of change to its defense posture during the next few years. In its efforts to respond to the emerging strategic environment, meet political guidelines, and adjust to domestic considerations, defense officials are seeking to make the Taiwan military more streamlined, efficient, and responsive to the people it defends. For budgetary, political, and bureaucratic reasons, however, many of the proposed changes are unlikely to take place exactly as planned. This paper focuses on major areas of change introduced and lays out some of the key challenges and implications for Taiwan's government, its people and its defense establishment.

Taiwan Quadrennial Defense Review: Changes and Challenges

Taiwan's first QDR, published in March 2009, is the result of a mandate by the Legislative Yuan (LY) for the Ministry of National Defense (MND) to produce a defense assessment and plan for the next four years, in part to help understand where the current administration is going and to facilitate resource planning efforts. Perhaps just as importantly, the QDR process also allows the president and the LY to reinforce civilian control over the military and enables the LY to further exercise its legislative prerogative vis-à-vis the executive branch, both important elements of Taiwan's continuing democratization.[1] The QDR's four sections lay out core defense challenges, the national defense strategy guidance, defense transformation, and joint warfighting capability development plans.

The defense assessment recognizes China's growing military capabilities as Taiwan's greatest security challenge. While the QDR discusses the improved state of relations between China and Taiwan, the lower probability of war and other transnational threats, PRC (People's Republic of China) advances in recent years also receive significant attention. The QDR highlights ongoing Chinese military modernization efforts, defense concept developments, force structure changes, and deployment preparations under way in demonstrating that Taiwan still faces a major military threat from China.

In the QDR, the MND demonstrates its commitment to supporting President Ma Ying-jeou's "Hard ROC" policy through the implementation of a national defense strategy composed of five key elements: war prevention, homeland defense, contingency response, conflict avoidance, and regional stability. Its supporting military strategy reemphasizes "resolute defense" and "credible deterrence" as core concepts. The military strategy is focused on maintaining the security of Taiwan's national territories, improving the armed forces' warfighting capabilities, and

---

[1] Quadrennial Defense Review Editing Group, Taiwan Ministry of National Defense, *Quadrennial Defense Review 2009*, Taipei: Ministry of National Defense, 2009, p. 6.

planning for joint counter-blockade and joint interdiction operations aimed at denying an enemy the ability to land and gain a foothold on Taiwan.[2] The proposed defense transformation effort and emerging defense posture are designed to credibly support these national defense and military strategies.

The defense transformation plan consists of several important proposals. The first is to streamline Taiwan's defense organization by consolidating MND policy staff, joint staff, and the military services to improve accountability and strengthen service specialties. Under the reorganization, ministry departments and work units were to be consolidated, and the army, navy, air force, combined logistics, reserve, and military police headquarters merged into three: army, navy, and air force. This consolidation is designed to improve efficiencies and allow the services to better manage service-specific issues much like the U.S. model. Potential concerns that service-centric changes may be at the expense of joint efforts are offset in the document by an entire chapter focused on the need for greater strides in joint warfighting capability development. There appears to be recognition by Taiwan's leadership that service consolidation must not detract from ongoing joint integration and operations efforts.

As expected, much debate and bargaining has already taken place as the MND and the services sorted out where consolidations and cuts would occur. For instance, there was significant controversy over resistance by the military police to being placed under one of the service headquarters. Veterans groups and local constituencies working with LY representatives eventually made their case, and, with Ma's support, the military police were placed directly under the control of the MND general staff rather than under the army command, as proposed in the QDR. It is important to note that public interest, constituent groups, and their representatives all played an important role in reversing this decision, reflecting the democratic influences at work in Taiwan and a defense establishment that must respond.

The second QDR proposal aimed at reducing the total statutory armed force structure from 275,000 to 215,000 by late 2014 will be accomplished by streamlining the defense organization discussed above and making additional cuts within the services, especially as they transition to a volunteer force. This force-reduction plan is a carryover from previous Chen administration efforts, although the timeline to completion has been extended. The plan is for the Army to have its total strength cut by about 30,000, with the navy and air force scheduled to lose 5,000 personnel each. The remaining cuts are to come from the stand-down of the marine corps base garrison brigade and other limited consolidations. As one recent report pointed out, however, Taiwan currently actually has only 235,000 personnel on active duty[3] and active billets filled may be less, so the number of troops to be cut to get to the 215,000 end state will likely be fewer in number, at only about 10 percent of the current force. One implication is that the savings may be far less than expected because fewer cuts will actually be realized.

---

[2] Quadrennial Defense Review Editing Group, Taiwan Ministry of National Defense, 2009, pp. 70–73.

[3] U.S.-Taiwan Business Council, *Defense and Security Report, Second Quarter 2009*, Arlington, Va., 2009, p. 12.

In response to political and public pressures, the force reduction will include a push to reduce the number of senior-level general/flag officers. With 387 general officer billets spread out through the MND, the services, the National Security Bureau, the National Security Council, and the Presidential Office, Taiwan has an extremely high senior officer–to–personnel ratio. The goal is to make cuts to get this number down to a total of slightly more than 200 and the ratio down from almost 2 percent to 0.7 percent. These senior-level cuts have also led to infighting among the services and with the MND as decisions are made on which general/flag officer slots should go and what the impact will be.[4]

The QDR also notes the need to increase the ratio of civilian officials in the MND, in part to reduce the number of officers and noncommissioned officers (NCOs) working in the MND and to get those currently in those positions back to the fielded force.[5] Ramping up the numbers of civilian officials with defense expertise would not only help move some military back to the force but would also open up additional opportunities to build civil-military expertise. Building a broader base of civilian defense experts allows Taiwan to improve continuity in the MND between administrations, creates greater depth in a host of defense-related areas, and allows Taiwan more opportunities to develop relationships with civilian defense counterparts elsewhere.

The force reductions proposed are critical to the transition to what the QDR calls the "all-volunteer force." The conscript service commitment period, which has been coming down since Chen Shui-bian first proposed reducing it in 2004, is now only one year in duration. The MND recognizes that there are significant budgetary implications for recruitment and retention of a volunteer force, especially tied to living facilities, benefits, retirement assistance, and insurance coverage, which is probably why these areas received much more attention in the subsequent 2009 NDR. Indeed, recognizing that the transition will be much more expensive and difficult than originally anticipated, Taiwan defense officials in recent speeches and conversations are no longer using the term "all-volunteer force," instead referring to the future active component simply as a "volunteer force."

Additional transformation objectives in the QDR focus on improving force planning and armaments development mechanisms in an effort to promote an improved foreign and domestic analysis and acquisition processes. In addition, joint operations are expected to receive more attention, particularly efforts to improve command, control, communications, computer, intelligence, surveillance, and reconnaissance integration; information operations and electronic warfare; mobilization, training, and logistics; and the use of political warfare centers to improve psychological operations capabilities. Human resources will be revamped to improve professional officer training, deemed especially important with the advent of a volunteer force. Part of this effort is to evaluate whether to reestablish a reserve officer training corps to improve advanced officer education, NCO

---

[4] U.S.-Taiwan Business Council, 2009; Fu Mei, "Taiwan's Defense Transition: Beyond Q.D.R.," paper presented at the US-Taiwan Defense Industry Conference, Charlottesville, Va., September 28, 2009.

[5] Quadrennial Defense Review Editing Group, Taiwan Ministry of National Defense, 2009, p. 82.

development and help grow a civilian defense force. Finally, the QDR puts forward proposals to improve the MND's ability to manage defense expenditures in a fiscally constrained environment and commits the defense establishment to finding new ways to work with civilian industry and local governments on land-use issues.

Taiwan's 2009 National Defense Report: Building on and Revising QDR Objectives

The NDR, released in late October 2009, expands on the QDR's proposed defense posture, addresses current MND challenges, and makes some important revisions. The NDR's subtitle, *Building an Elite Armed Forces—Voluntaryism* [sic],[6] indicates the dominant focus of the document and the plan. The "all-volunteer force" label, as mentioned earlier, has been dropped in favor of an active-duty volunteer/reserve conscript force mix. The goal is "100% active volunteer force by 2014,"[7] but there is an expectation that all young males will still be required to undergo minimal military training and go into the reserve force in order to support the active force and Taiwan's defense plans. The MND identifies areas needing attention by the civilian and military authorities in its Volunteer Force Buildup Plan, including "organization, manning and equipping; military service remuneration; reserve mobilization; human resource systems; operational training and preparation; legislative amendments; logistics preparation; military armaments production; defense financial resources; dispensary; dependent benefits; and integrated assessment."[8]

The cost of transitioning to the active volunteer force within five years will require funding and resources as yet not provided by the LY in the defense budget. In fact, it is increasingly likely that cutbacks in the defense budget will require a significant readjustment to the current plan, including an extension to completion or lowering of expectations as to what can be accomplished by 2014. Part of the challenge is that there will likely be a significant initial spike in costs as soldiers departing the force receive drawdown pay and allowances and as new programs are stood up and incentives put into place. The details of these plans have yet to be announced. A broader personnel welfare act to take care of troops and their families is also introduced in the NDR, recognizing that any successful retention strategy will require significant attention and money. Significant demographic changes underway will also have an impact, as Taiwan's population is declining and with it the number of young men available to serve in the armed forces.

Disaster prevention and relief also have been introduced in the NDR as a new core armed forces mission. Although the shift to take on this mission was begun earlier by the military, the NDR change is due in no small measure to the turmoil surrounding the slow response of the Taiwan government to Typhoon Morakot in August

---

[6] Taiwan Ministry of National Defense, *2009 National Defense Report: Building an Elite Armed Forces—Voluntaryism* [sic], Taipei, 2009).

[7] Taiwan Ministry of National Defense, 2009, p. 75.

[8] Taiwan Ministry of National Defense, 2009, p. 121.

2009. Besides making multiple proposals in the document to support President Ma's directive to treat this area as a primary focus, the MND also notes that it will "observe the guidance of the 'central disaster response center' of the government,"[9] alluding to the interagency struggle that took place following the onset of the typhoon and the need to subordinate its efforts to a civilian central authority. The costs of taking on this new mission and its support requirements have yet to be adequately addressed.

Of ongoing concern and in particular reaction to the recent corruption scandals, an intangible core value, discipline, receives attention. Perhaps in an effort to take back the reins from civilian agencies rooting out corruption in the military, the MND notes, "For corruption, legal violations, and relevant security crises, the MND has been capable of engaging the problems, identifying key difficulties, and formulating concrete measures for improvement . . . so that the Armed Forces may be ashamed of greed and proud of incorruptibility."[10] The recent spate of corruption accusations and pay-for-promotion convictions have had a negative effect on the reputation of the military and internal morale and have diverted attention from other critical areas.

Finally, the NDR makes note of Taiwan's efforts to initiate peace and seek out confidence-building measures (CBMs) to support the government's cross-Strait efforts at compromise and keeping the peace. Under the defense strategy objective of war prevention, specifically under the section on establishing cross-Strait military CBMs, the QDR notes that the goal is "lowering the probability of war."[11] The NDR, however, changes the goal to "lowering the probability of accidental provocation of war."[12] This interesting change appears to recognize that a relaxation in tensions is taking place across the Strait and that accidents or miscalculations are now the biggest potential threat to peace. Whether this means that there will be movement to initiate military CBMs or that this will effect changes in Taiwan military activities and operations remains to be seen.

Challenges and Implications

The ongoing and planned QDR and NDR changes have important challenges and implications for Taiwan, its military, and third parties, such as China and the United States. First, there is the question of whether the political will and funding exist to see these changes through. President Ma's initiatives across the Strait are changing the security environment, which is likely to have a corresponding effect on Taiwan's defense posture. Multiple domestic political challenges to Ma within his party, with the LY, and by the public could well weaken his commitment to see the changes through. A change in threat perceptions could lead to a commensurate change in the willingness of the public or its representatives to support the defense spending levels needed to see QDR and NDR changes through.

---

[9] Taiwan Ministry of National Defense, 2009, p. 78.

[10] Taiwan Ministry of National Defense, 2009, pp. 75–76.

[11] Quadrennial Defense Review Editing Group, Taiwan Ministry of National Defense, 2009, p. 66.

[12] Taiwan Ministry of National Defense, 2009, p. 80.

Second, continued reductions in defense spending will clearly affect the full implementation of the proposed changes related to defense posture transformation. Internal LY debates, external debates between the LY and the executive branch, and positioning in the lead-up to elections beginning this year are sure to have an impact as well. In particular, the spike in the cost of transitioning to a volunteer force requires not only a solid plan but also support by the government to see each phase through.

A third challenge with significant implications for military readiness and Taiwan's defense posture is the significant downturn in civil-military relations. Multiple discussions with Taiwan and U.S. officials indicate that the MND is not being kept in the loop about ongoing cross-Strait dialogue and the related security impacts of these discussions. Moreover, relations between the National Security Council and the MND are strained, and Ma and his advisers have reportedly been dismissive of MND advice and perspectives. This situation was further exacerbated during the Typhoon Morakot response, when civilian and military officials traded blame for the slowness of the government to respond. Some see Ma's decision to accede to the military police headquarters change due to resistance by veterans and other groups as another sign that the president is unwilling to stand up and fight for proposals he has approved. Outside observers almost unanimously agree that the military remains strongly committed to civilian rule and Taiwan's democratic values. At issue is not obedience to civilian control but the negative impact that civil-military tensions are likely having in addressing critical Taiwan defense reforms and, even more significantly, in ensuring good and reliable communications, coordination, and control, especially in a time of crisis.

Recent pay-for-promotion scandals, independent prosecutor investigations of Taiwan defense contractors, military accidents, charges of Taiwan navy personnel involvement in the murder of a prostitute, and the attempted suicide of Taiwan's former top marine have all further stressed the military's relationship with the president and other senior national security officials. These developments have also affected morale and diverted the attention of senior officials from the day-to-day business of running the military and working to execute new defense initiatives. As the MND leadership responds to these investigations, the ability of the government to focus on carrying out QDR and NDR priorities and maintaining military readiness may not receive the attention it deserves.

While the military appears committed to the QDR and NDR proposals, it is also recognized that large bureaucracies are resistant and slow to change, resulting in a fourth significant challenge. Some government officials in Taipei feel that, with a potentially major shift in the political relationship between Taiwan and China under way, the military is not adapting quickly enough to keep up with those changes. MND defenders, some of whom agree that the military may not be changing quickly enough in some areas, nonetheless believe that the military's obligation is to plan and prepare for worst-case scenarios. Some outside the government see the defense establishment trapped in a culture of victimization, often played out, for example, in its testy reactions to negative media reports and increasing frustration over dealing with the President's Office and changing government interagency realities. To its credit, the military recognizes the need to adapt to changing realities and is developing new means to help tell its story and make its case.

A fifth challenge associated with the changes described in the QDR and NDR is one familiar to most democracies that have transitioned to a volunteer military. Fundamental choices will have to be made about how to develop a new culture with incentives designed to bring on board the right kind of soldiers and keep them in for the long term. Recruitment and retention efforts will have to address service to the nation, a challenge particularly among many young people who see little incentive or significant security threats requiring their commitment. Soldiers who are trained up and remain for only one year are not around long enough to put their training to any real use. An additional problem is that many conscripts do not have a positive view of their short time in service. Enlisted conscript duties are often seen as menial, irrelevant to life plans, and offering little authority and influence while in the service. Creating opportunities and incentives in and beyond the military would be important to ensuring future success in recruiting and retention.

Family support is important, especially in deciding to make the military a career. Parents and spouses need to see the military as a respectable way of life, something they want their children, husbands, or wives to join. New plans that look at family housing, exchange, medical, and pay support are sure to attract supportive families, leading to greater retention. Providing financial support for these initiatives and changing the perceptions of military social status could prove critical in the coming transition.

Sixth, the consolidation of service headquarters and reduction in senior general/flag officer numbers bring the promise of greater cooperation and communication, but also the challenge of debilitating infighting, some of which has already taken place. The army, navy and air force are expected to assume some of the logistics and reserve missions in a way that may assist in peacetime and wartime preparation and transition. There are important opportunities with this move that will further promote a joint mindset and community. However, if the services do not see the need to join forces and commit to moving toward a mutually beneficial goal, especially in a severely resource-constrained environment, real and lasting success as proposed in the QDR and NDR may not be achieved.

A seventh area worth watching is the need identified in the reports to develop civilian defense expertise, an issue with potentially far-reaching implications. In part, this effort would allow officers currently in MND headquarters positions the opportunity to go back to the field. But it is also based on recognition that the continuity and experience that come from long-term service by civilians in the defense realm could significantly improve civil-military relations and an understanding of defense issues and concerns among the broader populace. Part of the requirement will be for military and civilian entities to develop mechanisms and opportunities to increase trust and understanding in order to overcome vast cultural differences. Although this will take years, establishing a civilian defense bureaucracy will provide needed perspective outside the military on defense issues and serve to develop future civilian leaders with long-term experience on defense issues.

Finally, the proposed defense posture changes, in order to be successful, will need to be augmented by a vigorous and persuasive campaign to continue to inform the public about threats to Taiwan. A mainstay should be continuing to highlight, in multiple venues, the perceived threat that generated the new QDR and NDR in the first place, making the case for why change is needed. Even as cross-Strait improvements are taking place, it is important that the Taiwan government articulates why a credible defense posture remains paramount.

Taiwan has already taken a significant step by outlining in its QDR and NDR what needs to be done to stay relevant, successfully adapt to the changing domestic situation, and meet the emerging regional environment. In doing so, it has outlined important changes that will help the government, its military, and its people transition to meet new realities. Hard choices will have to be made and resources applied. If those commitments are made and seen through, Taiwan's defense posture and its critical role in helping keep the peace and stability will be well served.

10. Taiwan's Long-Term Challenges and Strategic Preparations

Fu-Kuo Liu

Since the political change in Taiwan of May 2008, the cross-Strait relationship has made a big turn from tension to relief and provocation to conciliation. Change is not only taking place in the cross-Strait relationship, but also in Taiwan's domestic political structure and the threat factors of Taiwan's national security. As Taiwan's future national development is heavily dependent upon the readjustment of its relationship with China, it is right to believe that the cross-Strait relationship will be the top issue on Taiwan's policy agenda for many years to come. How much will changes in the cross-Strait relationship affect strategic defense planning and military development in Taiwan? This paper evaluates Taiwan's security challenges, strategic preparedness, and the prospects of U.S.-Taiwan security cooperation.

Over the past 17 months or so, during three rounds of SEF-ARATS (Straits Exchange Foundation–Association for Relations Across the Taiwan Strait) talks, Taipei has managed to sign nine agreements with Beijing (on mainland tourism, charter flights, direct air transport, direct sea transport, postal cooperation, food safety, crime-fighting and judicial assistance, financial cooperation, and regular flights) as well as reach a consensus on the inflow of Chinese investment in Taiwan. Progress in cross-Strait relations has generated positive momentum for a peaceful settlement to the Chinese civil war. The structural changes in the relationship across the Strait send a clear message to the region: China and Taiwan are beginning the process of cross-Strait reconciliation. In general, the process will require further efforts at economic normalization, political trust-building, and, eventually, the signing of a peace accord.

On the political front, since 2008, Taiwan and China have resumed their talks and institutionalized a number of cross-Strait links. Based on an understanding of the "1992 consensus," the two sides have managed to stabilize the relationship. The baseline is that Beijing and Taipei have to respect each other and not deny each other's existence. So far, many important issues have been brought to the negotiating table and resolved. On the bright side, it has become a common practice for the two sides to put pressing issues on the table for solution; on the strategic front, however, the cross-Strait agreements reached thus far do not necessarily constitute a real political discussion about how to resolve the ultimate sources of cross-Strait tension and conflict. Because mutual trust across the Strait remains weak, China's goodwill and concessions are always regarded as potential traps being used to lure the Taiwanese to lower their guard and pursue the course of peaceful unification, and thus as inevitably serving Beijing's strategic calculations. In this view of Beijing's strategy, it is in China's interest for the time being to help the Kuomintang (KMT) government stay in power for as long as possible so as to prevent the Democratic Progressive Party (DPP) from returning to power. It is clear that Beijing and Taipei have different political agendas.

For now, China has actively guided Taiwan toward a position in the domestic and international contexts that is closer to Beijing's strategic interests. In the early stages of cross-Strait cooperation that we have seen thus far, whatever demands Taiwan has made, China has by and large tried to accommodate. This reflects a certain sense of shared interests and perhaps even identity between policy circles in Beijing and Taipei, particularly between the Chinese Communist Party (CCP) and the KMT. The pace of cross-Strait progress is now considered by Beijing and Taipei to be an important part of the KMT's domestic performance. It seems that well before a negotiation round starts, surprisingly, Taipei has already revealed what negotiation outcomes would be acceptable. As Taipei has repeatedly set the near-term agenda, Beijing has tended to come up with accommodating approaches that work to shape the longer-term context in which cross-Strait relations will play out. For this reason, it is perhaps not surprising that President Ma has been continuously criticized by his political opponents as lacking strategic preparation vis-à-vis Beijing, even though clear progress in cooperation between the two sides of the Strait has been achieved. Although the two governments have so far been able to cooperate significantly on functional issues, in the domestic political arena, President Ma has been severely criticized for conceding too much to Beijing and not sufficiently guarding Taiwan's sovereignty.

Security Challenges

In spite of some doubts in Taiwanese society about the value of better cross-Strait ties, and disagreements as to the direction in which changes in the relationship with China should proceed, most observers of the recent progress in cross-Strait relations have seen it as encouraging. Several important factors have played a big part in this change.

First, the global financial tsunami that struck in September 2008 may have helped facilitate the progress of cooperation across the Strait, especially in the fields of economic and financial interactions. The issue of financial cooperation across the Strait took on greater prominence in the negotiation agenda in late 2008, as the KMT government reached the conclusion that it had to increase economic interactions with China as a way of reviving Taiwan's economy.

Second, Beijing's prolonged anxiety about the unpredictable conduct of Taiwan's government under Chen Shui-bian led it to welcome President Ma Ying-jeou's election. After eight years of confrontation with the DPP government, China realized that the KMT's return to power represented the best opportunity for making strategic advances in cross-Strait relations that it is likely to see. The period from 2008 to 2012, when both President Ma and President Hu Jintao are in power and pragmatic approaches prevail in the cross-Strait relationship, has been described by some observers as an important period of "strategic opportunity."[1]

---

[1] See Donald S. Zagoria, "Cross-Strait Relations: Cautious Optimism," summary of the Conference on Prospects for Relations Across the Taiwan Strait, a Trilateral Conference sponsored by the National Committee on American Foreign Policy, January 13–14, 2009. Several Chinese experts have also used this term. For example, see Liu Hong, "The Cross-Strait Relationship Has Entered an Era of Strategic Opportunity,"
「兩岸關係進入戰略機遇期」，《台聲雜誌》，第九期, September 15, 2008, p. 30.

Third, one of the fundamental goals for Taiwan in terms of building a better relationship with the mainland is the pursuit of greater "international space" for Taiwan. Taiwan has expressed a fairly high expectation of Chinese goodwill in allowing the island greater visibility vis-à-vis the international community, and Beijing has thus far responded by respecting Ma's policy on a "diplomatic truce" and by ceasing to block Taiwan's participation as an observer in the World Health Assembly (WHA).

In sum, the new relationship across the Strait has been characterized by substantial policy changes and expressions of goodwill. Several additional positive points deserve attention as well:

1. The scope of issues under negotiation has broadened, and the two sides have maintained a practical attitude. This indicates that Taipei and Beijing are becoming more pragmatic and taking an incremental approach to managing cross-Strait ties.
2. Interactions across the Strait have become more institutionalized and regularized in three layers: the formal channel of the SEF-ARATS talks; the political party channel, as conducted through the KMT-CCP Economic Forum; and official engagement in the SEF-ARATS talks process.
3. Before the two sides touch upon political issues, the leaders of the two sides have decided to focus on encouraging more interactions and a greater degree of functional cooperation. As usual, Beijing has clearly set guidelines (in the form of Hu Jintao's Six Points articulated on December 31, 2008) for the relationship to be developed further, while Taipei, due to the lack of a domestic consensus over relations with the mainland, has not been able to work up a comprehensive plan and has instead focused much more on near-term efforts to improve relations.

Nevertheless, Taiwan's leaders are clearly aware that China's ultimate goal remains unification. The key question now is, "How much longer will Beijing continue to offer concessions and policy enticements to Taipei?" Through multiple rounds of negotiation, observers have sought to assess what Beijing really wants from Taiwan. Does Taiwan have leverage over China? Will Beijing's support to President Ma Ying-jeou and future KMT leaders continue? Beijing was apparently surprised by Ma's plunging popularity after Typhoon Morakot struck in August 2009. In the aftermath of the typhoon, Beijing became more cautious in its approach to Taiwan, reviewing its contacts with the Taiwan political world and beginning to extend feelers to the DPP so as not to put all its eggs in one basket.

In light of the warming relationship with the mainland, the first and foremost security challenge for Taiwan is that mutual trust across the Strait remains weak. Without mutual trust in place, any given political incident may be misinterpreted and quickly increase tension in the Strait. The visit of the Dalai Lama to Taiwan in the aftermath of Typhoon Morakot in August 2009 demonstrated that some voices emanating from Beijing are still willing to criticize Ma for betraying cross-Strait understandings about how China's interests should be respected. This incident revealed the vulnerability of the relationship in the absence of mutual trust between

Beijing and Taipei. If the two sides cannot find a way to reach agreement on such fundamental issues of trust and understanding, this failure will increase the level of Taiwan's insecurity. The key question is how much can be done.

In addition, as the new relationship has gradually developed across the Strait, it has greatly affected Taiwan's overall security and defense policies. The immediate challenge is that while fully and openly engaging with its "rival," Taiwan has not yet been able to work out a new national security strategy to find a good balance between economic interactions and defense buildup. To respond to the new relationship across the Strait, Taiwan should review its outdated security strategy. So far, for obvious domestic political reasons, the government's policy remains sluggish, but Taiwan experts have attempted to help redefine the strategy. For Taiwan, China may either still be identified as an enemy or be considered a counterpart/partner. A redefined security strategy should clearly identify new strategic goals that will reflect the new relationship with China and at the same time put forward new thinking about how to strengthen the security relationship with the United States.

The third security challenge that Taiwan faces is exactly this question of how to strike a strategic balance between the importance it attaches to the cross-Strait relationship and its security cooperation with the United States. Since May 2008, the development of better cross-Strait relations has seen contributions from both sides. Much progress has been made and regular contacts between the two sides have been institutionalized. Of course, a general feeling is that cross-Strait relations are making up for lost time and catching up to where they would have been if not for the deterioration that occurred during the Chen administration. Further improvements are expected to come from the next few rounds of SEF-ARATS talks. In contrast, since President Obama took office in January 2009, U.S.-Taiwan relations have been characterized by a polite but clear distance. It seems that the two sides have done whatever they could to facilitate a better relationship, but the absence of a systematic effort to improve the bilateral U.S.-Taiwan relationship has been widely noted. Important issues, such as initiating the next arms sales program, upgrading defense cooperation, building a concept of shared strategic interest, and signing of a free-trade agreement, have made little progress. Unlike the situation in the past, there have not been any discussions between Washington and Taipei about how to help Taiwan advance in the international community and further enlarge Taiwan's international engagement.

From a diplomatic perspective, the progress of the bilateral relationship stagnated for quite some time as a result of the attitude of cautious politeness on the part of the Obama administration in general and as a result of the American beef issue in particular. The Legislative Yuan decision to amend its Food Safety Law resulted in Taiwan breaching a bilateral beef trade protocol signed with the United States in October 2009 and may have harmed ties.[2] Until satisfactorily resolved to both sides' satisfaction, this issue will test the importance of strategic

---

[2] Ko Shu-ling, Flora Wang, Jenny W. Hsu, and Shih Hsiu-chian, "Legislature Bans Some US Beef," *Taipei Times*, January 6, 2010.

interests that both sides share. Should the beef issue be settled smoothly, the two sides will likely be able to move forward with new initiatives more easily. At a fundamental level, the real concern is whether there is an action plan for promoting deeper cooperation going forward.

The fourth security challenge Taiwan faces is the increasing tendency of the United States to limit its arms sales to Taiwan as U.S.-China relations take on greater importance for Washington. Recently, many analysts suggested that President Obama's trip to Beijing in November would have a direct impact on the issue of arms sales to Taiwan.[3] Since the United States will have to face a hard choice between continuation of arms sales to Taiwan, especially in the case of F-16C/D fighter jets, and maintenance of relations with the mainland, U.S. arms sales policy toward Taiwan may gradually be constrained by its relationship with China. If so, it will fundamentally change the course of U.S. policy, which for decades has emphasized that U.S. arms sales to Taiwan will not be conditioned on relations with, or even discussed with, Beijing. Uncertainty about Taiwan's prospects for continuing to obtain advanced weapons from the United States continues to grow, even though a US$6 billion arms package went through in January 2010.

As a result of this increasing uncertainty facing Taiwan, the KMT government has continuously been questioned at home and abroad for tilting too much toward mainland China.[4] Some observers worry that the warm relations across the Strait have given rise to naïve thinking in some corners of Taiwan that the island does not need to invest further in strengthening its defense capabilities. Even if the relationship across the Strait were to improve significantly, the security challenges confronting Taiwan would still remain high. Instead of reducing the need to worry about overall security, the new situation in the Taiwan Strait has created the need for Taiwan analysts to consider all possible angles of a new, and much more complicated, cross-Strait environment and the challenges it presents.

Taiwan's Optimal Strategy

The KMT returned to power last year, assisted by widespread public perceptions of incompetence, corruption, and political gridlock associated with the DPP government during its eight years in power. As a result of the rapid progress in improving relations across the Strait, fundamental changes have occurred in the traditional antagonistic nature of the cross-Strait relationship. Taiwan's government decisionmaking system needs to catch up with the pace of changes and be more flexible. Currently, decisionmaking on cross-Strait issues is centered in the National Security Council, coordination of policy is carried out by the Mainland Affairs Council, and implementation is

---

[3] Josh Rogin, "Obama in No-Win Situation over Taiwan Arms Sale," *The Cable* (*Foreign Policy*), September 15, 2009. See also "Obama Will Have to Deal Soon with Arms Sales to Taiwan: Scholars," Central News Agency, October 29, 2009.

[4] The DPP's chairperson, Tsai Ing-wen, has expressed her party's suspicions about Ma's pro-China policy and has criticized the government's handling of relations with Washington. See Ko Shu-ling "MAC Rejects Criticism of Ma's Cross-Strait Policies," *Taipei Times*, February 3, 2009.

executed by the SEF. The government is also assisted by the KMT on a purely party basis but so far has not received much assistance from Taiwan's think-tank network. The decisionmaking system in Taipei appears to be overburdened by the cross-Strait progress, as many of the day's most pressing issues take up a great deal of energy and leave little time for long-term strategic planning. The official perspective would benefit from being broadened to include regional security concerns. What would Taiwan's optimal strategy be to protect its longer-term security interests?

First, while rapprochement with mainland China is likely to be the top issue on the Ma administration's policy agenda for years to come, the administration also intends to facilitate closer relations with the United States. Because the United States is developing closer relations with China under President Obama, it will be important for Taiwan to carefully balance its relationship with the both countries. If Taiwan is able to move forward with the proposed Economic Cooperation Framework Agreement (ECFA) this year, the relationship across the Strait will be further stabilized. Signing an ECFA would not only bring about economic benefits, but it would also serve as a preventive measure further reducing the likelihood of China using military force. It would be greatly in Taiwan's interest to reach a similar economic cooperation deal with the United States. By emphasizing its interest in concluding economic cooperation deals with both Beijing and Washington, Taiwan may be able to ensure peace in the Taiwan Strait while also achieving progress in improving cooperation with America. Thus, how to strike the most desirable balance between relations with the mainland and those with the United States should be at the center of Taiwan's new strategy.

Second, Taiwan's security and future can only be preserved and guaranteed through U.S. security assurance. No matter how positively the relationship develops across the Strait, China will definitely protest against any sort of U.S. arms sales to Taiwan. As such, the most critical effort Taiwan needs to undertake at the present moment is to work more actively with U.S. partners to explore joint strategic perspectives for enhancing cooperation on security and the future development of relations between Taipei and Washington, which are currently lacking. Through a more active approach, Taiwan can continue to modernize its outdated defense establishment and obtain advanced weapons systems that satisfy its defense needs. By doing so, a common strategic interest in maintaining defense cooperation between the United States and Taiwan would be strengthened. Taiwan would enjoy greater support from the United States on arms sales, and the United States would be more willing to help deflect China's protests.

Third, while the cross-Strait relationship is moving toward conciliation, uncertainty remains high at present. For China, the current trend toward reconciliation will hopefully lead to Beijing's ultimate goal of peaceful unification. It is therefore important that Taiwan's strategy enables it to fulfill enough of China's expectations while always leaving Taipei sufficient room for maneuver. Taiwan's optimal strategy should help prevent it from sailing completely to Beijing's preset course and thereby constitute a "smart strategy." Such a "smart strategy" should be based on strategic deliberation about the unfolding cross-Strait peace process. It would involve active use of comprehensive means to engage China, building solid mutual trust, and balancing strategic relations with the United States and China.

Fourth, for the first time in decades, both China and Taiwan have come to realize that they have a fresh opportunity to revisit and revise their strategic postures toward each other. On defense, although the Chinese military so far shows no signs of reshaping its strategy toward Taiwan, Taiwan should take this "strategic opportunity" to redefine its policy and strategy in response to a new cross-Strait relationship. Thus, a new policy approach can be developed on the basis of a more realistic assessment and could serve as a spur, forcing Beijing to respond by moderating the threat it poses to Taiwan. If Taipei does plays up its strategic reorientation, Taiwan's defense strategy and defense reform process will then conform more closely to its realistic requirements, and its defense development and strategy will be based on Taiwan's real needs. Currently, three possible factors—namely, China's military buildup and its threat posture, domestic political changes in Taiwan, and Taiwan's financial power—serve as the parameters of the defense reform process in Taiwan.

Taiwan and the United States: Upgrading the Partnership

The United States has been the guarantor of Taiwan's security for decades. If Taiwan moved to reorient its security strategy to cope with the new strategic environment in the Taiwan Strait, what would it need from the United States? In Taiwan's optimal strategy, what role would the United States play in the long term? Taiwan's national development, including economic and security development, is constrained by its relationships with China and the United States. What does Taiwan need from the region in the short term and longer term?

In searching for stability in the cross-Strait relationship, the first thing Taiwan needs from the United States is likely to be continuing security assurances. Even if the cross-Strait relationship continues to develop positively, China has not yet committed to changing its military posture against Taiwan. This leaves open the possibility that China may never opt to relinquish its military option against Taiwan as long as the two sides remain divided. Given the wide range of opportunities for bilateral and/or multilateral security cooperation present in the existing regional security context, defense modernization remains a pressing issue for Taiwan, as upgrading military capabilities can make Taiwan a more useful strategic partner to potential regional security actors and would also help increase its strategic value to the United States.

The second thing Taiwan should prioritize in its relations with the United States is the strengthening of its bilateral economic linkages, which will enable Taiwan to extend its engagement with international economic institutions. Under the context of diplomatic isolation, Taiwan will have to count on bilateral cooperation with the United States to develop new opportunities with partners in the international community. Taiwan's strength relies very much in its economic development and prosperity. By engaging China over the past two decades, Taiwan has gained tremendous economic advantages in global markets, but at the same time it has faced increasing economic competition at home and in U.S. markets. Taiwan's interests are not fully represented in international economic institutions today, even though its economy is currently ranked the 18th largest in the world. Its economic importance, technological innovations, and financial strength are not yet adequately recognized in all institutional settings. For example, despite the size and strength of its economy, Taiwan does not enjoy a seat at the G-20. Taiwan needs to expand its strategic outreach in the global economy, which will enhance Taiwan's security by ensuring that its security is of concern to the international community. In the longer term, the United States can help broaden the scope of bilateral economic cooperation open to Taiwan and push Taiwan to engage more with global economic institutions.

On the diplomatic front, the new cross-Strait relationship has led Beijing to accept Taiwan's observer status in the WHA. As Taiwan's participation in any significant international organization is still considered by Beijing as touching upon the issue of sovereignty, even in the longer term, China is not likely to yield on its opposition to greater participation by Taiwan in international institutions. After 17 months of rapprochement across the Strait, one positive result is that Beijing increasingly seems to acknowledge that it will have to do something to meet Taiwan's expectations that talks with Beijing will result in Taiwan enjoying greater opportunities for international engagement. However, Beijing's fundamental position on the issue of international representation remains unchanged, and it is still trying to figure out how to satisfy Taiwan without compromising this basic position.

In the case of Taiwan's participation as an observer in the WHA, Beijing's calculation appears to have been based on a calculation about how to gain ground in Taiwan's domestic arena and provide political support to the KMT government. However, Beijing's current policy on Taiwan's participation in international organizations still limits Taipei to joining only those bodies that do not require sovereignty for membership. Recent elaboration on Beijing's position by senior Chinese officials and think-tank experts shows that, so far, China does not have a comprehensive approach to dealing with this issue and at present it is likely to be very reluctant to allow Taiwan further opportunities for participation in international fora.[5] Observing President Ma's declining popularity in Taiwan, Beijing's constant concern is how best to prepare to respond if the DPP returns to power in 2012 or 2016. New initiatives for Taiwan's international outreach will be needed in the future if cross-Strait rapprochement is to maintain a base of popular support in Taiwan.

Conclusion

After the KMT returned to power in 2008, cross-Strait tensions diminished quickly. The most obvious change was that Taiwan was no longer seen as a troublemaker by either Beijing or Washington. Furthermore, the process of reconciliation across the Strait has brought about new hopes for peaceful development and regional cooperation. The rapid progress in cross-Strait relations that has occurred since last year nonetheless has created new concerns.

---

[5] A general guideline on the future cross-Strait relationship is outlined in "Hu Jintao's Six Points." In this speech, Hu encouraged cross-Strait cooperation and coordination on Taiwan's international participation, but in reality, after the WHA case, no talks on Taiwan's international space have been held. For more on this issue, see "President Hu Offers Six Proposals for Peaceful Development of Cross-Strait Relationship," Taiwan Affairs Office of the State Council, December 31, 2008.

The first concern derives from domestic politics. Because Taiwan holds presidential elections every four years, China's perception of Taiwan's future political development remains one of the most important uncertainties and concerns. Of course, if the DPP returns to power, the current rapprochement may be reversed. Although the DPP's chances of regaining the presidency seem rather low at present, it is nonetheless a worst-case scenario that China is compelled to grapple with. If the DPP does return to power in the future, would the progress made by the cross-Strait talks be reversed? Judging from the present progress and efforts made, it is almost impossible to turn the clock backward. At the same time, President Hu Jintao has adopted a pragmatic approach toward Taiwan. After his term as president concludes, will the next PRC leader continue to pursue this approach? Many observers believe that the next Chinese leader will be more subject to populist pressures from society, which may complicate future cross-Strait relations.

A second source of uncertainty is whether China will be willing to give up the option to use force. For decades, coercion has been considered the final means to defend China's integrity and sovereignty against Taiwan independence. If the two sides reach agreement on an ECFA next year, will Beijing be willing to give up its traditional threat of armed force against Taiwan? If so, when? Much will depend on how the ECFA negotiations play out. If the ECFA is signed in June 2010, as currently appears likely, further negotiations on the details of cross-Strait economic ties as stipulated by the ECFA will start immediately. It will definitely increase political pressure on Beijing to reduce the level of hostility against Taiwan. At this moment of uncertain development in Taiwan's politics, it seems unlikely that Beijing will renounce the use of force at any point within the next five to ten years; a new generation of leaders will take over in Beijing during this period and will presumably want to strengthen their authority and national security credentials, a development that leaves little room for flexibility on issues of sovereignty and military security.

On the strategic level, the current momentum of cross-Strait rapprochement suggests that Taiwan would be wise to engage more with the United States, which would increase Taiwan's confidence in further developing cooperative mechanisms across the Strait and increase its engagement with the international community.

11. Alternative Futures: Long-Term Challenges for the United States

Michael McDevitt

Introduction

This paper speculates about the future. It addresses the question, "What are the security implications for the United States if today's cooperative relationship between Taiwan and the mainland continues into the future?" Some Chinese commentators have claimed that the current state of cross-Strait relations is "an irreversible trend leading to reunification."[1] Whether this is true or not, and whether this is a positive development or not, depends on one's views regarding the future of Taiwan as a democracy and about the overall Sino-U.S. strategic balance in East Asia.

In any case, today, China's policy toward Taiwan remains focused on "peaceful" reunification. From Beijing's perspective, its policy approach based upon party-to-party relationships and increasingly robust economic engagement is working. Of course, it is also a policy backstopped by a powerful military capability that is able to "severely punish" Taiwan should it stray toward independence. Straying toward independence does not seem likely at the moment. The Ma administration is focused on rapprochement, not permanent separation—but importantly, not reunification.[2] Because Taipei has apparently turned its back on permanent separation from China, the prospect of conflict across the Strait is very low. That means that the potential for conflict between the United States and China over Taiwan is also very low. An unprovoked use of force by China against Taiwan that could trigger U.S. involvement seems remote, but as this paper explores, it cannot be totally discounted if Beijing grows impatient because of a lack of progress toward reunification.

Some Essential Realities

When speculating about the future, it is always good to start with a baseline based on "the reality on the ground." There are three essential geostrategic realities to keep in mind.

First, Taiwan is always going to be a small island existing in the shadow of the mainland. It is always going to be just 100 miles from China. It will always be between a 50th and a 60th of the size of China in terms of population. Taiwan will always be disadvantaged in terms of the size of its military establishment and, increasingly, in the qualitative superiority of its weapons systems. Certainly, it will always be disadvantaged by its long-term

---

1 Guo Zhongguan, "Scholar Says the Reunification Process Will Enter a Crucial Period as Cross Strait Exchanges Undergo Structural Changes," China News Agency, Hong Kong [*Zhongguo Tongxun*], October 12, 2009.

2 In his inaugural address, President Ma made the strategic pledge of "no unification, no independence, and no use of force," with the codicil that "Taiwan will maintain the status-quo in the Taiwan Strait." Ma has been quite explicit that reunification is something for the distant future, that unification is not his goal, and that is not on the agenda during his administration. His strategic objective is to "stabilize" the cross-Strait relationship.

military potential and the amount of resources available for defense. Taiwan cannot be towed out into the Pacific Ocean. It lacks the geographic blessing of either distance or strategic depth in a standoff with China.

On the other hand, being 100 miles away has also favored Taiwan. It has been just far enough away from the mainland to avoid the fate of Tibet. For the past half century, the Taiwan Strait has been a barrier to the decisive application of Chinese military power. The People's Liberation Army (PLA) cannot walk, drive, or swim to Taiwan. It is the PLA's inability to overcome the problem of projecting decisive power across a substantial body of water that has kept Taiwan from being incorporated into the People's Republic of China (PRC).

The second reality revolves around Beijing's belief that it must maintain the capability to use force as a prominent feature of its declaratory policy toward Taiwan. By figuratively keeping its finger on the trigger, China forces the United States, because of its policies that reject the use of force or military coercion, to plan for the possibility of conflict with China over Taiwan. Since Beijing understands that this is the case, it also considers how best to deal with U.S. intervention if it elects to employ force against Taiwan. As a result, another military dynamic comes into play—namely, the long-range planning efforts and resource allocation decisions made by both China and the United States that have one another as the target. Despite the possibility of conflict being very low, defense establishments by their very nature must plan for worst-case contingencies. As a result, all three militaries that could be directly involved in a conflict in the area around the Taiwan Strait are actively planning, exercising, and war-gaming in order to determine how best to prevail in such a conflict.

It has been almost a decade since Beijing issued a white paper that introduced another element into considerations surrounding the use of force. The 2000 China national defense white paper argued that the failure to begin the process of discussions leading to the reunification of Taiwan and mainland China could not be postponed indefinitely without Taiwan risking being compelled to reunify through the use of force. The 2000 white paper introduced an element of caprice to the Taiwan situation that had not existed before, because now the aspect of time was linked to eventual reunification.[3] In other words, Beijing does not intend to wait forever; the current situation of a de facto independent Taiwan cannot be allowed to drag on indefinitely. This should suggest to U.S. military planners that conflict can apparently be dictated by the whim of Beijing. Potentially, a Taiwan crisis could erupt at any moment—without obvious provocation. This is not likely, but because the use of force remains on the table, it is nonetheless a fact (if perhaps an inconvenient one) that must be taken into account when considering the future.

The third reality has to do with the seemingly inexorable pace of China's military modernization and how that modernization is changing the military balance of power in the vicinity of Taiwan in China's favor. During much of the Cold War, when China's military potential was either consumed by the Cultural Revolution or

---

[3] Information Office of the State Council, People's Republic of China, *China's National Defense in 2000*, Beijing, October 16, 2000, p. 6.

focused on the Soviet Union, the PLA never really had the means to surmount the barrier of the Taiwan Strait and apply military power against Taiwan. In effect, the PLA was a "paper tiger" when it came to threatening Taiwan with military punishment during these years.

This did not matter much, since the political leadership on both sides of the Strait sought the same end—eventual reunification of Taiwan and the mainland. The argument was over which party would be in charge of the "uniting." This changed dramatically almost 20 years ago with the advent of democracy and when notions of a *de jure* independent Taiwanese state began to politically resonate in Taiwan.

For the PLA, the prospect of permanent separation and an independent Taiwan provided a focus for military modernization that had not been present before. Taiwan became an operational *idée fixe* for the PLA as it introduced capabilities that would provide credibility to policy pronouncements regarding the use of force to prevent independence.[4]

This single-minded focus on the operational problem of Taiwan has resulted in PLA weapons and capabilities that allow it to "reach out and touch" Taiwan in a way that was not possible in earlier decades. Today, the PLA is able to match, or in some cases surpass, Taiwan's highest-end military capabilities with equal or better Russian, or Russian-based, systems.[5] Assessing whether the PLA could successfully seize Taiwan, and cause it to capitulate through bombardment and then invasion, is beyond the scope of this paper. Suffice it to say, to do this, the PLA has to accomplish two essential tasks—get the army safely across the Taiwan Strait and then defeat the ROC army defenders. According to most experts, the PLA is on the cusp of being able to gain and maintain air superiority over the Taiwan Strait, an essential prerequisite to any attempt to project the PLA across the Strait so it can physically seize Taiwan through invasion.[6]

These three realities—Taiwan's unfortunate geographic circumstances, Beijing's Taiwan policy that rests ultimately on the threat of force, and China's impressive military capabilities that are getting better by the day—must frame any speculation about the future.

---

[4] David M. Finkelstein, "PLA Modernization," Carnegie Endowment for International Peace, New Vision Program debate series, Washington, D.C., February 6, 2007, is the best succinct summation of the drivers behind PLA modernization. (Copy in author's possession.)

[5] See, for example, Carlo Kopp, *Sukoi Flankers: The Shifting Balance of Regional Air Power,* Australia Air Power Association, Technical Report APA-TR-2007-0101, September 2009.

[6] David A. Shlapak, David T. Orlesky, Toy I. Reid, Murray Scot Tanner, and Barry Wilson, *A Question of Balance: Political Context and Military Aspects of the China-Taiwan Dispute*, Santa Monica, Calif.: RAND Corporation, MG-888-SRF, 2009, pp. 31–84. This is the most complete unclassified analysis of the issue of gaining air superiority over the Taiwan Strait; its conclusions are not encouraging for Taiwan.

An Optimistic Future?

Experts generally agree that cross-Strait relations are now more stable and promising than they have been for decades and perhaps since 1949.[7] However, whether there is a historic and strategic opportunity to move forward and lay the foundations for a permanent framework for peace and security in the Taiwan Strait, as some suggest, depends upon one of the three parties in this strategic triangle making a fundamental change to its declared policy.

For example, China could give up the threat of force, betting that time and economic linkages are on its side, or it could simply declare that Taiwan was free to choose its own political destiny and that Beijing would not interfere since Taiwan would always be culturally and economically linked to the mainland. Alternatively, Taipei could decide to begin discussions with Beijing with the expressed aim of political reunification. Or it could declare independence and hope that, after much soul-searching, Beijing would decide to do nothing. Finally, Washington could actively work with Beijing to develop a plan that left Taipei with no choice but to reunify, or it could simply repeal the Taiwan Relations Act and declare that Taiwan is an internal affair of China's and America is no longer going to be involved.

Or, even more implausibly, the United States could recognize the ROC, establish formal relations, reestablish the alliance and hope Beijing does nothing.

Now, clearly none of these things seems likely to happen over the next five or so years, if ever—although among the examples listed above, the initiation of a cross-Strait reunification dialogue by Taipei is not completely far-fetched. Issues like public outrage, strategic credibility, worries about worse-case outcomes, and nationalism all stand in the way of any of these outcomes, despite the fact that long-term stabilization of cross-Strait relations would have enormous strategic benefits for the United States, China, and Taiwan and for regional and global security.

Assuming that none of these dramatic policy changes is likely to take place, any thinking about the future needs to be framed within variations on today's current situation. In other words, the context for speculation about the future is today's status quo. It is unlikely that Washington or Beijing would change policies in the ways suggested above, but policy choices by Taipei are possible and are, in analytic terms, the independent variable.

Taipei apparently has two basic choices. First, it could try to perpetuate today's current peaceful but politically unresolved situation into the indefinite future with the hope that Beijing will gradually evolve politically in a direction that would either make reunification desirable to Taiwan's population or make independence an issue not worth fighting about. Beijing is alert to this possibility and calls it "peaceful separation." Many in the United States have called this the "kick-the-can-down-the road" approach. It is based on hope—the hope that something good will turn up.

---

[7] For example, see Donald S. Zagoria, "Cross-Strait Relations: Cautious Optimism," summary of the Conference on Prospects for Relations across the Taiwan Strait, a Trilateral Conference sponsored by the National Committee on American Foreign Policy, January 13–14, 2009.

This seems to be the implicit objective of America's "no unilateral changes to the status quo" policy. Because none of the three parties is being forced under present circumstances to make tough political decisions, this may turn out to be the most likely outcome, despite Beijing's avowed unwillingness to wait forever. To change this dynamic by increasing incentives for the people of Taiwan to want reunification (for example, by compromising on the use of force issue), Beijing would have to suppress its anxiety over the Kuomintang (KMT) losing power to another Democratic Progressive Party (DPP) administration that would rekindle pro-independence momentum. Because Beijing thinks it has to hedge against this outcome, compromises involving its deterrent—its option to use force—will be hard to make.

There may be one possible exception: some sort of a grand bargain, probably underwritten by Washington, and perhaps Tokyo and Seoul, that is based on a perpetuation of the current geopolitical status quo with the exception that the use of force by Beijing is removed from the equation. It is based on the idea that a binding understanding is reached between Beijing and Taipei. Taipei pledges that it will not attempt to unilaterally change the status quo by declaring independence, and in return, Beijing removes the use of force from the table. But, importantly, there is no agreed-upon end state. The terms of the agreement would presumably hold for a long period of time—say, 30 years.[8]

For such an agreement to be credible, it would have to have broad political support in Taiwan, including from the DPP and/or similar independence-seeking parties that might appear on the Taiwan political stage over the years. Similarly, Beijing would have to repeal its Anti-Secession Law, revise its declaratory policies on the use of force, and put the breaks on aspects of its military modernization that are clearly targeted at Taiwan—including its development of short-range ballistic missile forces, amphibious shipping, and short-range air superiority fighters.

The United States would have a role in such an agreement. Besides somehow guaranteeing Taipei's good behavior, arms sales to Taiwan would probably have to be circumscribed, especially equipment associated with the future modernization of Taiwan's military. (Note that this would not mean that U.S. arms sales to Taiwan would be totally eliminated, as the United States would still need to provide spare parts and the like for what Taiwan already owns.) Arms sales could drop off, in any case, if Taipei came to believe that it no longer needed to make major modernization purchases.

Were this scenario to play out, the major advantage for the United States would be removing the most plausible source of conflict with China. If what I have called the "black cloud of war" over Taiwan were removed, the need to either deter the use of force by China or plan for intervention in support of Taiwan would no longer be a major planning factor in U.S. strategic calculations.

This would be of great value to the broader U.S.-China relationship, since so many of the irritants in the U.S.-China security relationship have their roots in the possibility of conflict over Taiwan. It would not, however,

---

[8] Kenneth Lieberthal, "Preventing a War over Taiwan," *Foreign Affairs*, Vol. 84, No. 2, March–April 2005.

result in nirvana. While Taiwan has been the focus of Beijing's anti-access/area-denial strategy, and the concomitant threat to U.S. freedom of action in the Western Pacific, it is important to remember that China has other strategic worries on its maritime frontier that make its anti-access concept equally germane.

Most importantly, from Beijing's perspective, the anti-access/area-denial concept of operations is how China defends itself more broadly against a conventional maritime-launched attack by the United States. China's economic center of gravity will remain on its eastern seaboard, and remain vulnerable to attack from the sea, for the foreseeable future. We are reminded frequently by Chinese interlocutors that they have not forgotten that the century of humiliation, starting with the Opium Wars, was caused by threats that came mainly from the sea. Anti-access/area denial has the potential to secure China's maritime approaches for the first time in China's long history. Unfortunately, the way Beijing has elected to solve this problem creates insecurity for U.S. allies and friends in the region, since China's concept is based upon keeping credible U.S. military power as far away from East Asia as possible.

Thus, while the United States would gain important strategic advantages by removing the most likely trigger for conflict with China as well as some associated irritants, such as arms sales, the underlying sense of military competition between the two militaries would probably live on. This seems inevitable as long as the United States finds it necessary to maintain a substantial military presence in East Asia to support its friends and allies and hedge against the possibility of a militarily assertive China.

The second alternative for Taiwan appears similar to the first but is actually quite different, because it would have an agreed-upon end state: Taipei could continue to do what it has been doing—political and economic rapprochement with the mainland rationalized by economic self-interest. Over time, the dialogue would morph into political-military issues, such as confidence-building and discussions over ending the Chinese civil war. This, of course, is what is going on today. What would be different from today would be an understanding by both parties that the agreed-upon end state—no matter how long it was in coming—would be reunification. Today, there is no such agreement, much to the frustration of Beijing.

This alternative would be the best outcome for better Sino-U.S. relations because it would, in theory, bring closure to U.S. involvement in the Chinese civil war. Once agreement was reached that reunification was the ultimate goal, issues such as arms sales and the Taiwan Relations Act would gradually move offstage. However, this would still not address the larger strategic question of the competing U.S.-China strategies—assured access versus access denial. These two diametrically opposed strategic concepts, which serve each country's most important interests in East Asia, will remain relevant in the future and, as a result, cause the continuation of today's ongoing capabilities competition.

The prospect of eventual reunification would also introduce another dynamic into the Sino-U.S. relationship: the geostrategic implications associated with the unsinkable aircraft carrier of Taiwan falling into the hands of China. While U.S. policy has long recognized the geostrategic implications of peaceful reunification, and is willing to accept the potentially adverse consequences of Taiwan in the PRC's hands, it may not have fully appreciated Japanese concerns about this outcome.

The Geostrategic Importance of Taiwan

The geostrategic importance of Taiwan has been part of Japan's *weltanschauung* since the late 1880s. It was the Imperial Japanese Navy (IJN) that insisted on the annexation of Taiwan when the Treaty of Shimonoseki, which ended the Sino-Japanese War, was being negotiated in 1895. The reasons that the IJN was so insistent are complex and beyond the scope of this paper except to note that both Japanese politicians and naval leaders were persuaded that if they did not take Taiwan, a European power might do so. Worries that Taiwan would fall into the hands of a Western maritime power were not unrealistic. Only a decade earlier, France had attacked and then blockaded Taiwan to coerce the Qing court into accepting French demands in Indochina.[9]

Concerns about Taiwan falling into the hands of a power that could be hostile to Japan are still relevant 110 years later. Geography and sea lanes have not changed. More contemporary evidence of Japan's concerns about Taiwan not being in the hands of a hostile, or a potentially hostile, power is found in a draft paper by Steven Goldstein and Randall Shriver. They uncovered the fact that the issue of Taiwan has been an element in the Japan–U.S. strategic relationship since 1950. During the 1960s and 1970s, the government of Japan was very worried about Taiwan falling into the hands of the communist mainland. Japan's economic viability depends on the maritime trade routes that pass through the waters around Taiwan.[10] For Japan, vulnerability to economic isolation is not simply a conceptual problem. The successful U.S. submarine and carrier air campaign in World War II to economically isolate Japan remains a real-world reminder to Tokyo regarding the importance preventing a disruption to maritime commerce and energy imports.[11]

One of Japan's leading strategists, Ambassador Hisahiko Okazaki, has written about the strategic implications of PRC annexation of Taiwan. He claims that it that would compromise the sea lanes in which Japan's Middle Eastern oil travels, and that it would also give China greater leverage over Southeast Asia—which could indirectly affect Japan's very large economic interests in that region.[12]

---

[9] Alan M. Wachman, *Why Taiwan? Geostrategic Rationales for China's Territorial Integrity*, Stanford, Calif.: Stanford University Press, 2007, p. 51; S. C. M. Paine, *The Sino-Japanese War of 1894–1895: Perceptions, Power, and Primacy*, New York: Cambridge University Press, 2003, p. 261; Edward I-te Chen, "Japan's Decision to Annex Taiwan: A Study of Ito-Mutsu Diplomacy," *Journal of Asian Studies*, Vol. 37, No. 1, November 1977, pp. 61–72.

[10] Steven M. Goldstein and Randall Schriver, "Japan and Conflict in the Taiwan Strait, 1951–2007: From Passive Observer to Active Participant," draft paper in author's possession.

[11] Theodore Roscoe, *U.S. Submarine Operations in World War II*, Annapolis, Md.: U.S. Naval Institute Press, 1949, pp. 410–439. See also H. P. Wilmont, *The Battle of Leyte Gulf: The Last Fleet Action*, Bloomington, Ind.: University of Indiana Press, 2006, pp. 6–10, for a discussion of the strategic implications of the destruction of Japan's merchant marine. In 1941, Japan imported some 48,720,000 tons of goods; when the war ended in August, tonnage for 1945 was only 7,710,000.

[12] David Fouse, "Japan-Taiwan Relations: A Case of Tempered Optimism," *A Special Assessment: Asia's Bilateral Relations*, Honolulu: Asia-Pacific Center for Security Studies, October 2004, p. 4-6.

In fact, Japan's case is indirectly made by the Chinese themselves. PRC strategists also appreciate the geostrategic position of Taiwan. In a mirror image to Japanese concerns, they fret that the combination of the Ryukyu Chain and Taiwan effectively acts as a picket fence around the East China Sea, potentially constraining access to the eastern seaboard of central and northern China—which, of course, includes Shanghai. Former U.S. Ambassador to China James Lilley accurately described Taiwan as "the cork in China's bottle." Reunification with the mainland would "end what China feels to be a blockade on its ability to control its surrounding seas."[13]

PLA strategists from the Academy of Military Sciences made this clear in their 2005 publication of an excellent work on strategy, titled *The Science of Military Strategy*. It states,

> Taiwan is located in the southeast of our sea area and is in the middle of the islands surrounding our coastline. It is in the key area of sea routes of the Pacific Ocean, and is thus crowned as "the key to the southeast coastal area of China," and "the fence to the seven provinces in the center of China." The sea routes from the East China Sea to the South China Sea, from Northeast Asia to Southeast Asia, as well as the route from the West Pacific to the Middle East, Europe and Asia, pass here.
>
> It is where we can breach the chain of islands surrounding us in the West Pacific to the vast area of the Pacific, as well as a strategic key area and sea barrier for defense and offense. If Taiwan should be alienated from the mainland, not only our natural maritime defense system would lose its depth, opening a sea gateway to outside forces, but also a large area of water territory would fall into the hands of others. What's more, our line of foreign trade and transportation which is vital to China's opening up and economic development will be exposed to the surveillance and threats of separatists and enemy forces and China will forever be locked to the west side of the first chain of islands in the West Pacific.[14]

This assessment makes clear that in PLA strategic thought, Taiwan in the hands of the PRC would provide an important element in the seaward defenses of mainland China—whereas a Taiwan in unfriendly hands would constrain China's access to the open ocean and could provide a base for attacks on the PRC.

In the end, it is unlikely that Japanese concerns about the possible consequences of reunification would have a decisive impact on U.S. policy choices, nor is it likely that Japan would elect to directly confront China by encouraging Taipei to avoid reunification. It most likely would have a positive impact on U.S.-Japan relations, however, which in turn could improve America's strategic position in East Asia. First, with Taiwan and the mainland reunified, Japan is likely to value its strategic partnership with the United States even more highly. So long as an element of competition and suspicion is a feature of the Sino-Japanese relationship, Japan is likely to value the hedge that its alliance with Washington provides.

---

[13] Ambassador James Lilley, cited in Nancy Bernkopf Tucker, "If Taiwan Chooses Unification, Should the United States Care?" *Washington Quarterly*, Vol. 25, No. 3, Summer 2002, p. 22.

[14] Peng Guangqian and Yang Youzhi, eds., *The Science of Military Strategy*, Beijing: Military Science Publishing House, Academy of Military Science of the People's Liberation Army, 2005, pp. 442–443.

Given trends in Chinese economic development, the aging of Japan, and its pacifist public mindset, Japan will increasingly count on the United States to balance China. Barring a disaster in China, Japan will increasingly be overshadowed by China in most areas related to power, including, of course, military power. When faced with the prospect that China could control the sea lanes on either side of Taiwan, Japan is likely to improve its own anti-submarine and other relevant capabilities—which would be an additive improvement to America's ability to assure access to the region.

Conclusion

Reducing or removing the risk of a U.S.-China conflict over Taiwan is in the strategic interest of the United States. There are likely to be other points of military contention between Beijing and Washington in the future, but none of them involves the interest of both states to such a degree that it could lead to major conflict. There could be minor dust-ups in the South China Sea involving U.S. friends and allies who might turn to Washington for assistance. But given that the United States has no important interests in the South China Sea, except that the sea lanes remain open, it is hard to imagine that Washington would choose to use force to reverse a Chinese occupation of a contested island or islet.

Obviously, things that increase the possibility of conflict across the Taiwan Strait are not in America's interest—nor for that matter are they in China's interest.

As we look to the future, a troubling wildcard is the possibility that impatience, when combined with a growing sense of Chinese triumphalism, could lead Beijing to decide to force the issue of reunification. Because of this possibility, and the fact that the United States and China will be engaged in a military capabilities competition, even if things turn out well in cross-Strait relations, is not a bad thing. As long as the United States chooses to keep competing to assure its access, and does not let Chinese capabilities gain the upper hand, there will continue to be a powerful deterrent to Chinese impatience.

The worst of all possible outcomes would be the dangerous brew of a China that calculates that it has achieved the military upper hand—i.e., that its anti-access/area-denial capabilities will deter U.S. intervention—combined with impatience with the progress of reunification with Taiwan and an overweening sense of confidence that the PRC can afford to throw its weight around in East Asia without regard to the consequences.

This situation represents the worst-case scenario because, in the absence of some provocation by Taipei, if China loses patience and elects to use force to settle unification once and for all, that decision could lead to a U.S.–China war. Today, it seems improbable that Beijing would be this reckless, but it is something that bears watching because even now there are press reports of PLA generals worrying that Taiwan's current policy will lead to a "peaceful split from China."[15] One of the issues U.S. experts will have to watch closely is Beijing's policy approach toward Taipei: Will it shift away from the "halting independence" focus, back to an emphasis on "completing reunification"? Such a policy switch could easily be the trigger for a "more impatient" policy debate in Beijing. Should perpetuation of today's status quo with no agreed-upon reunification plan create frustration among Beijing's policy elite and lead to a view rationalizing military action, or even simply saber-rattling, it would be very difficult for Washington to stand by and not intervene in some fashion. Not to do so would shred American credibility as a force for stability in East Asia by calling into question America's reliability as an ally when confronted by an assertive China.

[15] PLA Major General Luo Yuan, quoted by *China Times* senior reporter Che Le-yi in "An Analysis of Retired Chinese Military Leaders's Recent Talks on the Establishment of Cross-Strait Confidence Building Measures," Peace Forum, January 26, 2010.

12. Deeper Cross-Strait Rapprochement and PLA Modernization: Implications for China's Relations with Asia and the United States

Michael A. Glosny[1]

Since the mid-1990s, China's military modernization has focused on deterring Taiwan independence and preparing for a military response if deterrence fails. Given China's assumption of U.S. intervention in a Taiwan conflict, the People's Liberation Army (PLA) has been developing military capabilities to deter, delay, and disrupt U.S. military support operations. The 2008 election of Taiwan President Ma Ying-jeou, however, has contributed to improved cross-Strait economic and political cooperation and dramatically reduced the threat of Taiwan independence and war across the Taiwan Strait. Cooperation has included full restoration of direct shipping, flights, and mail across the Taiwan Strait; Taiwan's participation in the World Health Assembly (WHA); regularized cross-Strait negotiation mechanisms that have already reached several agreements; and the recent signing of the Economic Cooperation Framework Agreement (ECFA).[2]

This decrease in cross-Strait tension and tentative rapprochement has raised the prospect of fundamental changes in China's security challenges. If China and Taiwan sustain this positive cooperation over the next five to ten years and continue to deepen rapprochement, how would this affect regional stability, China's diplomatic grand strategy, and China's military modernization? Other analysts have examined the implications of an ultimate political resolution to the Taiwan issue, but this paper analyzes the implications of deeper cross-Strait rapprochement, a much more likely scenario over the next five to ten years.[3] This deeper rapprochement would probably not resolve the issue of Taiwan's political status, but it would greatly reduce the chances that the People's Republic of China (PRC) would use force. Sustained cross-Strait stability would make the Taiwan issue less important in Chinese domestic politics and much less prominent in China's relations with others. This could occur as a result of a peace agreement or through a series of cooperative measures by both sides that put the relationship on a course toward peaceful resolution. Experts devote a great detail of attention to scenarios of crisis and conflict in the Taiwan Strait, but the implications of deeper cross-Strait cooperation also deserve analytical

---

[1] The author is indebted to Roger Cliff, Scott Harold, David Finkelstein, Michael Kiselycznyk, Isaac Kardon, Phillip Saunders, Andrew Scobell, and Christopher Twomey for comments on earlier drafts.

[2] For a review of these developments, see Alan D. Romberg, "Cross-Strait Relations: First the Easy, Now the Hard," *China Leadership Monitor*, No. 28, Spring 2009; Bonnie S. Glaser, *Building Trust Across the Taiwan Strait: A Role for Military Confidence-Building Measures*, Washington, D.C.: Center for Strategic and International Studies, January 2010; and other papers in this volume.

[3] For earlier analyses of the implications of resolution of the Taiwan issue, see Nancy Bernkopf Tucker, "If Taiwan Chooses Unification, Should the United States Care?" *Washington Quarterly*, Vol. 25, No. 3, Summer 2002; Roger Cliff and David A. Shlapak, *U.S.-China Relations After Resolution of Taiwan's Status*, Santa Monica, Calif.: RAND Corporation, MG-567-AF, 2007; and Andrew Scobell, "How China Manages Taiwan and Its Impact on PLA Missions," in Roy Kamphausen, David Lai, and Andrew Scobell, eds., *Beyond the Strait: PLA Missions Other Than Taiwan*, Carlisle, Pa.: Strategic Studies Institute, U.S. Army War College, 2009, pp. 29–38.

attention. This discussion of potential future implications of deeper cross-Strait rapprochement is speculative in nature.

Deeper rapprochement across the Taiwan Strait would clearly be a positive development. It would remove the most likely source of war between the United States and China, or at least greatly reduce the chances of such a war breaking out over the Taiwan issue. China would also no longer need to issue threats or conduct coercive military exercises to intimidate Taiwan. These provocative acts often undermined regional stability, damaged China's relations with Asian countries, and led to concerns about China's future intentions. As any deeper rapprochement will include a clearer understanding about Taiwan's international space, the United States and other Asian countries would welcome the removal of the irritant of Beijing's sensitivity and angry responses to interactions with Taiwan. Sustained cross-Strait stability would also remove the "nightmare scenario," in which regional countries may have to choose whether to support the United States or China in the event of a war over Taiwan. For China, deeper rapprochement would remove a threat to the regime and make it easier to manage relations with the United States and with Asian countries. In military terms, cross-Strait rapprochement would also remove concerns about Taiwan being used by outside powers as a potential base to exert strategic pressure on China and make it easier for China to break out of the first island chain.

However, stability across the Taiwan Strait will not remove all concerns that a rising China may destabilize the region. Analysts have not fully considered the new challenges that deep rapprochement will produce in China's relations with Asia and the United States. Asian countries will be relieved, but many will worry that a rising China no longer constrained by a focus on Taiwan will use its increased power to challenge their interests elsewhere in Asia. The United States will have similar concerns about an unconstrained China challenging its interests, and will face demands for enhanced, credible defense commitments from regional countries.

The United States and Asian countries will worry about the continued rise of China regardless of the situation across the Taiwan Strait. Former U.S. Ambassador to China James Lilley referred to Taiwan as "the cork in China's bottle."[4] Deeper rapprochement will remove the cork, enabling China to focus less on the Taiwan issue, devote more attention and resources to other issues, and transfer capabilities that had been focused on Taiwan to other contingencies. This will lead other countries in the region to worry that an unconstrained, rising China may become more assertive elsewhere in the region.

For China, stabilizing the cross-Strait political situation will "free up" resources devoted to military preparations for Taiwan contingencies and give the PLA new options. China's potential choices for its military modernization include (1) relaxed modernization, (2) domestic and continental concerns, (3) an anti-access focus, (4) assertive pursuit of regional maritime claims, and (5) extra-regional activities. New pressures from China's integration into the world economy and expanding interests are already leading to new pressures to take on some

---

[4] Tucker, 2002, p. 22.

missions in addition to preparing for a Taiwan contingency, but deeper rapprochement will likely lead to a more thorough evaluation of the proper mix of roles and missions for the PLA.

Deeper rapprochement across the Strait will produce new uncertainties and apprehension over how an unconstrained China will use its increased power. The direction of PLA modernization can help alleviate these concerns or further exacerbate them. If China pursues a path of relaxed modernization, or a combination of limited investments in the other options, China's reassurance may alleviate some of these worries and maintain a stable international environment. If China follows an assertive course, especially if it combines significant investments in a combination of assertive areas for PLA modernization, it will help make potential concerns become realities and more likely trigger strong countervailing balancing responses from the United States and the region.

This paper proceeds as follows. First, I briefly lay out China's overall grand strategy. Then, I analyze the new challenges and difficulties that China will face in its relations with the region and the United States as a result of stable cross-Strait relations. Third, I briefly discuss the potential choices for PLA modernization after deeper rapprochement provides more resources and new options. Lastly, I conclude.

China's Grand Strategy and Military Modernization

Through cooperation and attempts to demonstrate its benign intentions, China's grand strategy of reassurance aims to prevent the formation of balancing coalitions as China rises. For China's leaders, the next five to ten years correspond to the important "period of strategic opportunity" (*zhanlue jiyuqi*) for China's economic modernization and development, during which the leadership hopes to focus its efforts on building a "moderately well-off society" (*xiaokang shehui*).[5] During this "period of strategic opportunity," China's grand strategy is focused on maintaining a peaceful and stable international environment that will allow it to increase the country's "comprehensive national power" (*zonghe guoli*), focus on economic modernization and development, and rise to great-power status.

Scholars have characterized this grand strategy in different terms, but my own view is that it would best be conceptualized as one of reassurance.[6] The goal of this diplomatic strategy is to prevent complications in China's

---

[5] At the 16th Party Congress in 2002, the Chinese Communist Party (CCP) leadership formally declared the first 20 years of the 21st century to be a period of strategic opportunity that needed to be effectively grasped. For more on the diplomatic aspects, see Chu Shulong, "Quanmian Jianshe Xiaokang Shiqi de Zhongguo Waijiao Zhanlue" ["China's Diplomatic Strategy in the Period of Building a Well-Off Society in an All-Around Way"], *Shijie Jingji yu Zhengzhi* [*World Economics and Politics*], No. 8, 2003, pp. 8–13, and Shi Yinhong, "Zhongguo Heping Jueqi de Zhanlue Jiyu he ruogan Jiben Tiaojian" ["The Strategic Opportunity of China's Peaceful Rise and Several Fundamental Conditions"], *Guoji Guancha* [*International Survey*], No. 3, 2004, pp. 22–23, 26.

[6] The official characterization is one of a strategy of peaceful development (*heping fazhan*). For the official white paper, see Information Office of the State Council, People's Republic of China, *China's Peaceful Development Road*, Beijing, December 2005. For analysis of China's grand strategy, see Huang Renwei, *Zhongguo Jueqi de Shijian he Kongjian* [*The Time and Space for China's Rise*], Shanghai: Shanghai Academy of Social Sciences Press, 2003; Ye Zicheng, *Daguo DaZhanlue: Zhongguo Chengwei Shijie Daguo de Zhuyao Wenti ji Zhanlue Xuanze* [*China's Grand Strategy: Important Issues and Strategic Choices for China in Becoming a World Great Power*], Beijing: Chinese Academy of Social Sciences Press, 2003; Yan Xuetong et al.,

international environment that may distract attention from this focus on development and force China to divert resources to deal with external challenges. For a rising China, the goal is to increase power and influence without provoking a balancing coalition. In implementing this grand strategy of reassurance, China will continue to cooperate with major powers and regional powers in an effort to demonstrate that it has benign intentions and show that as it gets more powerful it will not threaten the interests of these countries, but will use its increased power to help protect those interests.

Some may argue that if China continues its rise for the next five to ten years, the government will likely shift its grand strategy. However, any fundamental change in China's grand strategy will likely occur only after fundamental reassessments of key Chinese judgments about the international environment and China's international position—they include the "trend of the times" (*shidai zhuti*), "international structure" (*guoji geju*), and China's "orientation" (*dingwei*).[7] As these judgments are unlikely to fundamentally shift during this period, China's grand strategy of reassurance will likely endure. Moreover, as China will remain focused on economic modernization and increasing its power, Chinese experts argue that deeper cross-Strait rapprochement would also not lead to a shift in grand strategy.[8]

Although the broad contours of China's grand strategy have not changed substantially in the last decade, and are not likely to in the next five to ten years, China's deeper embrace of globalization and engagement with the world is leading to new challenges and pressures for China's foreign and security policy. Its economic integration and increased global activism have led to an unprecedented expansion of national interests. As new actors and new interests have become more prominent in China's global engagement, coordinating and managing China's foreign affairs has become much more difficult.[9] Recent diplomatic meetings (such as the summer 2006 Foreign Affairs

---

"'Daguo de Jueqi yu Zhongguo de Xuanze' Bitan" ["Pen Discussions on 'The Rise of Great Powers and China's Choices'"], *Zhongguo Shehui Kexue* [*Social Sciences in China*], Vol. 5, 2004. For a thorough English-language analysis of China's grand strategy, see Avery Goldstein, *Rising to the Challenge: China's Grand Strategy and International Security*, Stanford, Calif.: Stanford University Press, 2005, and Michael D. Swaine and Ashley J. Tellis, *Interpreting China's Grand Strategy: Past, Present, and Future*, Santa Monica, Calif.: RAND Corporation, MR-1121-AF, 2000.

[7] On the importance of these assessments for Chinese foreign policy, see Wang Jisi, "International Relations Theory and the Study of Chinese Foreign Policy: A Chinese Perspective," in Thomas W. Robinson and David Shambaugh, eds., *Chinese Foreign Policy: Theory and Practice*, Oxford, UK: Oxford University Press, 1994, pp. 481–505, and David M. Finkelstein, *China Reconsiders Its National Security: "The Great Peace and Development Debate of 1999,"* Alexandria, Va.: CNA Corporation, December 2000.

[8] Author's interviews, Beijing, spring 2010.

[9] For discussions of the background and drivers of these expanding interests, see Men Honghua, "Zhongguo Guojia Zhanlue Liyi de Tuozhan" ["The Expansion of China's National Strategic Interests"], *Zhanlue yu Guanli* [*Strategy and Management*], No. 2, 2003; Wang Yizhou, "Heping Fazhan Jieduan de Guojia Anquan" ["National Security During the Stage of Peaceful Development"], *Shijie Zhishi* [*World Affairs*], No. 23, 2006; and Su Changhe, "Lun Zhongguo Haiwai Liyi" ["On China's Overseas Interests"], *Shijie Jingji yu Zhengzhi* [*World Economics and Politics*], No. 8, 2009. For analysis of expanding interests in a military context, see Wang Lidong, *Guojia Haishang Liyi Lun* [*On China's National Maritime Interests*], Beijing: Guofang Daxue Chubanshe, 2007, and Yang Mingshu, chief ed., *Haishang Tongdao Anquan yu Guoji Hezuo* [*SLOC Security and International Cooperation*], Beijing: Shishi Chubanshe, 2005.

Work Conference and the 2009 Ambassadorial Meeting) have addressed how to manage these expanding overseas interests (*haiwai liyi*).[10]

These expanding interests have also created new requirements for the military to protect Chinese national interests. As part of implementing the "new historic missions," which were first outlined in 2004, Hu Jintao has tasked the PLA to prepare to conduct "diversified military tasks" (*duoyanghua junshi renwu*) and develop an improved capability to conduct "non-war military operations" (*feizhanzheng junshi huodong*).[11] These new formulations highlight the continued importance of domestic operations to maintain regime security, social stability, and border security, but they also include a new emphasis on international operations, such as peacekeeping, disaster relief, and military diplomacy, that are designed to protect China's expanding global interests.

No matter how the cross-Strait political situation develops, new pressures on the PLA to take on a more diverse set of missions are likely to continue, but if deeper rapprochement is achieved, the PLA will be able to conduct a more comprehensive review of the proper mix of roles and missions.

China's Relations with Asia

Regional states worry that a more powerful China, especially if it is no longer constrained by a focus on the Taiwan issue, may pursue new opportunities to expand its regional power and influence at their expense. Although they have taken notice of China's rapid post–Cold War military modernization, Asian countries have been somewhat reassured that these efforts have been focused on preventing Taiwan independence and coercing Taiwan. Many

---

[10] See Bonnie S. Glaser, "Ensuring the 'Go Abroad' Policy Serves China's Domestic Priorities," *China Brief*, May 9, 2007, and Bonnie S. Glaser and Benjamin Dooley, "China's 11th Ambassadorial Conference Signals Continuity and Change in Foreign Policy," *China Brief*, November 4, 2009.

[11] Hu Jintao first laid out these missions in a December 24, 2004, speech, and they were repeated in the 2006 and 2008 defense white papers. These tasks include the following: "Providing an important source of strength for consolidating the ruling position of the CCP, providing a solid security guarantee for sustaining the important period of strategic opportunity for national development, providing a strong strategic support for safeguarding national interests, and playing a major role in maintaining world peace and promoting common development."

For authoritative Chinese-language analysis, see Song Guocai, Shi Limin, and Yang Shu, chief eds., *Feizhanzheng Junshi Xingdong Shili Yanjiu* [*Case Studies on Non-War Military Operations*], Beijing: Guofang Daxue Chubanshe, military circulation only, 2009; Shou Xiaosong and Xu Jingnian, chief eds., *Jundui Yingdui Feichuantong Anquan Weixie Yanjiu* [*Research on the Military's Responses to Nontraditional Security Threats*], Beijing: Jiefangjun Chubanshe, 2009; Wang Mingwu et al., chief eds., *Feizhanzheng Junshi Xingdong* [*Non-War Military Operations*], Beijing: Guofang Daxue Chubanshe, 2006; and Xiao Tianliang, *Junshi Liliang de Feizhanzheng Yunyong* [*Non-War Uses for Military Power*], Beijing: Guofang Daxue Chubanshe, 2009. For English-language analysis, see Daniel M. Hartnett, "The PLA's Domestic and Foreign Activities and Orientation," testimony before the U.S.-China Economic and Security Review Commission, March 4, 2009; James Mulvenon, "Chairman Hu and the PLA's 'New Historic Missions,'" *China Leadership Monitor*, No. 27, Winter 2009; and Roy Kamphausen, David Lai, and Andrew Scobell, eds., *The PLA at Home and Abroad: Assessing the Operational Capabilities of China's Military*, Carlisle, Pa.: Strategic Studies Institute, U.S. Army War College, June 2010. For analysis of how the PLA is trying to balance traditional combat missions and these newer, nontraditional missions, see Michael S. Chase and Kristen Gunness, "The PLA's Multiple Military Tasks: Prioritizing Combat Operations and Developing MOOTW Capabilities," *China Brief*, January 21, 2010.

Asian officials, while still expressing concerns about the long-term implications of PLA modernization, believe that China is not likely to launch a significant challenge to their interests in the short term if the Taiwan issue, China's first priority, remains unresolved.[12] If cross-Strait relations continue to improve, however, a rising, unconstrained China will produce heightened regional concerns that China may turn its attention to them next. These worries will be further exacerbated because much of the force structure developed to deter Taiwanese independence and complicate U.S. intervention could be transferred for use in other regional contingencies.[13]

If China were no longer constrained by its focus on Taiwan, it could undermine regional stability and challenge the interests of countries in the region. Maritime Southeast Asian states would worry that China might seize the Spratly Islands, given China's expansive South China Sea claims, the islands' potential energy reserves, and their importance for sea lines of communication (SLOCs). China might try to seize the Senkaku/Diaoyutai Islands or challenge Japan's exclusive economic zone (EEZ) claims. India would worry that China might take a more aggressive stance on unresolved land border disputes. Russia would fear that an unrestrained China could mount an aggressive move into the Russian far east, both to reclaim territory and to try to seize energy resources in Siberia. A more powerful and less constrained China might abrogate recent territorial agreements with India, Russia, and Vietnam and try to reclaim historic territories once it is stronger. Improved Chinese naval capabilities could also provoke worries that it may try to threaten SLOCs in the western Pacific, South China Sea, or Indian Ocean to pressure other countries; many Asian countries worry about this possibility as China's modernization continues.[14]

Some Chinese rhetoric, new developments in military doctrine, and recent assertive behavior in the region show that Asian countries have reason to be concerned about the potential threat from a rising, unconstrained China. Fudan University Professor Shen Dingli famously commented on what China might do after settling the Taiwan issue. In a 2002 interview with the *New York Times*, he said, "Once the Taiwan front is closed, we may turn to the South China Sea," adding that beyond the South China Sea, "we have a third issue to resolve [referring

---

[12] Three Asia experts similarly argue that "Asian elites regard China's military buildup as primarily aimed at Taiwan but harbor a residual wariness about China's long-term intentions." See Ellen L. Frost, James J. Przystup, and Phillip C. Saunders, "China's Rising Influence in Asia: Implications for U.S. Policy," *Strategic Forum*, No. 231, April 2008.

[13] For other, similar assessments, see Michael A. Glosny, "Heading toward a Win-Win Future? Recent Developments in China's Policy Toward Southeast Asia," *Asian Security*, Vol. 2, No. 1, 2006, and Jonathan D. Pollack and Richard H. Yang, eds., *In China's Shadow: Regional Perspectives on Chinese Foreign Policy and Military Development*, Santa Monica, Calif.: RAND Corporation, CF-137-CAPP, 1998. Judgments are also based on the author's interviews with Asian embassy officials in Beijing, fall 2005–spring 2006.

[14] For discussions of these concerns, see Pollack and Yang, 1998; Alastair Iain Johnston and Robert S. Ross, *Engaging China: The Management of an Emerging Power*, London: Routledge, 1999; David Shambaugh, ed., *Power Shift: China and Asia's New Dynamics*, Berkeley, Calif.: University of California Press, 2006; and Kevin Cooney and Yoichiro Sato, eds., *The Rise of China and International Security: America and Asia Respond,* New York: Routledge, 2009.

to the Diaoyutai Islands]."[15] Although this statement is not official PRC government policy, several Asian officials and experts have invoked Shen's statement and comments from other Chinese officials and scholars that have led to suspicions about China's long-term intentions.[16]

There is already evidence of PLA preparations for potential operations in the East China Sea and South China Sea, including exercises that appear aimed at such contingencies. The 2006 version of the *Science of Campaigns* [*Zhanyixue*] included a new type of naval campaign called "attacks against coral islands and reefs" (*dui shanhu daojiao jingong zhanyi*) that the PLA must prepare to fight.[17] Another book from a regional PLA institution refers to "large-scale island attack operations" (*daxing daoyu jingong zuozhan*) as an type of important combat operation.[18]

Recent evidence of Chinese assertiveness and willingness to challenge the interests of regional countries highlights the potential future threat from China. If China is willing to take such actions while it is still somewhat dissatisfied with the progress of cross-Strait reconciliation and still worried about the possibility of the Democratic Progressive Party (DPP) returning to office and pushing Taiwan independence, an unconstrained China would be much more likely to directly challenge regional powers. Recent examples have included patrols by submarines, survey ships, and surface combatants in Japan's EEZ and territorial waters, as well as near the Senkaku/Diaoyutai Islands. China has tried to strengthen its maritime claims in the South China Sea through patrols and intimidation of oil companies that have tried to operate in the area. It has also challenged Indian claims to disputed territory.[19]

Regional countries have certainly followed PLA modernization in recent years, but China's focus on Taiwan has meant that modernization efforts have not been seen as an imminent threat to the countries of the region. After cross-Strait rapprochement, continued military modernization will force Asian countries to be much more attentive and vigilant. In the next five to ten years, weaknesses in power projection capability will place limits on the threat that China can pose to the region, but regional countries will not only devote greater attention to the acquisition of new capabilities but also closely monitor PLA training, deployments, and doctrine.

---

15 Craig Smith, "China Reshaping Military to Toughen Its Muscle in the Region," *New York Times*, October 16, 2002. Other Western analysts have voiced similar concerns. According to one Defense Intelligence Agency analyst, "Resolution of the Taiwan issue may lead China's leaders to move on to the last remaining territorial disputes in the East and South China Sea." See Mark Cozad, "China's Regional Power Projection: Prospects for Future Missions in the South and East China Seas," in Kamphausen, Lai, and Scobell, 2009, p. 304.

16 Author's interviews, Beijing, spring 2006.

17 Zhang Yuliang, chief ed., *Zhanyi Xue* [*The Science of Campaigns*], Beijing: Guofang Daxue Chubanshe, 2006, pp. 535–538.

18 Gai Shijin and Zhang Peizhong, *Duoyanghua Junshi Renwu Lun* [*On Diverse Military Tasks*], Beijing: Changzheng Chubanshe [Long March Press], 2009, pp. 64–65.

19 For reports on these examples, see Peter J. Brown "China's Navy Cruises into Pacific Ascendancy," *Asia Times*, April 21, 2010; John Pomfret, "U.S.-China Talks End Without Accords on Key Issues," *Washington Post*, May 26, 2010; "As China Swaggers, Neighbors Embrace U.S.," *Wall Street Journal*, May 25, 2010; and Rahul Singh, "Indian Army Fears Chinese Attack by 2017," *Hindustan Times*, March 26, 2009.

To date, regional states have been reluctant to pressure China to explain its rising defense budget and defense modernization plans. The removal of the Taiwan issue, however, will make regional countries more likely to demand such explanations, as well as greater military transparency. This is likely to make China's relations with its neighbors more acrimonious and make it more difficult to reassure its neighbors that it has peaceful and cooperative intentions.

Potential threats from a rising, unconstrained China will likely force the United States to clarify its defense commitments to regional allies and friends. American allies and friends are likely to press for clearer commitments in the South China Sea and East China Sea, areas where U.S. commitments have been limited and sometimes ambiguous. In the face of China's rising power and a global diffusion of power, these states are likely to ask the United States to make its commitments more credible. If worries about China cause a strengthened U.S. commitment to the region and strengthened defense ties between the United States and Asian countries, this will complicate China's security environment, damage China's relations with its neighbors, and potentially unleash spirals of hostility.

If the U.S. response to demands for a clearer commitment to the region is insufficient, or if its commitments are no longer seen as credible, this could have various implications for China. If America's alliances collapse and the United States reduces its presence in Asia, this could greatly improve China's international environment, as it would face several weaker powers that may have difficulty cooperating to oppose it. On the other hand, this could also lead to an independent Japan that acquires nuclear weapons and devotes more resources to military modernization. Regional powers, even without cooperation with the United States, are powerful enough to complicate China's international environment, especially if they work together to prevent China's dominance.

China's Relations with the United States

The most important consequence of a sustained cross-Strait rapprochement is the removal of the most likely source of war between the United States and China. Alan Romberg writes, "It is hard to conjure up a scenario that would pit the PLA against another major power, including the United States, in all-out conflict other than one relating to Taiwan."[20] Stability across the Taiwan Strait, however, will not necessarily ensure smooth U.S.-China relations. The deeper structural issues between a declining hegemon and a rising power will remain. Historical experience has shown that these shifting power dynamics often lead to friction, competition, and conflict. These structural

20 See Alan D. Romberg, "Future East Asian Security Architecture: Implications for the PLA," in Swaine et al., 2007, p. 314.

pressures may drive the United States and China into competition over spheres of influence, relative status, and regional hegemony.[21]

Although conflict is not structurally determined, a rising China no longer constrained by a focus on Taiwan will produce similar concerns for American leaders about where China will focus its attention next.[22] China could use its increased military power and enhanced leverage to break apart America's regional alliance network. American leaders would worry that China might not only try to drive U.S. forces away from China's coastal waters, but also try to push the United States out of East Asia. China might also devote significant resources to wage a global battle with the United States for military and political influence around the world. In the face of a wide range of potential threats from a rising, unconstrained China, the United States would likely need to reexamine how it defines its interests in East Asia and decide what commitments to make and with what degree of clarity. Although appeasement has taken on a bad name, the United States will likely need to begin to consider the relative costs and merits of adjusting some of its policies, in the form of either burden sharing or reducing commitments. In the face of a rising autocratic China, U.S. leaders should also consider which interests in the region are nonnegotiable and worth responding to potential Chinese challenges with great vigilance.

How the Taiwan issue is resolved will also affect Sino-U.S. relations. Cliff and Shlapak argue that "almost any type of peaceful resolution implies that subsequent relations between the United States and China will be cooperative and peaceful."[23] This is generally correct, but China's perception of the U.S. role in either facilitating or obstructing this deepening rapprochement will affect the future of bilateral relations and Beijing's perception of the United States. If the United States is seen as helpful or neutral in this process, then U.S.-China relations will likely be relatively positive. If China perceives the United States as having worked to obstruct rapprochement, this could damage relations and produce a more competitive bilateral relationship. There is already deep suspicion in China that despite U.S. official support for "peaceful resolution," the United States will never accept unification.[24] Some PRC scholars and think-tank researchers view the 2008 and 2010 U.S. arms sales to Taiwan as especially provocative because they were viewed as part of an effort to derail cross-Strait rapprochement. If China believes that the United States tried to obstruct cross-Strait reconciliation, this would be seen as further evidence that the true U.S. intentions are to split (*fenhua*) and weaken China, which would likely lead to a more contentious bilateral

---

[21] For a discussion of these dynamics and their application to U.S.-China relations, see Aaron L. Friedberg, "The Future of U.S.-China Relations: Is Conflict Inevitable?" *International Security*, Vol. 30, No. 2, Fall 2005, and John J. Mearsheimer, "China's Unpeaceful Rise," *Current History*, Vol. 105, No. 690, April 2006.

[22] According to one scholar, "For Washington, this change [resolution] means a less predictable, flexible, and potentially less-burdened opponent, though one still noted for its lack of transparency." See Tucker, 2002, p. 21.

[23] See Cliff and Shlapak, 2007, p. 21.

[24] Several PRC interlocutors have referenced Nancy Tucker's 2002 *Washington Quarterly* article as evidence that the U.S. government would never support unification even if Taiwan wants it. Author's interviews, Beijing, Shanghai, summer 2002.

relationship. The PRC's perception of the U.S. role in cross-Strait rapprochement is likely to affect the state of U.S.-China relations both during and after the resolution of Taiwan's status.

New Options for PLA Modernization

Deepening cross-Strait rapprochement is beginning to reduce the centrality of Taiwan contingencies in PLA modernization. If the cross-Strait rapprochement continues to deepen, this will give China the opportunity to consider new options and mixes of forces as it continues its military modernization. Mark Cozad argues, "Resolution of the Taiwan issue would certainly clear the way for an expanding review of the PLA's missions."[25] According to Nancy Tucker, "Unification could release a significant percentage of China's resources. The PLA would be free to change its priorities, redeploy its forces, and reconceptualize its strategic objectives."[26] These authors have analyzed the implications of political resolution of the Taiwan issue, but the deeper cross-Strait rapprochement discussed in this paper will also likely reduce the PLA's need to focus on Taiwan contingencies and will allow the PLA to adjust its mix of missions and forces.[27] In this section, I briefly describe five different options for China's future military modernization. Each involves changes in PLA capabilities, Chinese behavior, or both. Some of these options are also not mutually exclusive. To a limited extent, the PLA has already begun to conduct some of the missions contained in these five options. No matter what happens with Taiwan, there will be pressure to take on more of these missions, but cross-Strait stability will likely lead to deeper reassessment of the relative priority placed on these missions and free up resources to make larger investments in moving down one or more of these modernization paths.

Option #1: Relaxed Modernization

After the cross-Strait situation stabilizes, China could adopt a more relaxed approach to military modernization, allowing the annual military budget to grow but by a much smaller percentage than it has recently. Eminent PLA expert Ellis Joffe argued, "Without Taiwan as the driving force, the scope and pace of the future build-up might be reduced."[28] Deeper rapprochement will produce a new "guns vs. butter" debate inside China, and the civilian leadership may decide to divert resources toward domestic issues as part of a "peace dividend." China's leaders may see a stronger connection between reduced defense spending and regime security; after the Taiwan issue has

---

25 Cozad, in Kamphausen, Lai, and Scobell, 2009, p. 287.

26 Tucker, 2002, p. 21.

27 For an insightful analysis of the effect of cross-Strait political dynamics on the PLA, see the interview with Major General Peng Guangqian, "Liang'an Baofa Junshi Chongtu Weixian Dajian" ["The Danger of Cross-Strait Military Conflict Breaking Out Has Dropped Greatly"], *Da Gongbao*, December 24, 2008.

28 See Ellis Joffe, "China's Military Buildup: Beyond Taiwan?" in Andrew Scobell and Larry M. Wortzel, *Shaping China's Environment: The Role of the People's Liberation Army,* Carlisle, Pa.: Strategic Studies Institute, U.S. Army War College, October 2006, p. 43.

improved substantially, the regime may conclude that its security and legitimacy would be enhanced by diverting resources away from the military and toward addressing China's difficult economic and social problems.

Traditional missions, such as internal security, border security, and defense of maritime claims, will require continued investments in manpower, training, and equipment. Demands to protect China's overseas interests as part of China's "new historic missions" will also drive improvements in the PLA's ability to project limited power overseas and participate in peacekeeping operations, humanitarian assistance/disaster relief, and noncombatant evacuation operations, as well as provide public goods. There would no longer be a need, however, to develop capabilities to coerce Taiwan or develop robust anti-access capabilities to defeat U.S. intervention. The rapid buildup of submarines, cruise missiles, fighters, and cyberwarfare would likely slow as well. China would also be relatively restrained in using its military capabilities in a coercive manner. The overall picture is one of continued military modernization, but at a much slower pace.

In a "post-Taiwan" world, there will likely be powerful domestic forces supporting cuts in the defense budget. As a result of the immense social, economic, and political problems China is currently facing, Susan Shirk argues that "a subterranean 'guns vs. butter' debate is beginning among the policy elite."[29] Stability across the Taiwan Strait would remove the imminent threat of Taiwan independence, which Chinese hardliners have used to justify rapid military modernization. After deeper rapprochement, the PLA would be forced to make different arguments for why high levels of defense spending should continue. Slowing the growth of the defense budget and diverting resources to address growing domestic challenges would have many domestic supporters.[30]

Relaxed modernization would also have military and domestic benefits. Civilian experts and PLA officers recognize that building a force designed to protect global SLOCs, vie for regional dominance, or project power around the globe with multiple aircraft carrier battle groups requires a huge financial investment. Such missions can be costly and also strain China's diplomatic relations and complicate its international environment, as this type of modernization would make China more threatening. A more moderate military modernization would be less expensive and also serve China's diplomatic interest in keeping friendly and cooperative relations with important countries in the region. It would likely take a strong civilian leader to reduce defense spending, as he would face opposition from both the PLA and political opponents trying to portray him as weak on defense. Relaxed modernization is not the most likely future trajectory for the PLA, but continued high levels of defense spending will likely come under new domestic pressure if the need to prepare for Taiwan contingencies disappears.

---

[29] Susan L. Shirk, *China: Fragile Superpower,* New York: Oxford University Press, 2008, p. 74.

[30] Shirk, 2008, pp. 74–75.

Option #2: Domestic and Continental Concerns[31]

Although much commentary on recent developments in the PLA emphasizes the new international activities and missions, maintaining internal stability and regime security continues to be the PLA's most important tasking. After the achievement of deeper rapprochement, and the reduced importance of Taiwan contingencies, China may decide to devote more resources to strengthening the PLA's capabilities to respond to domestic security threats and potential threats around China's land borders. There is an important domestic component to official PLA discussions of the "new historic missions" and "non-war military operations" that could become even more important over time.[32] The leadership may conclude that strengthening China's domestic coercive capacity would be the best way to strengthen regime security and legitimacy.

China faces several potential threats to its security—internally and on its land borders. As unbalanced economic development continues, the dangers of economic and political instability are prominent concerns for the regime. The Chinese military would be responsible for maintaining order and stability in the face of large-scale mass protests. The recent uprisings in Xinjiang and Tibet have reminded the leadership that disaffected ethnic and religious minorities could undermine regime legitimacy and must be swiftly controlled and repressed. The PLA must also maintain border security, and many PLA analysts worry about the potential for instability in neighboring regions spilling into China.[33] Some analysts highlight that, as a continental power, China must not lose sight of the potential threats from Russia and India.[34] Preparation for this range of missions, in addition to the PLA's role in domestic disaster relief operations, will require substantial resources, and the PLA could decide to prioritize these domestic and continental concerns.

If China decides to prioritize domestic and continental security in its future modernization, investments in international military activities and operations will likely continue as interests expand, but even after deeper cross-Strait rapprochement, these investments would only increase slowly. There would be increased investments in capabilities to maintain control of China's borders and in the face of potential large-scale riots. An open question for this modernization option is whether there would be a change in the division of labor between local police forces, the People's Armed Police, and the PLA. Currently, these other forces play the leading role, with the PLA serving as the "last line of defense."[35]

---

[31] I am grateful to Andrew Scobell for suggesting the addition of this section.

[32] M. Taylor Fravel, "Economics and Security: The Effect of Economic Growth on China's Military Strategy" unpublished draft, 2010; Andrew Scobell, "Discourse in 3-D: The PLA's Evolving Doctrine, Circa 2009," in Kamphausen, Lai, and Scobell, 2010, pp. 103–138.

[33] M. Taylor Fravel, "Securing Borders: China's Doctrine and Force Structure for Frontier Defense," *Journal of Strategic Studies*, Vol. 30, No. 4, August 2007.

[34] Robert S. Ross, "China's Naval Nationalism: Sources, Prospects, and the U.S. Response," *International Security*, Vol. 34, No. 2, Fall 2009.

[35] Murray Scot Tanner, "How China Manages Internal Security and its Impact on PLA Missions," in Kamphausen, Lai, and Scobell, 2009, pp. 39–98.

Option #3: Anti-Access Focus

A third choice for the PLA would be to focus on developing anti-access capabilities and preventing hostile military forces from operating near China's coast or in its EEZ. In recent years, China's anti-access strategy has been associated with complicating U.S. wartime intervention to enable China to defeat Taiwan, but anti-access is a much broader concept.[36] It can include preventing an adversary from operating in the air and sea area around a country and can extend to peacetime as well as wartime. Increased attention to anti-access will require changes in the way the PLA operates. It would likely require much more aggressive peacetime air and sea challenges to surveillance operations near China's coast and in its EEZ in an effort to deter these activities, or at least push them further away from China's coast. Moreover, if China wanted to deter such activities and be prepared to quickly meet such challenges, it would also require more aggressive patrols of the sea and airspace of its EEZ. Some of these activities are already occurring, with the EP-3 and *Impeccable* incidents as examples, but a focus on anti-access would include a much more aggressive posture and require greater investments.[37]

Although some assets that were focused on Taiwan could be diverted to the anti-access operations, this anti-access focus would also include demands for new capabilities. The PLA would require a greater number of surface ships to be able to challenge maritime incursions, and it would need an aggressive building campaign to be able to sustain round-the-clock patrols of its EEZ to keep potential challengers out. Increased investment in the number of aircraft would be needed to maintain a strong presence in the sky as well. Chinese investments in aerial refueling would also enable the PLA to maintain aerial patrols with fewer airplanes. To prevent submarine incursions in its EEZ and territorial waters, China would also need to strengthen its anti-submarine warfare capabilities. Continued development of cruise missiles, surface-to-air missiles (SAMs), and anti-shipping ballistic missiles (ASBMs) would likely continue. These assets would be less useful, however, in deterring or responding to peacetime incursions.

These anti-access capabilities could also enable some limited offensive operations. If China wanted to extend its anti-access capabilities to deter or disrupt third-party intervention during a potential seizure of islands in the East China Sea or South China Sea, however, this would require a significant investment in capabilities. This type of operation would require much greater anti-access and power projection capabilities than those in support of operations against Taiwan. To be prepared for the intervention of a third party, China would need to deny or restrict the ability of others to project power in defense of the island. This would require a combination of surface ships, airplanes, and submarines operating far from Chinese ports to limit the effectiveness of such an intervention.

---

[36] See Roger Cliff, Mark Burles, Michael S. Chase, Derek Eaton, and Kevin L. Pollpeter, *Entering the Dragon's Lair: Chinese Antiaccess Strategies and Their Implications for the United States*, Santa Monica, Calif.: RAND Corporation, MG-524-AF, 2008, and RADM Michael McDevitt "The PLA Navy Anti-Access Role in a Taiwan Contingency," unpublished manuscript, 2010.

[37] For more on EEZ operations, see Peter A. Dutton, "The Implications of China's Naval Modernization for the United States," testimony before the U.S.-China Economic and Security Review Commission, June 11, 2009.

Cruise missiles, SAMs, and ASBMs could also be required, but depending on the location, they would have insufficient range to reach the area. Moreover, China will require power-projection capabilities to attack, seize, and hold the island, which would require a significant investment, given the long-range requirements of such operations.

Option #4: Assertive Pursuit of Regional Maritime Claims

After the Taiwan mission becomes less central, the PLA could adopt a posture geared toward pursuit of regional maritime claims in the East China Sea and South China Sea. This includes at least the ability to defend maritime claims and could also include the ability to seize and control disputed islands. This mission requires the procurement of more surface combatants with advanced air defense capabilities, which would enable the ships to operate beyond the reach of land-based air power. Surface combatants would need to respond to any detected challenges by other countries to China's maritime claims, which would likely require patrols of the areas surrounding the disputed islands to deny others from seizing the islands or their resources. Greater numbers of fighters with extended range or helicopters could also help deter challenges to China's maritime claims and chase potential challengers away. Naval and air patrols aimed at deterring or preventing other countries from operating in the surrounding area would also strengthen Chinese claims to disputed areas and weaken the claims of other countries.

The ability not only to more aggressively defend maritime claims and prevent challenges but also to be able to seize and occupy disputed islands would require substantial increases in regional power projection. In addition to the naval and air force elements to maintain sea control and air control, requirements will include enhanced combat lift and expeditionary capability. Projecting sustained combat power to the disputed territories of the East China Sea and South China Sea would require a significant increase in resources.

In addition to capabilities, the biggest change in this defense posture is in deployment patterns. In recent years, the PLA has increasingly operated naval and air assets out in the region, but such a posture would require it to do this on a more sustained basis. Moreover, the posture implies much more assertive and aggressive patrolling of these disputed areas and more assertive challenges to the navies and fishing vessels of other countries operating near these disputed areas. In recent years, the PLA has begun to pay more attention to defense of maritime claims and maritime rights and interests, but a more assertive pursuit of these aims would require investments in forces and changes in operations.

Option #5: Extra-Regional Activities

This option is the broadest and least well defined. The capabilities required to implement it depend on the types of military operations and activities envisioned. Constructive and cooperative missions, such as peacekeeping operations, humanitarian assistance/disaster relief, noncombatant evacuation operations, anti-terrorism, and anti-piracy are within this category, with the PLA's deployment of surface ships to the Gulf of Aden to assist in anti-piracy efforts as an example. These are part of the "new historic missions" dictated by Hu Jintao, and most of these types of operations give China an opportunity to demonstrate that it is a force for peace and stability and a "responsible stakeholder." Constructive extra-regional activities also include military diplomacy efforts, such as port visits and joint exercises.

This modernization option, however, could also include more assertive power-projection missions that undermine international peace and stability and provoke deeper suspicion about a rising China. Projecting capabilities outside of East Asia could allow China to threaten or pressure other countries in its own form of "gunboat diplomacy." If China tries to develop global SLOC defense capabilities, many of these capabilities could also be used to threaten or interdict the key SLOCs for other countries as well. These capabilities could allow China to extend its sphere of influence into the Indian Ocean and beyond, potentially challenging important areas of U.S. and European influence.

Given that sustaining extra-regional military operations will likely require improved logistical support, many have focused on whether China is trying to establish overseas bases. Based on a 2005 report commissioned by the U.S. Department of Defense, many have begun to refer to China's improved relations with and assistance in developing port facilities in Pakistan, Bangladesh, Burma, Thailand, and Sri Lanka as a "string of pearls" strategy that will enable China to project military power in South Asia and the Middle East. Although these reports of establishing military bases are usually exaggerated, there is some evidence that the anti-piracy deployments in the Gulf of Aden are pushing some within China to begin to consider the need for overseas supply facilities and bases. In February 2009, PLA Air Force Colonel Dai Xu began his call for bases by asking rhetorically, "Can one supply ship allow two combat ships to provide long-term escort for the commercial ships of the world?" Colonel Dai continued that establishing "Chinese 'bases on the high seas' (*yuanyang jidi*)" is a logical extension of this thinking.[38] In a December 2009 interview on Chinese television focused on the Gulf of Aden deployments, retired Rear Admiral Yin Zhuo offered his views on the potential utility of overseas bases. He highlighted that the decision rested with the central government but that, "if China wanted to have a relatively stable and fixed supply and repair and maintenance base (*buji xiuzheng jidi*), I think that would be appropriate."[39]

The Chinese Ministry of National Defense immediately ruled out the establishment of overseas naval bases; Rear Admiral Yin argued that foreign media exaggerated his original statement, once again repeating that the

---

[38] Dai Xu, "Zhongguo Ying Jianli Yuanyang Jidi" ["China Should Establish Bases on the High Seas"], *Huanqiu Shibao* [*Global Times*], February 3, 2009. Some have translated *yuanyang jidi* as "overseas bases," but "bases on the high seas" is more accurate. The usual Chinese phrase for the broader concept of "overseas bases" is *haiwai jidi*.

[39] "Zhuanjia: Zhongguo Haijun ke Tantao Jianli Changqi Anji Buji Jidi" ["Expert: PLAN May Explore Establishing a Long-Term Coastal Supply Base"], ChinaReviewNews.com, date unknown. Several other Chinese-language news outlets summarized the content of the interview, but the citation above includes the full text of the interview.

decision rested with the central government, and denied the rumors that China was building overseas bases.[40] Although the government has been very strong in denying these rumors, there appears to be the beginnings of a debate over whether or not China needs some improved overseas supply and logistics capability. If China increases its focus to extra-regional activities, either constructive or aggressive, it will need to improve its ability to project power far away from China and sustain such operations.

The required changes in capability will depend on the types of extra-regional activities China wants to be able to conduct, how long it hopes to sustain its power projection, and how permissible an environment it needs to be able to operate. At a minimum, any increased focus on extra-regional activities will require investments in lift capacity, replenishment, and refueling. Operating out of the region for short durations during peacetime, such as for port visits, will not require too great an investment of resources.

Fighting long-duration wars far from China will require huge investments in logistics and combat power. The need to project limited combat power for relatively short durations is less demanding and would require smaller investments in capabilities. The size of the investment, the types of power-projection forces developed, and how these forces are used are the major issues that will distinguish which of these types of extra-regional activities China focuses on.

Conclusion

In this paper, I have analyzed the implications of deeper cross-Strait rapprochement for regional stability, China's foreign policy, and PLA modernization. As other analysts have pointed out, cross-Strait rapprochement would be a positive development, as it would remove a long-standing source of regional tension and the most likely source of war between the United States and China. I argue, however, that this would also produce new challenges in China's relations with Asia and the United States. Asian countries have certainly paid attention to China's military modernization over the last two decades, but the focus of this modernization on Taiwan contingencies as the number-one priority has made this threat less imminent. Once China no longer needs to focus on the Taiwan issue, many Asian countries will perceive the rise of China as a more imminent threat and will worry that it might challenge their interests next. The United States and China will continue to deal with the structural contradictions of the ongoing power transition. The United States, moreover, will have similar concerns as the rest of Asia concerning the potential for a rising, unconstrained China to challenge its interests in Asia and elsewhere.

Stability across the Taiwan Strait will also allow China to make different choices in its military modernization and alter the mix of its military forces. New pressures as a result of China's deeper international engagement and expanding interests have already begun pushing the PLA to adopt a more diversified set of

---

[40] "China Rules Out Overseas Naval Base Now," *China Daily*, January 1, 2010; "Haijun Zhuanjia Fouren Haiwai Jian Junshi Jidi Chuanwen" ["Naval Expert Denies Rumor that China Is Establishing Military Bases Overseas"], *Zhongguo Qingnianbao* [*China Youth Daily*], March 5, 2010.

missions. These pressures to diversify will likely continue even if cross-Strait relations deteriorate, but deeper cross-Strait rapprochement would "free up" resources and provide an opportunity for a different mix of roles and missions.

I introduced five potential options for future PLA modernization over the next five to ten years: (1) relaxed modernization, (2) domestic and continental concerns, (3) an anti-access focus, (4) assertive pursuit of regional maritime claims, and (5) extra-regional activities. Although "relaxed modernization" is probably the least likely trajectory, the potential for a new "guns vs. butter" debate in China is underappreciated. The PLA will have to make new arguments that do not focus on Taiwan to continue to receive high budgets after Taiwan becomes less central; the "new historic missions" have become the basis for these new arguments. Domestic and continental concerns will remain important, but unless there are several major riots or incidents, this mission will not likely become the focus of PLA modernization, especially as it does not require an expensive force structure. The most likely future trajectory is a combination of limited investments in an anti-access focus, assertive pursuit of regional maritime claims, and extra-regional activities, without China "picking" one. Changes in China's external environment, such as other regional states trying to seize disputed territory or an increased need to operate out of area, could push the PLA in one direction. But absent that, the PLA will continue to face pressures to execute all of these missions and will likely develop some capability to execute each mission at the same time.

Over the next five to ten years, as China's rise continues, other states are likely to become more worried about the possibility of a threatening China, which will make China's grand strategy of reassurance more difficult to implement successfully. For Asia and the United States, deeper rapprochement across the Strait will remove one major problem, but it will also add a new layer of apprehension and concern about China's future behavior on top of the existing uncertainties. The direction of China's military modernization and the new mix of forces and missions can help alleviate these concerns about a rising, unconstrained China, or they can further exacerbate them. If China is restrained in how it modernizes and employs its military, such as through relaxed modernization, a focus on constructive and cooperative regional and extra-regional activities, or a combination of limited investments in the other options, China's reassurance may alleviate some of these worries and help maintain a stable international environment. If it follows a more assertive course in PLA modernization and makes significant investments in anti-access, assertive pursuit of regional maritime claims, or aggressive extra-regional activities, China will help make potential concerns become realities and likely trigger strong countervailing balancing responses from the United States and the region. The most threatening course for the United States and the region would be if China simultaneously made significant investments in these three areas. More aggressive courses for PLA modernization will undermine China's reassurance strategy by making it more difficult to credibly demonstrate its benign intentions.

13. A New Taiwan Strategy to Adapt to PLA Precision Strike Capabilities

Michael J. Lostumbo[1]

The relative military strength between China and Taiwan is shifting rapidly to Beijing's advantage. This is a problem for Taiwan to the extent that China thinks there are military solutions to cross-Strait differences. While the dynamic relationship between China and Taiwan produced dramatic growth in cross-Strait economic and social links, bringing more stability to the area, the underlying differences have not been resolved. The strong military counter-trend cannot be ignored. This paper considers options for Taiwan to revise its defense program to address the qualitative edge that the mainland is investing to achieve. Taiwan does not have to match the mainland's level of military spending, provided it can invest sufficiently in military capabilities that exploit People's Liberation Army (PLA) operational challenges to make military solutions seem less appealing and therefore deter an attack.

In this paper, I identify the operational challenges facing Taiwan, provide historical examples of combatants who faced similar challenges, identify operational challenges for the PLA, and discuss the implications for Taiwan's future force structure and the factors that Taiwan should consider in evaluating the utility of particular capabilities.

Mainland Military Capabilities of Concern to Taiwan

The mainland's sustained investments are yielding impressive military forces. From Taiwan's perspective, the most significant developments appear to be the multiplicity of long-range precision strike capabilities because of the potential damage they could inflict on Taiwan. While Taiwan has been concerned about the threat of ballistic missiles for years now, the growing number and accuracy of these weapons makes them much more threatening than they were in the past. PLA ballistic missiles are becoming so accurate that they have moved from instruments of terror to potentially having a seminal role in PLA strategy because of their utility in striking many of Taiwan's defensive forces.[2] A number of fixed targets, which previously would have played major roles in the defense of Taiwan, now sit vulnerable. As David Shlapak has written, it would take about 75 ballistic missiles with accuracies in the range of 25 meters to close all the military air bases in Taiwan for a period of time.[3] The base closures would leave a much more permissive environment for fixed-wing attacks against

[1] The ideas presented in this paper draw heavily from conversations over several months with my colleagues David Frelinger and Barry Wilson. I would also like to thank Alan Vick for his comments on an earlier draft.

[2] William S. Murray, "Revisiting Taiwan's Defense Strategy," *Naval War College Review*, Summer 2008, p. 18.

[3] David Shlapak, David T. Orlesky, Toy I. Reid, Murray Scot Tanner, and Barry Wilson, *A Question of Balance: Political Context and Military Aspects of the Cross-Strait Dispute*, Santa Monica, Calif.: RAND Corporation, MG-888-SRF, 2009, p. 43. Depending on the intensity of the attack, type of aircraft operating from the airfield, and airfield repair capabilities, closure might be for hours, days, or weeks.

stranded aircraft, maintenance, and refueling facilities. Aircraft in mountain shelters would likely survive but could be kept out of the war by periodic attacks focused on taxiways leading to the mountain entrances. Thus, in a relatively short period of time and with a relatively small fraction of their ballistic missiles, the PLA could be in control of Taiwan's air space and still able to employ hundreds of accurate missiles to target a wide range of Taiwanese defense forces. Naval port facilities have similar vulnerabilities. A variety of fixed sensor sights and communications facilities could also be destroyed in this way.

The PLA's precision strike capabilities are not limited to ballistic missiles. Cruise missiles, rockets, and air-launched precision weapons provide the PLA with the ability to direct long-range precision strikes against a large number of targets, both fixed and mobile. Striking mobile targets requires a dynamic targeting ability. In addition to precision weapons, the PLA needs to connect sensors that can identify mobile targets and a control element that can direct both sensors and shooters quickly enough to strike observed mobile targets before they disappear. The PLA has recently begun to make investments in airborne command aircraft and operates a large number of sensors that appear to give it the hardware required to conduct dynamic targeting.

The PLA is also developing joint doctrine and capabilities to forge a 21st-century air force. As the most recent U.S. Department of Defense report states,

> The PLA Air Force (PLAAF) is converting from a limited territorial defense force to a more flexible and agile force able to operate off-shore in both offensive and defensive roles, using the U.S. and Russian air forces as models. Mission focus areas include: strike, air and missile defense, early warning and reconnaissance, and strategic mobility.[4]

Taiwan certainly takes note of this new conversion by the PLAAF to offshore operations in an offensive role. In doctrinal terms, the PLA considers precision air strikes part of an "air offensive campaign," which can support more comprehensive campaigns, such as a "joint blockade campaign" or a "joint landing campaign." In a joint blockade campaign, the targets would be the ports (military and commercial) and ships at sea, as well as air bases and aircraft attempting to interfere with or break the blockade. In the case of a joint landing campaign, the PLA air offensive campaign would be focused on adversary air defenses, including attacking aircraft on the ground, Taiwan's ground forces and naval bases, and deployed maritime forces (exclusive to the PLA Naval Air Force).[5] Doctrinally, the PLA has the bare elements of a more modern air employment strategy now, but it will need to develop them further in order to contemplate the kinds of operations that the United States began demonstrating in the 1990s.

---

[4] U.S. Department of Defense, *Military Power of the People's Republic of China, 2009*, Washington, D.C.: Office of the Secretary of Defense, 2009, p. 13.

[5] This material on PLA doctrine comes from unpublished research conducted by Roger Cliff and others at RAND.

While developing doctrine and training to conduct dynamic targeting has proven a nontrivial challenge, looking to the future, it appears within PLA competence to achieve this capability.[6] If this assessment proves accurate, the implications for Taiwan's security will be profound, as the PLA could hold at risk not just fixed targets but also Taiwan's fielded forces. Essentially, Taiwan could be facing an adversary imitating U.S. air operational concepts. Several writers have noted the profound impact that the 1991 Persian Gulf War had on the PLA. Since then, its record of investment in precision capabilities suggests that it is paying the United States the compliment of imitation. If so, Taiwan needs to prepare to fight while under precision air attack, like U.S. adversaries have had to do since 1991.

If the PLA has a well-developed dynamic targeting capability and large numbers of precision weapons with sufficient sensors and controllers to use them effectively, Taiwan must seriously question the viability of its current defense concept because it was drawn up without taking such a PLA capability into account. To set a new direction for Taiwan's strategy, policymakers in Taipei should look to recent conflicts in which combatants faced opponents with similar capabilities.

Lessons from Recent Conflicts

Taiwan gets its most sophisticated military equipment from the United States, but in terms of its strategy, it should probably be drawing insights from recent U.S. adversaries and other conflicts in which a weaker power tried to hold territory in the face of an enemy with air superiority and precision weapons. The conflicts in Kosovo in 1999 and Lebanon in 2006 meet these criteria.[7]

In 1999, the United States and the North Atlantic Treaty Organization (NATO) sought to use air superiority and precision firepower to coerce Serbia into withdrawing its forces from Kosovo. Despite the huge disparity in capabilities between NATO and Serbia, NATO was not able to stop Serb operations in Kosovo completely. The Serbs adopted a strategy of dispersal and concealment of their forces, using camouflage, trees, and buildings to hide heavy equipment to survive against NATO air operations while continuing to press Kosovar

[6] RADM Eric McVadon (U.S. Navy, ret.) has also suggested that Taiwan consider the possibility of future advanced air operations from the PLA coordinated by AWACs. See Eric A. McVadon, "Joint Air and Missile Defense for Taiwan: Implications for Deterrence and Defense," in Martin Edmonds and Michael M. Tsai, eds., *Taiwan's Security and Air Power: Taiwan's Defense Against the Air Threat from Mainland China,* London: Routledge Curzon, 2004, p. 121.

[7] Other examples exist. However, they were either unsuccessful or involved in countering the opponent's air superiority with guerilla warfare tactics, which are unlikely to be adopted as the primary strategy in Taiwan. Operation Enduring Freedom (OEF) and Operation Iraqi Freedom (OIF) are examples of failed responses to persistent precision air campaigns. Chechnya and post-OEF and -OIF operations in Afghanistan and Iraq are examples where guerilla tactics were used to present fewer lucrative targets when facing persistent, precision air attack capabilities. Finally, the experience of Sweden, Switzerland, and Yugoslavia offer salient examples of small countries adopting defensive strategies and equipping and training their militaries to exploit rugged, complex terrain to deter attacks by vastly superior forces.

militias.[8] The Serb forces were divided into company- and battalion-sized units, operating autonomously with a mix of motorized infantry, tanks, artillery, and some support forces.[9]

Although Serbia had an air force, with few exceptions, its aircraft were hidden and did not fly against NATO forces; however, limited Serb surface-to-air missile (SAM) challenges to NATO aerial forces kept NATO fliers cautious. The SAM limitations were primarily due to the antiquated SAM force that the Serbs operated. They fired 665 radar-guided SAM rounds, and these SA-2s, SA-3s, and SA-6Bs brought down two aircraft.[10] Had they been more modern systems, the results would likely have been dramatically different. Even so, NATO pilots flew at medium altitudes as a result of the Serb SAM threat, which, in turn, reduced their air-to-ground effectiveness.[11] As one RAND analysis of the war summarized, "Operation Allied Force demonstrated that U.S. air forces could not inflict much damage on fielded forces if those forces dispersed and employed cover and concealment techniques in rugged terrain."[12] U.S. forces had difficulty finding Serb forces that hid under trees, next to buildings, and in villages. The U.S. sensor-to-shooter loop was also shown to be too slow in some cases to attack exposed forces before they could reach another hiding place.

The early NATO strategy of striking Serb forces in the field to stop the ethnic violence failed, forcing NATO to switch strategy and focus on coercing the Serb government more directly. While it is true that in the end NATO prevailed after putting pressure directly on the Serb government by striking targets in Belgrade, that does not make the experience of the Serb army's response to NATO tactics irrelevant for Taiwan.[13] Serb strategies to keep the U.S. precision attacks from destroying the Serb army in the field should help give Taiwan insights to prepare for potential future conflict.

The Serbs are not the only forces to have come under attack by a modern air force with precision weapons. In the summer of 2006, provoked by the capture of two Israeli soldiers, Israel entered Lebanon with the intention of creating a *cordon sanitaire*. Despite Israeli air supremacy, Hezbollah chose to operate in the face of a concerted air campaign rather than concede southern Lebanon. It used precision weapons from hidden, prepared defensive locations, including tunneling and fortified urban positions, to counter Israeli operations. This strategy proved effective in resisting the Israeli invasion, even though the Israelis operated numerous unmanned aerial vehicles

---

[8] Alan Vick, Richard M. Moore, Bruce R. Pirnie, and John Stillion, *Aerospace Operations Against Elusive Ground Targets* Santa Monica, Calif.: RAND Corporation, MR-1398-AF, 2001, p. 19.

[9] Bruce R. Nardulli, Walter L. Perry, Bruce R. Pirnie, John Gordon IV, and John G. McGinn, *Disjointed War: Military Operations in Kosovo, 1999,* Santa Monica, Calif.: RAND Corporation, MR-1406-A, 2002, p. 30.

[10] Martin Andrew, "Revisiting Lessons of Operation Allied Force," Air Power Australia, Analysis 2009-04, June 14, 2009.

[11] If NATO ground forces had invaded Kosovo, NATO air forces would have been forced to go much lower to conduct effective close-air support. NATO air losses would have been much higher as a result.

[12] Nardulli et al., 2002, p. 48.

[13] See, for example, Stephen T. Hosmer, *The Conflict Over Kosovo: Why Milosevic Decided to Settle When He Did,* Santa Monica, Calif.: RAND Corporation, MR-1351-AF, 2001, for an analysis of the reasons for Serbian capitulation.

(UAVs) and fixed-wing aircraft seeking to detect and attack these sites. The well-equipped Hezbollah forces defended against Israeli maneuver forces with anti-tank guided missiles,[14] rocket-propelled grenades (RPGs), and rockets. Hezbollah's anti-tank teams consisted of two soldiers well trained on the weapons system and two or three others to help carry equipment to operate the anti-tank weapon.[15] Some of these weapons were launched remotely, making them difficult to find before their launch and leaving nothing of value to attack after their launch. Hezbollah even managed to execute a successful anti-ship cruise missile strike on an Israeli ship.[16]

The Israeli Winograd Committee final report on the conduct of the war concluded that,

> A semi-military organization of a few thousand men resisted, for a few weeks, the strongest army in the Middle East, which enjoyed full air superiority and size and technology advantages. The barrage of rockets aimed at Israel's civilian population lasted throughout the war, and the [Israel Defense Forces] did not provide an effective response to it. . . . After a long period of using only standoff firepower and limited ground activities, Israel initiated a large-scale ground offensive, very close to the Security Council resolution imposing a cease-fire. This offensive did not result in military gains and was not completed.[17]

Hezbollah operated in small units and used a command-and-control system equipped with encrypted radios and landlines to direct operations. Its command system stayed operational, and commanders appear to have chosen where to hold and fight and where to concede territory. Israeli air supremacy made it difficult for Hezbollah to maneuver, so it could not capitalize on counterattack opportunities.[18] If it had an ability to temporarily clear the air space over a battlefield, it may have been able to maneuver to reinforce threatened sectors or to exploit weaknesses in Israeli deployments.

The picture that emerges from studying recent, relevant conflicts is that precision strikes can be very deadly to larger formations of mechanized forces moving in the open and to easily identifiable fixed targets; however, small groups of mobile or concealed forces can evade detection. Furthermore, if these hidden forces have precision weapons, they can be very effective, even against much more capable forces.

The experiences of the Serb and Hezbollah forces highlight the importance of both the survivability of fielded forces and the need for those forces to maintain employable combat power. Even if Taiwan's forces develop strategies to operate in the face of these precision air attacks, they will still need weapons and employment concepts to keep challenging PLA forces. The huge disparity between the size of the two forces means that Taiwan cannot

---

[14] These were primarily Russian-made AT-3 Saggers and AT-14 Kornet-Es. Other anti-tank weapons included the RPG-29, AT-14 Metis-M, AT-4 Spigot, TOW, AT-5 Spandrel. See Andrew Exum, *Hizballah at War: A Military Assessment*, Washington, D.C.: Washington Institute for Near East Policy, Policy Focus No. 63, December 2006.

[15] Exum, 2006, p. 11.

[16] Stephen Biddle and Jeffrey A. Friedman, *The 2006 Lebanon Campaign and the Future of Warfare: Implications for Army and Defense Policy*, Carlisle, Pa.: Strategic Studies Institute, U.S. Army War College, 2008.

[17] "English Summary of the Winograd Commission Report," *New York Times,* January 30, 2008.

[18] Biddle and Friedman, 2008.

afford to just plan to hide underground. Instead, it needs to field very high-leverage defensive strategies. To do this, it needs to understand some of the operational challenges the PLA will face in trying to take Taiwan.

PLA Operational Challenges

While the PLA has made heavy investments in its military forces in recent years, it is nevertheless not invulnerable. For Taiwan to bolster its deterrent posture, it needs to identify capabilities that can pose difficult operational challenges for the PLA to overcome. While the mainland can inflict a lot of damage on Taiwan using its ballistic missiles and other long-range weapons, in order to take control of the island definitively, it would have to land forces there. In the context of a possible invasion, the PLA will be concerned about protecting its vulnerable forces both as they cross the Strait and early in the invasion when the number of PLA forces will be relatively small. Therefore, Taiwan should focus on efforts that threaten those forces to the point of deterring the PLA from risking its forces in such a way.[19]

PLA forces can come across the Strait in a variety of ways: large transport ships that unload at a dock, amphibious ships that either unload on the beach or disgorge smaller vessels close to the shore, fast ferries, or from the air. During the crossing, PLA forces are particularly vulnerable, and the PLA will be concerned about not only getting its combat forces across the Strait initially but also sustaining and reinforcing them. To protect these forces as they traverse the Strait and when they arrive on Taiwan, the PLA will need to have confidence in its air forces being able to decimate opponents they encounter and interdict reinforcing Taiwanese forces to prevent the landing forces from being overwhelmed. Once on Taiwan, these forces face the challenge of fighting through complex terrain. The attacking forces would rely heavily on roads that go through dense urban areas and are elevated, cross rivers, and travel through narrow, mountain passes. Contemplating fighting through such territory against forces trained and equipped to use the natural advantages to defend it would be very daunting for PLA commanders. In addition, typically successful urban operations require combined arms assaults using sophisticated urban tactics. The constraints of the cross-Strait maneuver will likely result in the early attacking forces being composed of rather light forces and thus not likely to have the full mix of combined arms capabilities that tend to be required for success.[20]

Taiwan needs to develop capabilities that could threaten these delivery modes and the aircraft protecting them, and that appear capable of surviving the expected relentless PLA attack on those forces from the air, while using the strong defensive advantages of its urban, mountainous landscape.

---

[19] The mainland could use its precision strike capabilities to facilitate a blockade, but the implications of the development of dynamic targeting are more profound if applied to a joint landing campaign, which is the focus of this paper. For an analysis of a blockade campaign against Taiwan, see Michael A. Glosny, "Strangulation from the Sea? A PRC Submarine Blockade of Taiwan," *International Security*, Vol. 28, No. 4, Spring 2004.

[20] Russell W. Glenn, *Combat in Hell: A Consideration of Constrained Urban Warfare*, Santa Monica, Calif.: RAND Corporation, MR-780-A/DARPA, 1996. See also the historical appendix in Vick et al., 2001.

Implications for Taiwan

With these PLA operational constraints in mind, we can now consider some possible responses from Taiwan to exploit these weaknesses. This section focuses on ways in which Taiwan might counter amphibious forces as they cross the Taiwan Strait, forces that have landed on Taiwan, and the air campaign meant to protect them.

Anti-ship cruise missiles offer a ready option to counter large ships transporting troops across the Strait. While other options may be feasible, the few cruise missiles that have been used in combat have a very high effective rate against large ships.[21] The long range of the cruise missiles would put PLA forces in jeopardy for a long period of time as they crossed the Strait. Cruise missiles can be launched from a variety of platforms: trucks, fast-attack boats, aircraft, or ships. In selecting the most appropriate launcher from among these options, Taiwan should consider the survivability of the platforms as the overriding concern. To be effective, these missiles must survive until they can be launched. The throughput of the platform in terms of the number of weapons it can launch in a given time and the attendant costs should be additional considerations.

To be effective, anti-ship cruise missiles need to be cued by a survivable sensor. Taiwan could consider sensor aircraft, UAVs, and passive ground-based sensors to play this role. The importance of these sensor capabilities to the overall defense of Taiwan warrants investing in multiple sensors and multiple platforms and locations in order to ensure that some of these sensors can remain operational at key times during the battle. Only a small number of sensors need to be operational in order to be effective. If one successful sensor can cue scores of missiles, it will be worth the expense and trouble to field and protect these capabilities. In addition, Taiwan needs a command system that can link the sensors and the shooters, even while under concerted attack. Again, the survivability of these systems is the paramount concern in considering these alternatives, and redundancy is prudent.

As the attacking force nears Taiwan's shores, it is possible that it will consist of many smaller vessels and could even include groups of individual amphibious tanks. For those targets, Taiwan will want something smaller than an anti-ship cruise missile. Potential candidates include small precision unitary warheads designed to attack moving armored vehicles, weapons that dispense anti-armor submunitions, and area-denial weapons (such as mines). Short-range missiles or rockets can carry these weapons, and some can be fired from artillery guns. These same weapons could also be effective against the landed PLA forces.

Taiwan would probably initially face a rather light ground force comprising mostly dismounted infantry and light tanks supported by some attack helicopters and an air force with complete air superiority over the battlespace. As the attack evolved, heavier forces would almost certainly be brought in. In preparing to confront an enemy with these kinds of capabilities, Taiwan should draw insights from relevant recent conflicts. In Lebanon, Hezbollah's advanced preparation of its defenses often paid off. Numerous caves, safe houses, and concealed

---

21 For instance, in the Falklands war, Argentina had only five Exocet cruise missiles and was able to use them to sink two ships (Shlapak et al., 2009, p. 99).

locations helped its forces evade detection. Land mines and geography channeled Israeli forces into areas where concealed positions with interlocking fields of fire could exact a heavy toll on attacking forces. The defenders used a combination of small-arms weapons and anti-tank munitions to halt the Israeli forces. In Kosovo, the Serbs used a mix of armor, infantry, and air defenses—enough capability to deal with the Kosovar militias, but a small enough footprint to evade attack from the air.

Taiwan will obviously be facing more formidable forces than militias; however, the strategy is comparable in that Taiwan needs a force that is potent enough to meet the PLA ground forces and survivable enough to operate under air attack. These forces should be designed, trained, and equipped in order to take advantage of the complex urban terrain that it will defend. Such terrain can negate the advantages that the PLA might otherwise enjoy, making it difficult for them to mass forces in an effective way or consistently use combined-arms tactics. Taiwan could prepare numerous challenges in advance, from concealed firing positions to combat engineering obstacles, such as dropped roads and other barriers.

Taiwan needs some heavy forces but also needs to adopt operational concepts that recognize its forces are vulnerable to air attack when moving out in the open. In contrast, infantry forces are not very lucrative targets from the air. Infantry with anti-tank precision weapons could elude PLA air attacks while thinning the landed PLA ground forces. This would be an important and challenging role for the infantry, one that is best suited to professional active-duty forces that can be highly trained and proficient in such operations. This is not a role for reservists.

To hold at risk the PLA aircraft helping to defend the amphibious forces as they cross the Strait and once they land, Taiwan should consider using its SAMs as a way to enable its defensive strikes on the attacking vessels and landed forces. Taiwan currently has several SAM systems, its most sophisticated being the Patriot air defenses. The PLA will likely have a rather large air component devoted to the attack. Taiwan's efforts to counter the attack could be more effective if coupled with air defense operations. Even a small capability, like the Serbs had in Kosovo, could impede the effectiveness of the PLA's air-to-ground operations. In Kosovo, the Serbs did not use their SAMs to defend assets at all costs; instead, they used an opportunistic strategy in which they attacked NATO aircraft under favorable conditions. For Taiwan, a strategy of using its air defenses to protect its forces for short periods of time so as to allow them to conduct operations against attacking forces is an important component to fielding a fighting force that is both survivable and effective.

Conclusion

The PLA has not only made large investments in modernizing its forces, but in many cases it seems to have chosen its investments well. For its size, Taiwan makes significant investments in its own defense. The key question is, over the coming years, will Taiwan invest those resources in a way that seeks to exacerbate the operational challenges faced by the PLA?

The biggest challenges the PLA faces are in getting its forces across the Taiwan Strait and protecting them once they are there. These forces will be supported by an impressive precision strike capability. Therefore, Taiwan needs to consider two criteria in assessing new military capabilities: lethality and survivability. In other words, will the investment enable a capability to target vulnerable PLA forces, and can they withstand formidable precision strike capabilities?

If Taiwan can field substantial forces that meet these criteria, it will call into question the success of a PLA invasion and make the cost of military action by the mainland appear too high to be worthwhile. Such changes, coupled with support from friendly countries, can serve as powerful deterrents against mainland hopes of an easy victory over Taiwan. The defenses outlined above have some political advantages as well, inasmuch as they are clearly defensive forces and adaptations solely intended to thwart a violent attack on Taiwan. By posing unacceptable risks to an attacking force, but not posing a risk directed against the mainland itself, such forces offer the unique benefit of being effective without being threatening. In the past, some potential platforms, such as land-attack cruise missiles, have been criticized as overly provocative because of their potential to threaten targets on the mainland. While such an argument probably has a sound rebuttal, in this case, the point is moot.

Perhaps the biggest political hurdle to overcome in developing a consensus around such a strategy in Taiwan is the fact that none of these investments would be seen as a marquee defense acquisition items. Anti-ship cruise missiles and shorter-range precision weapons cued by mobile sensors are likely to be both obtainable and affordable for Taiwan, but would they also be salable politically? By comparison to efforts by Taiwan to acquire submarines and F-16C/Ds, the acquisition of the capabilities proposed above is not likely to capture the political imagination of the Taiwan military to as great an extent. Nevertheless, such items could be defended by Taiwan's leaders as essential components of the defense of the island that are effective, cost-efficient, and less politically destabilizing to the cross-Strait and Taiwan-U.S. relationships.

Like other small states living next to large and potentially hostile neighbors, Taiwan needs to be seen as neither threatening nor inviting. A defense strategy built around survivable platforms that can deliver solid stopping power to the attacking force is just the kind of strategy that Taiwan's military forces should adopt. Such a change could be salable politically within the island by noting that the kinds of precision weapons and sophisticated air defenses described above can be accurately characterized as investments in truly new, modern, and asymmetric defenses, as opposed to simply minor upgrades of legacy platforms.

The vast defense spending differential between China and Taiwan also suggests that similar considerations about lethality and survivability should guide efforts to reform Taiwan's existing force structure. Existing forces are not free, as they continue to require investments to operate and maintain. Ideally, Taiwan will make its investment decisions based on a long-range plan to exploit PLA operational challenges and will assess not only whether its new forces meet these criteria but also whether its current forces do so as well. Forces that are not both lethal and survivable in the modern environment should be divested, even if they have not reached the end of their expected service life. In a constrained resource environment, divestitures are a necessity. Such an approach would provide

Taiwan with a military deterrent consistent with its defense spending limitations and sufficiently capable to give it a chance of deterring its main opponent.

References

Adams, Jonathan, "Exuberance in Taiwan as Ties with China Warm," *New York Times*, May 13, 2009. As of December 23, 2010: http://www.nytimes.com/2009/05/14/business/global/14bulls.html

Allen, Kenneth W., "China's Approach to Confidence-Building Measures," in Michael Krepon, Khurshid Khoja, Michael Newbill, and Jenny Drezin, eds., *Global Confidence Building: New Tools for Troubled Regions*, New York: St. Martin's Press, 1999, pp. 43–59.

Allison, Graham, and Philip Zelikow, *Essence of Decision: Explaining the Cuban Missile Crisis*, New York: Addison-Wesley Longman Publishers, 1999.

Andrew, Martin, "Revisiting Lessons of Operation Allied Force," Air Power Australia, Analysis 2009-04, June 14, 2009.

"As China Swaggers, Neighbors Embrace U.S.," *Wall Street Journal*, May 25, 2010.

Biddle, Stephen, and Jeffrey A. Friedman, *The 2006 Lebanon Campaign and the Future of Warfare: Implications for Army and Defense Policy*, Carlisle, Pa.: Strategic Studies Institute, U.S. Army War College, 2008.

Brooks, Stephen G., *Producing Security: Multinational Corporations, Globalization, and the Changing Calculus of Conflict,* Princeton, N.J.: Princeton University Press, 2007.

Brown, Peter J., "China's Navy Cruises into Pacific Ascendancy," *Asia Times*, April 21, 2010.

Chase, Michael S., and Kristen Gunness, "The PLA's Multiple Military Tasks: Prioritizing Combat Operations and Developing MOOTW Capabilities," *China Brief*, January 21, 2010.

Che Le-yi, "An Analysis of Retired Chinese Military Leaders's Recent Talks on the Establishment of Cross-Strait Confidence Building Measures," Peace Forum, January 26, 2010. As of December 23, 2010: http://www.peaceforum.org.tw/onweb.jsp?webno=3333333573&webitem_no=2373

Chen, Edward I-te, "Japan's Decision to Annex Taiwan: A Study of Ito-Mutsu Diplomacy," *Journal of Asian Studies*, Vol. 37, No. 1, November 1977, pp. 61–72.

Chen Hanxi, "Xin anquan jian shijian: Zhongguo di jianli xinren cuoshi zhengce jiqi yingxiang" ["The New Security View: China's Policy of Confidence-Building Measures and Its Influence"], *Guoji guanxi xueyuan xuebao*, No. 5, 2005, pp. 31–35.

Chen Wanjun and Cao Junping, "PLA Navy Develops Combat Software for Surface Vessels," Xinhua, November 14, 2005.

Chen Xiancai, "Liang'an junshi huanxin jizhu: lilun jian'gou yu shixian lujing" ["Cross-Strait Military Mutual Trust Mechanisms: Theoretical Design and Path of Realization], *Taiwan yanjiu jigan*, No. 103, January 2009.

"China Rules out Overseas Naval Base Now," *China Daily*, January 1, 2010.

"China Tells Tourists to Boycott Taiwan City over Dalai Lama: Report," Agence France Presse, September 17, 2009. As of December 23, 2010: http://www.google.com/hostednews/afp/article/ALeqM5gGWa06u_m5gcBznCiyoW_P1qP5uQ

Christensen, Thomas J., U.S. Deputy Assistant Secretary for East Asian and Pacific Affairs, "A Strong and Moderate Taiwan," speech to the U.S.-Taiwan Business Council, September 11, 2007.

Chu Shulong, "Quanmian Jianshe Xiaokang Shiqi de Zhongguo Waijiao Zhanlue" ["China's Diplomatic Strategy in the Period of Building a Well-Off Society in an All-Around Way"], *Shijie Jingji yu Zhengzhi* [*World Economics and Politics*], No. 8, 2003.

Cliff, Roger, Mark Burles, Michael S. Chase, Derek Eaton, and Kevin L. Pollpeter, *Entering the Dragon's Lair: Chinese Antiaccess Strategies and Their Implications for the United States*, Santa Monica, Calif.: RAND Corporation, MG-524-AF, 2008. As of December 23, 2010: http://www.rand.org/pubs/monographs/MG524.html

Cliff, Roger, and David A. Shlapak, *U.S.-China Relations After Resolution of Taiwan's Status,* Santa Monica, Calif.: RAND Corporation, MG-567-AF, 2007. As of December 23, 2010: http://www.rand.org/pubs/monographs/MG567.html

"A Clue to PLA Fine-Tuning of Cross-Strait Mutual Confidence," *Xinhua Aobao*, August 3, 2009.

Cole, Bernard D., *The Great Wall at Sea: China's Navy in the Twenty-First Century*, Annapolis: U.S. Naval Institute Press, 2010.

Cole, J. Michael, "Paradigm Shift: Expanded Opportunities for Chinese Espionage Against Taiwan," Taipei: MacArthur Center for Security Studies, October 19, 2009. As of December 23, 2010: http://www.mcsstw.org/www/research2.php?article_id=145

Cooney, Kevin, and Yoichiro Sato, eds., *The Rise of China and International Security: America and Asia Respond,* New York: Routledge, 2009.

Council for Security Cooperation in the Asia-Pacific, "Asia Pacific Confidence and Security Building Measures," Memorandum 2, undated. As of December 23, 2010: http://www.cscap.org/index.php? page=memorandum-no-2---asia-pacific-confidence-and-security-building-measures

"Curbing 'Taiwan Independence' Most Urgent Task," *People's Daily Online*, May 17, 2004. As of December 23, 2010: http://english.people.com.cn/200405/17/eng20040517_143467.html

Dai Xu, "Zhongguo Ying Jianli Yuanyang Jidi" ["China Should Establish Bases on the High Seas"], *Huanqiu Shibao* [*Global Times*], February 3, 2009.

DeLisle, Jacques, "Taiwan in the World Health Assembly: A Victory, with Limits," Washington, D.C.: Brookings Institution, Brookings Northeast Asia Commentary No. 29, May 2009.

Desjardins, Marie-France, *Rethinking Confidence Building Measures,* Adelphi Paper No. 307, Oxford: Oxford University Press, December 1, 1996.

Dutton, Peter A., "The Implications of China's Naval Modernization for the United States," testimony before the U.S.-China Economic and Security Review Commission, June 11, 2009.

"ECFA with China to Help U.S. FTA: Yuan," *China Post*, April 16, 2009. As of December 23, 2010: http://www.chinapost.com.tw/taiwan/china-taiwan relations/2009/04/16/204389/ECFA-with.htm

Election Study Center, National Chengchi University, "Changes in the Unification-Independence Stances of Taiwanese as Tracked in Surveys by Election Study Center," undated. As of December 23, 2010: http://esc.nccu.edu.tw/english/modules/tinyd2/content/tonduID.htm

"English Summary of the Winograd Commission Report, *New York Times*, January 30, 2008.

"Establishing Military Mutual Trust Mechanisms for Cross-Strait Consultations" (in Chinese), *Xinhua Aobao*, August 2, 2009. As of December 23, 2010:
http://www.waou.com.mo/detail.asp?id=37275

Exum, Andrew, *Hizballah at War: A Military Assessment*, Washington, D.C.: Washington Institute for Near East Policy, Policy Focus No. 63, December 2006.

Finkelstein, David M., *China Reconsiders Its National Security: "The Great Peace and Development Debate of 1999*," Alexandria, Va.: CNA Corporation, December 2000. As of December 23, 2010:
http://www.cna.org/sites/default/files/D0014464.A1.pdf

———, "PLA Modernization," Carnegie Endowment for International Peace, New Vision Program debate series, Washington, D.C., February 6, 2007.

Fisher, Cathleen S., "The Preconditions of Confidence Building: Lessons from the European Experience," in Michael Krepon, Michael Newbill, Khurshid Khoja, and Jenny S. Drezin, eds., *Global Confidence Building: New Tools for Troubled Regions*, New York: St. Martin's Press, 1999, pp. 291–312.

"Four-Point Guideline on Cross-Strait Relations Set Forth by President Hu Jintao," March 14, 2005. As of December 23, 2010:
http://www.fmprc.gov.cn/ce/cedk/eng/zt/AcrossTaiwanStraits/t187246.htm
Chinese version, as of December 23, 2010:
http://news.xinhuanet.com/newscenter/2005-03/04/content_2649780.htm

Fouse, David, "Japan-Taiwan Relations: A Case of Tempered Optimism," *A Special Assessment: Asia's Bilateral Relations*, Honolulu: Asia-Pacific Center for Security Studies, October 2004.

Fravel, M. Taylor, "Securing Borders: China's Doctrine and Force Structure for Frontier Defense," *Journal of Strategic Studies*, Vol. 30, No. 4, August 2007, pp. 705–737.

———, "Economics and Security: The Effect of Economic Growth on China's Military Strategy," unpublished draft, 2010.

Friedberg, Aaron L., "The Future of U.S.-China Relations: Is Conflict Inevitable?" *International Security*, Vol. 30, No. 2, Fall 2005, pp. 7–45.

Friedman, Thomas L., *The World is Flat: A Brief History of the Twenty-First Century*, New York: Farrar, Straus and Giroux, 2005.

Frost, Ellen L., James J. Przystup, and Phillip C. Saunders, "China's Rising Influence in Asia: Implications for U.S. Policy," *Strategic Forum*, No. 231, April 2008.

"Full Text of Hu Jintao's Report at 17th Party Congress," Xinhua, October 24, 2007. As of December 23, 2010: http://news.xinhuanet.com/english/2007-10/24/content_6938749.htm

Gai Shijin and Zhang Peizhong, *Duoyanghua Junshi Renwu Lun* [*On Diverse Military Tasks*], Beijing: Changzheng Chubanshe [Long March Press], 2009.

Gartzke, Erik, Quan Li, and Charles Boehmer, "Investing in the Peace: Economic Interdependence and International Conflict," *International Organization*, Vol. 55, No. 2, Spring 2001, pp. 391–438.

Glaser, Bonnie S., "Cross-Strait Confidence Building: The Case for Military Confidence-Building Measures," in Fugarino, Chris, and Donald S. Zagoria, eds., *Breaking the China-Taiwan Impasse*, Westport, Conn.: Praeger, 2003, pp. 155–182.

———, "Ensuring the 'Go Abroad' Policy Serves China's Domestic Priorities," *China Brief*, May 9, 2007.

———, *Building Trust Across the Taiwan Strait: A Role for Military Confidence-Building Measures*, Washington, D.C.: Center for Strategic and International Studies, January 2010.

Glaser, Bonnie S., and Benjamin Dooley, "China's 11th Ambassadorial Conference Signals Continuity and Change in Foreign Policy," *China Brief*, November 4, 2009.

Glaser, Bonnie S., and Brad Glosserman, *Promoting Confidence Building Across the Taiwan Strait*, Washington, D.C.: Center for Strategic and International Studies, September 2008.

Glenn, Russell W., *Combat in Hell: A Consideration of Constrained Urban Warfare*, Santa Monica, Calif.: RAND Corporation, MR-780-A/DARPA, 1996. As of December 23, 2010: http://www.rand.org/pubs/monograph_reports/MR780.html

Global Views Survey Research Center, "Survey on President Ma Ying-jeou's Approval Rating," January 21, 2011. As of February 24, 2011: http://www.taiwansecurity.org/2011/GVMaApproval-012111.pdf

Glosny, Michael A., "Strangulation from the Sea? A PRC Submarine Blockade of Taiwan," *International Security,* Vol. 28, No. 4, Spring 2004, pp. 125–160.

———, "Heading Toward a Win-Win Future? Recent Developments in China's Policy Toward Southeast Asia," *Asian Security*, Vol. 2, No. 1, 2006, pp. 24–57.

Glosserman, Brad, "Cross-Strait Confidence Building Measures," *Issues and Insights*, Vol. 5, No. 2, February 2005.

Godement, Francois, "Confidence Building Measures: Can Taiwan Learn from European Experiences," draft manuscript, 2006. As of December 23, 2010: http://www.peaceforum.org.tw/filectrl/121506.doc

Goldstein, Avery, *Rising to the Challenge: China's Grand Strategy and International Security,* Stanford, Calif.: Stanford University Press, 2005.

Goldstein, Steven M., and Randall Schriver, "Japan and Conflict in the Taiwan Strait, 1951–2007: From Passive Observer to Active Participant," draft paper.

Guo Zhongguan, "Scholar Says the Reunification Process Will Enter a Crucial Period as Cross Strait Exchanges Undergo Structural Changes," China News Agency, Hong Kong [*Zhongguo Tongxun*], October 12, 2009.

"Haijun Zhuanjia Fouren Haiwai Jian Junshi Jidi Chuanwen" ["Naval Expert Denies Rumor that China Is Establishing Military Bases Overseas"], *Zhongguo Qingnianbao* [*China Youth Daily*], March 5, 2010.

Hamrin, Carol Lee, and Zheng Wang, "The Floating Island: Change of Paradigm on the Taiwan Question," *Journal of Contemporary China*, Vol. 13, No. 39, 2004, pp. 339–349.

Hartnett, Daniel M., "The PLA's Domestic and Foreign Activities and Orientation," testimony before the U.S.-China Economic and Security Review Commission, March 4, 2009.

Hiali, A. Z., "Confidence- and Security-Building Measures for India and Pakistan," *Alternatives,* Vol. 30, 2005, pp. 91–122.

Higgins, Holly, "Applying Confidence-Building Measures in a Regional Context," in Holly Higgins, ed., *Building Nuclear Confidence on the Korean Peninsula: Proceedings of the July 23–24, 2001 Workshop*, Washington, D.C.: Institute for Science and International Security, 2001, pp. 23–35. As of December 23, 2010: http://www.isis-online.org/publications/dprk/higgins.pdf

Hosmer, Stephen T., *The Conflict Over Kosovo: Why Milosevic Decided to Settle When He Did*, Santa Monica, Calif.: RAND Corporation, MR-1351-AF, 2001. As of December 23, 2010: http://www.rand.org/pubs/monograph_reports/MR1351.html

"Hu Puts Forward Six Points to Further the Development of Cross-Strait Relations" (in Chinese), SINA, December 31, 2008. As of December 23, 2010: http://news.sina.com.cn/c/2008-12-31/132716956876.shtml

Huang Renwei, *Zhongguo Jueqi de Shijian he Kongjian* [*The Time and Space for China's Rise*], Shanghai: Shanghai Academy of Social Sciences Press, 2003.

Hughes, Wayne P., *The New Navy Fighting Machine: A Study of the Connections Between Contemporary Policy, Strategy, Sea Power, Naval Operations, and the Composition of the United States Fleet*, Monterey, Calif.: Naval Postgraduate School, NPS-OR-09-002-PR, August, 2009.

Information Office of the State Council, People's Republic of China, *China's National Defense*, Beijing, July 1998. As of December 23, 2010: http://www.fas.org/nuke/guide/china/doctrine/cnd9807/

———, *China's National Defense in 2000*, Beijing, October 16, 2000. As of December 23, 2010: http://www.china.org.cn/e-white/2000

———, *China's Peaceful Development Road*, Beijing, December 2005.

"An Interview with President Ma Ying-jeou," *New York Times*, June 19, 2008.

Jacobs, J. Bruce, and I-hao Ben Liu, "Lee Teng-Hui and the Idea of 'Taiwan,'" *China Quarterly*, Vol. 190, 2007, pp. 375–393.

"Jianli liang'an junshi huanxin shuangfang dou you qianglie yiyuan," *Aomen Bao*, January 3, 2009.

"Jiefangjun wei liang'an huxin weitiao lu duanni" ["A Clue to PLA Fine-Tuning of Cross-Strait Mutual Confidence"], *Xinhua Aobao*, August 3, 2009.

Johnston, Alastair Iain, and Robert S. Ross, *Engaging China: The Management of an Emerging Power*, London: Routledge, 1999.

Kahler, Miles, and Scott L. Kastner, "Strategic Uses of Economic Interdependence: Engagement Policies on the Korean Peninsula and Across the Taiwan Strait," *Journal of Peace Research*, Vol. 43, No. 5, September 2006, pp. 523–541.

Kamphausen, Roy, David Lai, and Andrew Scobell, eds., *Beyond the Strait: PLA Missions Other Than Taiwan*, Carlisle, Pa.: Strategic Studies Institute, U.S. Army War College, 2009.

———, eds., *The PLA at Home and Abroad: Assessing the Operational Capabilities of China's Military*, Carlisle, Pa.: Strategic Studies Institute, U.S. Army War College, June 2010.

Kastner, Scott L., "Does Economic Integration Across the Taiwan Strait Make Military Conflict Less Likely?" *Journal of East Asian Studies,* Vol. 6, No. 3, Fall 2006, pp. 319–346.

———, *Political Conflict and Economic Interdependence Across the Taiwan Strait and Beyond*, Stanford, Calif.: Stanford University Press, 2009.

———, "Drinking Poison to Quench a Thirst? The Security Consequences of China-Taiwan Economic Integration," paper presented at the Association for Asian Studies annual meeting, Philadelphia, Pa., March 2010.

Kelly, James, Assistant Secretary, Bureau of East Asian and Pacific Affairs, U.S. Department of State, statement before the Committee on International Relations, U.S. House of Representatives, at the hearing "The Taiwan Relations Act: The Next Twenty-Five Years," April 21, 2004.

Keng, Shu, and Gunter Schubert, "Agents of Taiwan-China Unification? The Political Roles of Taiwanese Business People in the Process of Cross-Strait Integration," *Asian Survey*, Vol. 50, No. 2, 2010, pp. 287–310.

Keohane, Robert O., and Joseph S. Nye, *Power and Interdependence*, New York: Longman Publishers, 2001.

Kiesow, Ingolf, *Confidence Building Measures in Europe During the Cold War: Possible Relevance for Asia Today*, Beijing: Institute for American Studies, China Institutes of Contemporary International Relations, 2005. As of October 2009:
http://www.foi.se/FOI/templates/Page____4536.aspx

Ko Shu-ling, "MAC Rejects Criticism of Ma's Cross-Strait Policies," *Taipei Times*, February 3, 2009. As of December 23, 2010:
http://www.taipeitimes.com/News/taiwan/archives/2009/02/03/2003435153

Ko Shu-ling, Flora Wang, Jenny W. Hsu, and Shih Hsiu-chian, "Legislature Bans Some US Beef," *Taipei Times*, January 6, 2010. As of December 23, 2010:
http://www.taipeitimes.com/News/front/archives/2010/01/06/2003462809

Kopp, Carlo, *Sukhoi Flankers: The Shifting Balance of Regional Air Power,* Australia Air Power Association, Technical Report APA-TR-2007-0101, September 2009. As of December 23, 2010:
http://www.ausairpower.net/APA-Flanker.html

Krepon, Michael, ed., *Chinese Perspectives on Confidence Building Measures*, Washington, D.C.: Stimson Center, Report No. 23, May 1997.

Krepon, Michael, Khurshid Khoja, Michael Newbill, and Jenny Drezin, eds., *A Handbook of Confidence-Building Measures for Regional Security*, 3rd ed., Washington, D.C.: Stimson Center, 1998.

Lee, Chyungly, "Maritime Confidence Building Measures Across the Taiwan Strait: Technical Collaboration for Human Security at Sea," Albuquerque, N.M.: Sandia National Laboratories, Cooperative Monitoring Center Occasional Paper No. 26, SAND 2003-0753, March 2003.

Levy, Jack S., "Loss Aversion, Framing Effects, and International Conflict," in Manus I. Midlarsky, ed., *Handbook of War Studies II*, Ann Arbor, Mich.: University of Michigan Press, 2000.

———, "Economic Interdependence, Opportunity Costs, and Peace," in Edward D. Mansfield and Brian M. Pollins, eds., *Economic Interdependence and International Conflict: New Perspectives on an Enduring Debate*, Ann Arbor, Mich.: University of Michigan Press, 2003, pp. 127–147.

Li Jianzhong, "Jiajin cuohao jianli liang'an junshi huanxin jizhu" ["Speed Up the Establishment of Cross-Strait Military Trust Mechanisms"], *Fazhi yu shehui*, No. 13, 2009.

Li Li, "Dongmeng diqu luntan yu yufang xin waijiao" ["The ASEAN Forum and the Foreign Policy of Preventing War"], *Jiangnan shehui xueyuan xuebao*, Vol. 3, No. 4, 2001, pp. 12–15.

Li Yonghui, "Shuyuan di linju" ["Alienated Neighbors"], *Eluosi zhonyga dongou yanjiu,* No. 2, 2005, pp. 66–72.

"Liang'an Baofa Junshi Chongtu Weixian Dajian" ["The Danger of Cross-Strait Military Conflict Breaking Out Has Dropped Greatly"], *Da Gongbao*, December 24, 2008.

"Liang'an junshi huanxin Taiwan fangnian yu san da misi" ["The Taiwan Side Has Three Big Myths in Regard to Cross-Strait Military Trust"], PhoenixNews.com, September 3, 2009. As of December 23, 2010: http://news.ifeng.com/opinion/phjd/zh/200909/0903_1925_1333173.shtm

Lieberthal, Kenneth, "Preventing a War over Taiwan," *Foreign Affairs*, Vol. 84, No. 2, March–April 2005, pp. 53–63.

Lin, Chiung-chu, "The Role of Issue in Taiwan's Politics, 1996–2004," *Issues and Studies*, Vol. 44, No. 1, 2008, pp. 71–104.

Lin, Chong-pin, "More Carrot Than Stick: Beijing's Emerging Taiwan Policy," *China Security*, Vol. 4, No. 1, Winter 2008, pp. 1–27.

Lin Chuan, "Both Sides of the Taiwan Strait Wish to Establish a 'Mechanism of Mutual Trust in Military and Security Affairs," Zhongguo Pinglun Tongxun She [China Review News Agency], January 5, 2009.

Liu Hong, "The Cross-Strait Relationship Has Entered an Era of Strategic Opportunity," 「兩岸關係進入戰略機遇期」，《台聲雜誌》，**第九期,** September 15, 2008. As of December 23, 2010:
http://www.tailian.org.cn/n1080/n288226/n288317/295655.html

Liu Huaqiu, "Step by Step Confidence and Security Building for the Asian Region," in Ralph A. Cossa, ed., *Asia Pacific Confidence and Security Building Measures*, Washington, D.C.: Center for Strategic and International Studies, 1995, pp. 119–136.

Liu Huaqiu and Zhang Hua, "Confidence Building in Asia," in Michael Krepon, ed., *Chinese Perspectives on Confidence Building Measures,* Washington, D.C.: Stimson Center, Report No. 23, May 1997.

Liu, Shih-chung, "Convergence and Divergence in Taiwan's U.S. Policy, 2004–2008," Washington, D.C.: Brookings Institution, CNAPS Visiting Fellow Working Paper, November 2009.

Luo Yuan, "Chance to Establish Cross-Strait Military Security Mutual Confidence Building System Should Not Be Missed," *Guoji Xianqu Daobao Online*, January 5, 2009a.

———, "Cross-Strait Military Mutual Trust Needs to Analyze and Solve Three Mysterious Ideas," Zhongguo Pinglun Tongxun She [China Review News Agency], August 12, 2009b.

Mainland Affairs Council, *Liang'an Jingji Tongji Yuebao* [*Cross-Straits Statistics Monthly*], various issues. As of December 23, 2010:
http://www.mac.gov.tw/lp.asp?ctNode=5934&CtUnit=4152&BaseDSD=7&mp=3

Mason, Margaret, "Confidence Building in the Asia Pacific Region: Prospects and Problems," in Ralph A. Cossa, ed., *Asia Pacific Confidence and Security Building Measures*, Washington, D.C.: Center for Strategic and International Studies, 1995.

McDevitt, RADM Michael, "The PLA Navy Anti-Access Role in a Taiwan Contingency," unpublished manuscript, 2010.

McVadon, Eric A., "Joint Air and Missile Defense for Taiwan: Implications for Deterrence and Defense," in Martin Edmonds and Michael M. Tsai, eds., *Taiwan's Security and Air Power: Taiwan's Defense Against the Air Threat from Mainland China,* London: RoutledgeCurzon, 2004, pp. 116–139.

Mearsheimer, John J., *The Tragedy of Great Power Politics*, New York: W. W. Norton and Company, 2001.

———, "China's Unpeaceful Rise," *Current History*, Vol. 105, No. 690, April 2006, pp. 160–162.

Mei, Fu, "Taiwan's Defense Transition: Beyond Q.D.R.," paper presented at the US-Taiwan Defense Industry Conference, Charlottesville, Va., September 28, 2009.

Men Honghua, "Zhongguo Guojia Zhanlue Liyi de Tuozhan" ["The Expansion of China's National Strategic Interests"], *Zhanlue yu Guanli* [*Strategy and Management*], No. 2, 2003, pp. 83–89.

Ministry of National Defense, People's Republic of China, "Regional Cooperation," web page, undated. As of December 23, 2010:
http://eng.mod.gov.cn/Database/RegionalCooperation/

Mulvenon, James, "Chairman Hu and the PLA's 'New Historic Missions,'" *China Leadership Monitor*, No. 27, Winter 2009.

Murray, William S., "Revisiting Taiwan's Defense Strategy," *Naval War College Review,* Vol. 61, No. 3, 2008.

Nardulli, Bruce R., Walter L. Perry, Bruce R. Pirnie, John Gordon IV, and John G. McGinn, *Disjointed War: Military Operations in Kosovo, 1999*, Santa Monica, Calif.: RAND Corporation, MR-1406-A, 2002. As of December 23, 2010:
http://www.rand.org/pubs/monograph_reports/MR1406.html

"Obama Will Have to Deal Soon with Arms Sales to Taiwan: Scholars," Central News Agency, October 29, 2009.

Paal, Douglas, remarks prepared for the Carnegie Congressional Series on China: Taiwan Policy, Washington, D.C., March 26, 2008. As of December 23, 2010: http://carnegieendowment.org/files/Paal.pdf

Paine, S. C. M., *The Sino-Japanese War of 1894–1895: Perceptions, Power, and Primacy,* New York: Cambridge University Press, 2003.

"Panamanian Ship's Captain, 2 Crew Member [sic] Rescued," Central News Agency, October 5, 2009. As of March 10, 2011: http://www.etaiwannews.com/etn/news_content.php?id=1074357&lang=eng_news&cate_img=49.jpg&cate_rss=news_Society

Pape, Robert, *Bombing to Win: Air Power and Coercion in War*, Ithaca, N.Y.: Cornell University Press, 1996.

Pederson, M. Susan, and Stanley Weeks, "A Survey of Confidence and Security Building Measures," in Ralph A. Cossa, ed., *Asia Pacific Confidence and Security Building Measures*, Washington, D.C.: Center for Strategic and International Studies, 1995.

Peng Guangqian and Yao Youzhi, eds., *The Science of Military Strategy,* Beijing: Military Science Publishing House, Academy of Military Science of the People's Liberation Army, 2005.

Permanent Mission of the People's Republic of China to the United Nations, "Practical Confidence-Building Measures in the Field of Conventional Arms," October 15, 2003. As of December 23, 2010: http://www.mfa.gov.cn/ce/ceun/eng/chinaandun/disarmament_armscontrol/qtxx/t29278.htm

Polachek, Solomon William, "Conflict and Trade," *Journal of Conflict Resolution*, Vol. 24, No. 1, March 1980, pp. 55–78.

Pollack, Jonathan D., and Richard H. Yang, eds., *In China's Shadow: Regional Perspectives on Chinese Foreign Policy and Military Development*, Santa Monica, Calif.: RAND Corporation, CF-137-CAPP, 1998. As of December 23, 2010: http://www.rand.org/pubs/conf_proceedings/CF137.html

Pomfret, John, "U.S.-China Talks End Without Accords on Key Issues," *Washington Post*, May 26, 2010.

"PRC Pundit Views Cross-Strait Military Trust, Rebuffs Calls to Redeploy Troops," *Zhongguo Qingnian*, 2009. Chinese version, as of December 23, 2010: http://mil.eastday.com/m/20090814/u1a4581493.html

"PRC Scholar Urges Confidence Building with Taiwan Military" (in Chinese), *Guoji Xianqu Daobao*, January 5, 2009.

"President Hu Offers Six Proposals for Peaceful Development of Cross-Strait Relationship," Taiwan Affairs Office of the State Council, December 31, 2008.

Quadrennial Defense Review Editing Group, Taiwan Ministry of National Defense, *Quadrennial Defense Review 2009*, Taipei, 2009.

Robinson, Thomas W., and David Shambaugh, eds., *Chinese Foreign Policy: Theory and Practice*, Oxford, UK: Oxford University Press, 1994.

Rogin, Josh, "Obama in No-Win Situation over Taiwan Arms Sale," *The Cable* (*Foreign Policy*), September 15, 2009. As of December 23, 2010: http://thecable.foreignpolicy.com/posts/2009/09/15/obama_in_no_win_situation_over_taiwan_arms_sale

Romberg, Alan D., "Cross-Strait Relations: First the Easy, Now the Hard," *China Leadership Monitor*, No. 28, Spring 2009.

Roscoe, Theodore, *U.S. Submarine Operations in World War II*, Annapolis, Md.: U.S. Naval Institute Press, 1949.

Rosen, Daniel, "What Are the Implications of Taiwan-China Economic Liberalization?" Washington, D.C.: Center for Strategic and International Studies, Freeman Report, September 2009.

Ross, Robert S., "Taiwan's Fading Independence Movement," *Foreign Affairs,* Vol. 85, No. 2, March–April 2006a, pp. 141–148.

———, "Explaining Taiwan's Revisionist Diplomacy," *Journal of Contemporary China,* Vol. 15, No. 48, August 2006b, pp. 443–458.

———, "China's Naval Nationalism: Sources, Prospects, and the U.S. Response," *International Security,* Vol. 34, No. 2, Fall 2009.

Saunders, Phillip C., and Scott L. Kastner, "Bridge over Troubled Water? Envisioning a China-Taiwan Peace Agreement," *International Security*, Vol. 33, No. 4, Spring 2009, pp. 87–114.

Schaub, Gary, Jr., "Deterrence, Compellence, and Prospect Theory," *Political Psychology*, Vol. 25, No. 3, 2004, pp. 389–411.

Schelling, Thomas C., *Arms and Influence*, New Haven, Conn.: Yale University Press, 1966.

Scobell, Andrew, and Larry M. Wortzel, *Shaping China's Environment: The Role of the People's Liberation Army*, Carlisle, Pa.: Strategic Studies Institute, U.S. Army War College, October 2006.

Shambaugh, David, "China Engages Asia: Reshaping the Regional Order," *International Security,* Vol. 29, No. 3, 2004, pp. 64–99.

———, ed., *Power Shift: China and Asia's New Dynamics*, Berkeley, Calif.: University of California Press, 2006.

Shear, David B., Deputy Assistant Secretary, Bureau of East Asian and Pacific Affairs, "China-Taiwan: Recent Economic, Political and Military Developments Across the Strait and Implications for the United States," testimony before the U.S.-China Economic and Security Review Commission, Washington, D.C., March 18, 2010.

Shi Jiazhu, "Nanhai jianli xinren cuoshi yu quyu anquan" ["South Seas CBMs and Regional Security"], *Guoji guancha*, January 2004, pp. 42–47.

Shi Yinhong, "Zhongguo Heping Jueqi de Zhanlue Jiyu he ruogan Jiben Tiaojian" ["The Strategic Opportunity of China's Peaceful Rise and Several Fundamental Conditions"], *Guoji Guancha* [*International Survey*], No. 3, 2004.

Shirk, Susan L., *China: Fragile Superpower*, New York: Oxford University Press, 2007.

Shlapak, David A., David T. Orlesky, Toy I. Reid, Murray Scot Tanner, and Barry Wilson, *A Question of Balance: Political Context and Military Aspects of the China-Taiwan Dispute*, Santa Monica, Calif.: RAND Corporation, MG-888-SRF, 2009. As of December 23, 2010: http://www.rand.org/pubs/monographs/MG888.html

Shlapak, David A., David T. Orletsky, and Barry Wilson, *Dire Strait? Military Aspects of the China-Taiwan Confrontation and Options for U.S. Policy*, Santa Monica, Calif.: RAND Corporation, MR-1217-SRF, 2000. As of December 23, 2010: http://www.rand.org/pubs/monograph_reports/MR1217.html

Shou Xiaosong and Xu Jingnian, chief eds., *Jundui Yingdui Feichuantong Anquan Weixie Yanjiu* [*Research on the Military's Responses to Nontraditional Security Threats*], Beijing: Jiefangjun Chubanshe, 2009.

Singh, Rahul, "Indian Army Fears Chinese Attack by 2017," *Hindustan Times*, March 26, 2009.

Smith, Craig, "China Reshaping Military to Toughen Its Muscle in the Region," *New York Times*, October 16, 2002.

Song Guocai, Shi Limin, and Yang Shu, chief eds., *Feizhanzheng Junshi Xingdong Shili Yanjiu* [*Case Studies on Non-War Military Operations*], Beijing: Guofang Daxue Chubanshe, military circulation only, 2009.

Su Changhe, "Lun Zhongguo Haiwai Liyi" ["On China's Overseas Interests"], *Shijie Jingji yu Zhengzhi* [*World Economics and Politics*], No. 8, 2009, pp. 13–20.

Swaine, Michael D., and Ashley J. Tellis, *Interpreting China's Grand Strategy: Past, Present, and Future*, Santa Monica, Calif.: RAND Corporation, MR-1121-AF, 2000. As of December 23, 2010: http://www.rand.org/pubs/monograph_reports/MR1121.html

Swaine, Michael D., Andrew N. D. Yang, and Evan S. Medeiros, with Oriana Skylar Mastro, eds., *Assessing the Threat: The Chinese Military and Taiwan's Security*, Washington, D.C.: Carnegie Endowment for International Peace, 2007.

Taiwan Ministry of National Defense, *2009 National Defense Report: Building an Elite Armed Forces—Voluntaryism* [sic], Taipei, 2009.

Tanner, Murray Scot, *Chinese Economic Coercion Against Taiwan: A Tricky Weapon to Use*, Santa Monica, Calif.: RAND Corporation, MG-507-OSD, 2007. As of December 23, 2010: http://www.rand.org/pubs/monographs/MG507.html

Teng Jianqun, "Zhongguo jianli xinren cuoshi shijian yu zhanwang" ["The Practice and Promise of Chinese Confidence-Building Measures"], *Guoji guanxi yanjiu*, No. 3, 2008, pp. 12–18.

"There Are Three Myths in Taiwan Cross-Strait Military Trust," Phoenix News, September 3, 2009. In Chinese, as of December 23, 2010: http://news.ifeng.com/opinion/phjd/zh/200909/0903_1925_1333173.shtml

Tsai Ing-wen, "CECA Comes with Big Hidden Costs," *Taipei Times*, March 1, 2009, p. 8.

Tucker, Nancy Bernkopf, "China-Taiwan: US Debates and Policy Choices," *Survival*, Vol. 40, No. 4, January 1998, pp. 150–167.

———, "If Taiwan Chooses Unification, Should the United States Care?" *Washington Quarterly*, Vol. 25, No. 3, Summer 2002, pp. 15–28.

U.S. Department of Defense, *Military Power of the People's Republic of China, 2009*, Washington, D.C.: Office of the Secretary of Defense, 2009.

U.S.-Taiwan Business Council, *Defense and Security Report, Second Quarter 2009*, Arlington, Va., 2009.

Vellucci, Frederic, "Recent Trends in PLA Navy Training and Education," testimony before the U.S.-China Economic and Security Review Commission, Washington, D.C., June 11, 2009. As of March 1, 2011: http://www.uscc.gov/hearings/2009hearings/written_testimonies/09_06_11_wrts/09_06_11_vellucci_statement.php

Vick, Alan, Richard M. Moore, Bruce R. Pirnie, and John Stillion, *Aerospace Operations Against Elusive Ground Targets*, Santa Monica, Calif.: RAND Corporation, MR-1398-AF, 2001. As of December 23, 2010: http://www.rand.org/pubs/monograph_reports/MR1398.html

Wachman, Alan M., *Why Taiwan? Geostrategic Rationales for China's Territorial Integrity*, Studies in Asian Security, Stanford, Calif.: Stanford University Press, 2007.

———, "Ensnared by Beijing: Washington Succumbs to the PRC's Diplomacy of Panic," *China Security*, Vol. 4, No. 1, Winter 2008, pp. 68–91.

Wallensteen, Peter, *Understanding Conflict Resolution*, 2nd ed., Los Angeles, Calif.: Sage Publications, 2007.

Wang Lidong, *Guojia Haishang Liyi Lun* [*On China's National Maritime Interests*], Beijing: Guofang Daxue Chubanshe, 2007.

Wang Mingwu et al., chief eds., *Feizhanzheng Junshi Xingdong* [*Non-War Military Operations*], Beijing: Guofang Daxue Chubanshe, 2006.

Wang, T. Y., "The Perception of Threats and Pragmatic Policy Choice: A Survey of Public Opinion in Taiwan," *Issues and Studies*, Vol. 41, No. 1, March 2005a, pp. 87–111.

———, "National Identity and Democratization in Taiwan: An Introduction," *Journal of Asian and African Studies*, Nos. 1–2, April 2005b, pp. 5–12.

Wang Yizhou, "Heping Fazhan Jieduan de Guojia Anquan" ["National Security During the Stage of Peaceful Development"], *Shijie Zhishi* [*World Affairs*], No. 23, 2006, pp. 48–51.

Wilmont, H. P., *The Battle of Leyte Gulf: The Last Fleet Action*, Bloomington, Ind.: University of Indiana Press, 2006.

Xiao Tianliang, *Junshi Liliang de Feizhanzheng Yunyong* [*Non-War Uses for Military Power*], Beijing: Guofang Daxue Chubanshe, 2009.

Yan Xuetong et al., "'Daguo de Jueqi yu Zhongguo de Xuanze' Bitan" ["Pen Discussions on 'The Rise of Great Powers and China's Choices'"], *Zhongguo Shehui Kexue* [*Social Sciences in China*], Vol. 5, 2004, pp. 51–63.

Yang Mingshu, chief ed., *Haishang Tongdao Anquan yu Guoji Hezuo* [*SLOC Security and International Cooperation*], Beijing: Shishi Chubanshe, 2005.

Ye Zicheng, *Daguo DaZhanlue: Zhongguo Chengwei Shijie Daguo de Zhuyao Wenti ji Zhanlue Xuanze* [*China's Grand Strategy: Important Issues and Strategic Choices for China in Becoming a World Great Power*], Beijing: Chinese Academy of Social Sciences Press, 2003.

Zagoria, Donald S., "Cross-Strait Relations: Cautious Optimism," summary of the Conference on Prospects for Relations across the Taiwan Strait, a Trilateral Conference sponsored by the National Committee on American Foreign Policy, January 13–14, 2009.

Zartman, I. William, "Ripeness," *Beyond Intractability*, August 2003. As of December 23, 2010: http://www.beyondintractability.org/essay/ripeness

Zhai Kun, "Junshi huanxin jizhi yu liang'an de heping fazhan" ["Military Confidence Building Mechanisms and the Peaceful Development of Cross-Strait Relations"], China Internet Information Center, October 1, 2006. As of December 23, 2010:
http://big5.china.com.cn/gate/big5/zhaikun.blog.china.com.cn/art/show.do?dn=lipeng&id=9318&agMode=1&com.trs.idm.g

Zhang Yuliang, chief ed., *Zhanyi Xue* [*The Science of Campaigns*], Beijing: Guofang Daxue Chubanshe, 2006.

"Zhuanjia: Zhongguo Haijun ke Tantao Jianli Changqi Anji Buji Jidi" ["Expert: PLAN May Explore Establishing a Long-Term Coastal Supply Base"], ChinaReviewNews.com, date unknown.

Contributors

Roger Cliff is an independent researcher specializing in East Asian security issues. His areas of research include China's force employment concepts, China's military capabilities, China's aerospace industry, and U.S.-China security relations. He has authored or co-authored several RAND research documents and more than a dozen journal articles and book chapters. Cliff was a researcher at the RAND Corporation until 2011. From 1999 to 2001, he was assistant for strategy development in the Office of the Deputy Assistant Secretary of Defense for Strategy. He speaks and reads Mandarin Chinese and has spent a total of over four years living in China and Taiwan. He received his Ph.D. in international relations from Princeton University's Woodrow Wilson School of Public and International Affairs. He also has an M.A. in Chinese studies from the University of California, San Diego, and a B.S. in physics from Harvey Mudd College.

Bernard D. Cole (Captain, U.S. Navy, retired) is a professor of international history at the National War College in Washington, D.C., where he concentrates on Chinese military and Asian energy issues. He served for 30 years as a surface warfare officer in the U.S. Navy, all in the Pacific, and commanded the USS *Rathburne* (FF1057) and Destroyer Squadron 35. He also served as a naval gunfire liaison officer in Vietnam with the Third Marine Division. Cole has written numerous articles and six books—most recently, *The Great Wall at Sea: China's Navy in the Twenty-First Century*, which was published in December 2010. He has a Ph.D. in history from Auburn University, an M.P.A. in national security affairs from the University of Washington, and an A.B. in history from the University of North Carolina.

Bonnie Glaser is a senior fellow with the CSIS Freeman Chair in China Studies at the Center for Strategic and International Studies (CSIS). She works on issues related to Chinese foreign and security policy. She is concomitantly a senior associate with CSIS Pacific Forum and a consultant for the U.S. government on East Asia. Glaser has written extensively on Chinese threat perceptions and views of the strategic environment, China's foreign policy, U.S.-China relations, U.S.-China military ties, cross-strait relations, Chinese assessments of the Korean peninsula, and Chinese perspectives on missile defense and multilateral security in Asia. Her writings have been published in the *Washington Quarterly, China Quarterly, Asian Survey, International Security, Problems of Communism, Contemporary Southeast Asia, American Foreign Policy Interests, Far Eastern Economic Review, Korean Journal of Defense Analysis, New York Times,* and *International Herald Tribune*, as well as various edited volumes on Asian security. She is currently a board member of the U.S. Committee of the Council for Security Cooperation in the Asia Pacific and a member of the Council on Foreign Relations. Glaser received her M.A. with concentrations in international economics and Chinese studies from the Johns Hopkins School of Advanced International Studies. She also has a B.A. in political science from Boston University.

Michael A. Glosny is an instructor in the Department of National Security Affairs at the Naval Postgraduate School in Monterey, California. He is also an adjunct senior research fellow at the Institute for National Strategic Studies (INSS) at the National Defense University in Washington, D.C. He is completing his Ph.D. at the Massachusetts Institute of Technology and is a member of MIT's Security Studies Program. He has also been an international security program fellow at Harvard University's Belfer Center for Science and Technology and a fellow at Harvard's John M. Olin Institute for Strategic Studies. His research interests include international relations and international security, with a focus on Chinese foreign and security policy and U.S. alliances in East Asia. His publications on various aspects of China's foreign and security policy have appeared in *International Security, Asian Security, Polity, Strategic Asia 2003–4: Fragility and Crisis,* and the China Policy Series from the National Committee on U.S.-China Relations, as well as edited volumes.

Steven M. Goldstein is the Sophia Smith Professor of Government at Smith College and a research associate at the John K. Fairbank Center for Chinese Studies at Harvard University. His research interests have been largely related to issues of Chinese domestic and foreign policy. Goldstein has published studies on U.S.-China relations, Sino-Soviet relations, the emergence of a Chinese communist view of world affairs, and the reform process in post-Mao China. His current research focus is on the relations between the mainland and Taiwan, as well as the evolution of U.S.-Taiwan relations.

Scott W. Harold is an associate political scientist at the RAND Corporation, where he specializes in Asian security and international affairs. In addition to his work at RAND, Harold is an adjunct professor in the Security Studies Program at Georgetown University's Edmund A. Walsh School of Foreign Service, where he has taught since 2006. He has also taught Chinese politics at Columbia University. Prior to joining RAND, Harold worked at the Brookings Institution's John L. Thornton China Center from 2006 to 2008. He has a Ph.D. in political science from Columbia University, where he wrote a thesis on China's foreign policy decisionmaking with respect to joining the World Trade Organization. Harold is fluent in Mandarin Chinese. His latest publication, with co-author Cheng Li, was "China's New Military Elite" (*Chinese Security*, Winter 2007).

Kwei-Bo Huang is an associate professor in the Department of Diplomacy at National Chengchi University in Taipei. He was on public service leave as chairman of the Research and Planning Committee, Republic of China Ministry of Foreign Affairs, between February 2009 and January 2011. His recent research interests include third-party mediation and U.S. foreign policy toward the Asia Pacific. He has a Ph.D. from the Department of Government and Politics, University of Maryland, College Park.

Scott L. Kastner is an associate professor in the Department of Government and Politics at the University of Maryland, College Park. He has a Ph.D. in political science from the University of California, San Diego, and an A.B. in history and government from Cornell University. In 2005–2006, he was a visiting research fellow in the

Princeton-Harvard China and the World Program, and in 2007–2008, he was a China security fellow at the Institute for National Strategic Studies, National Defense University. He is the author of *Political Conflict and Economic Interdependence Across the Taiwan Strait and Beyond* (Stanford University Press, 2009). His articles have appeared in such journals as *International Studies Quarterly*, *International Security*, the *Journal of Conflict Resolution*, *Comparative Political Studies*, *Security Studies*, and the *Journal of Peace Research*.

Fu-Kuo Liu is currently a research fellow and chair of the Research Division of American and European Studies at the Institute of International Relations, National Chengchi University. He is concurrently an adjunct professor in regional security at the International Doctoral Program in Asia Pacific Studies, College of Social Science, National Chengchi University. Liu also serves as executive director of the National Committee of the Council for Security Cooperation in the Asia Pacific in Taiwan and is executive director of the newly established Center for Security Studies at the Institute of International Relations. In addition to his work on regional security dialogues, he oversees the publication of a policy-oriented monthly and serves as a chief editor of *Strategic and Security Analyses Monthly* (published in Chinese) at the Institute of International Relations. Liu was chair of the Research and Planning Committee at the Republic of China Ministry of Foreign Affairs from 2002 to 2004 and consultative adviser to the Mainland Affairs Council from 2004 to 2006. In 2009, he received a three-year research grant from the MacArthur Foundation, which was used to establish the Center for Security Studies. His current research focuses on Taiwan security, U.S.-Taiwan relations, and cross-Strait cooperation. He has a Ph.D. in politics from the University of Hull in the United Kingdom.

Michael J. Lostumbo is the associate director of the International Security and Defense Policy Center at the RAND Corporation. His research focuses on defense policy and Asian security issues. Prior to joining RAND, he served as the special assistant to the Under Secretary of Defense for Policy, Walter B. Slocombe, and was involved in policy formulation on a variety of national security topics, including U.S. military strategy, national missile defense, and numerous bilateral security issues. Previously, he spent six years as senior foreign policy adviser to U.S. Senator Daniel Patrick Moynihan. Lostumbo has a master's degree in public policy from the Johns Hopkins School for Advanced International Studies and a bachelor's degree in South Asian studies from the University of Wisconsin, Madison.

Michael McDevitt (Rear Admiral, U.S. Navy, retired) is a vice president and director of CNA Strategic Studies, a division of CNA (Center for Naval Analyses), a not-for-profit, federally funded research center in Washington, D.C. CNA Strategic Studies conducts research and analyses that focus on strategy, political-military issues, and regional security studies. He was the director of the East Asia Policy Office in the Office of the Secretary of Defense during the first Bush administration. He also served for two years as the director of Strategy, War Plans, and Policy (J5), Commander in Chief, U.S. Pacific Command. McDevitt concluded his 34-year active-duty career as the commandant of the National War College in Washington, D.C. He has been an active participant in conferences and workshops on security issues in East Asia and has had a number of papers published in edited volumes on this subject.

Alan D. Romberg is a distinguished fellow and director of the East Asia Program at the Stimson Center. He has worked and written extensively on U.S. policy in East Asia for many years. A foreign service officer for more than 20 years, his assignments included positions as director of the U.S. State Department Office of Japanese Affairs and as National Security Council staff member for China. He was Principal Deputy Assistant Secretary of State for Public Affairs and deputy spokesman of the department; he later served as principal deputy director of the State Department's policy planning staff. He held the C. V. Starr Senior Fellowship for Asian Studies at the Council on Foreign Relations for almost ten years.

Phillip C. Saunders is director of studies and distinguished research fellow at the Center for Strategic Research, part of National Defense University's Institute for National Strategic Studies. He also serves as director of the Center for the Study of Chinese Military Affairs. Saunders has worked on China and Asian security issues at National Defense University since January 2004. He previously worked at the Monterey Institute of International Studies, where he served as director of the East Asia Nonproliferation Program from 1999 to 2003 and taught courses on Chinese politics, Chinese foreign policy, and East Asian security. He has conducted research and consulted on East Asian security issues for Princeton University and the Council on Foreign Relations and worked on Asia policy issues as an officer in the U.S. Air Force. Saunders has published numerous articles and book chapters on China and Asian security issues; his recent publications include "Bridge over Troubled Water? Envisioning a China-Taiwan Peace Agreement" in *International Security*, the INSS Strategic Forum "Managing Strategic Competition with China," and two monographs (*Assessing Chinese Military Transparency* and *Civil-Military Relations in China: Assessing the PLA's Role in Elite Politics*). Saunders attended Harvard College and received his Ph.D. and M.P.A. in international relations from the Woodrow Wilson School of Public and International Affairs at Princeton University.

David A. Shlapak is a senior defense analyst at the RAND Corporation. During his nearly three decades in the national security field, he has led studies on topics ranging from nuclear strategy to counterterrorism and homeland defense. For more than ten years, he has worked extensively on issues relating to Asian security and the U.S. defense posture in the Pacific region. He is author or co-author of numerous reports and monographs, including *The United States and a Rising China; The United States and Asia: Toward a New U.S. Strategy and Force Posture; Dire Strait? Military Aspects of the China-Taiwan Confrontation and Options for U.S. Policy; U.S.-China Relations After Resolution of Taiwan's Status*; and *A Question of Balance: Political Context and Military Aspects of the China-Taiwan Dispute,* all published by RAND.

Christopher P. Twomey joined the faculty of the Department of National Security Affairs at the Naval Postgraduate School as an assistant professor in November 2004. He has also served as associate chair for research in the department and as director of the Center for Contemporary Conflict from 2007 to 2009. In March 2010, he was named a research fellow with the National Asia Research Program at the National Bureau of Asian Research. His research interests center on security studies, Chinese foreign policy, modern nuclear affairs, strategic culture, statecraft, and East Asian security in theory and practice. His book *The Military Lens: Doctrinal Differences and Deterrence Failure in Sino-American Relations* (Cornell University Press, 2010) explains how differing military doctrines make diplomatic signaling, interpretations of those signals, and assessments of the balance of power more difficult. His edited volume *Perspectives on Sino-American Strategic Nuclear Issues* was published in 2008, and his work has appeared in journals such as *Asian Survey*, *Security Studies*, *Arms Control Today*, *Contemporary Security Policy*, *Asia Policy*, *Current History*, and the *Journal of Contemporary China*. For six years, Twomey has managed a track II diplomatic exchange on U.S.-China nuclear issues involving several PLA flag officers, academics, and civilian policymakers. He consults for the Office of Net Assessment and the Office of the Secretary of Defense on various contemporary and future issues related to Asian security. He received his Ph.D. in political science from the Massachusetts Institute of Technology.

Albert S. Willner is the director of the China Security Affairs Group at CNA (the Center for Naval Analyses) in Alexandria, Virginia. Before joining CNA, he was an associate dean at Georgia Gwinnett College. A retired U.S. Army colonel, Willner completed his service as the first active-duty U.S. defense attaché-equivalent since 1979 assigned to Taiwan. He has served in various positions in the U.S. Department of Defense, coordinating Asia-Pacific strategy, plans, and policy, and was the director of international relations and national security studies in the Department of Social Sciences at West Point. His research interests include Chinese defense policy, China-Taiwan security, and U.S.-China military relations. He co-edited *China's Nuclear Future* (Lynne Rienner, 2006) and is the author or co-author of numerous papers. Willner received his Ph.D. in foreign affairs from the University of Virginia.